0003943110
336.39 STEW
AF750624

CORPORATE FINANCE AND FISCAL POLICY IN IRELAND

394311
336.39 STEW

Corporate Finance and Fiscal Policy in Ireland

J. C. STEWART
Trinity College,
Dublin

WITHDRAWN FROM THE LIBRARY
OF UNIVERSITY COLLEGE CORK

UNIVERSITY COLLEGE CORK
Library

Avebury

Aldershot · Brookfield USA · Hong Kong · Singapore · Sydney

© J. C. Stewart, 1987

All rights reserved. No part of this publication may be reproduced, stored in a retrieval system, or transmitted in any form or by any means, electronic, mechanical, photocopying, recording, or otherwise without the prior permission of Gower Publishing Company Limited.

Published by

Avebury
Gower Publishing Company Limited,
Gower House,
Croft Road,
Aldershot,
Hants GU11 3HR,
England

Gower Publishing Company
Old Post Road,
Brookfield,
Vermont 05036
USA

British Library Cataloguing in Publication Data

Stewart, J.
Corporate finance and fiscal policy in Ireland.
1. Fiscal policy——Ireland
336.3'09415 HJ1043

Library of Congress Cataloging-in-Publication Data

Stewart, J., 1949-
Corporate finance and fiscal policy in Ireland.

Based on the author's thesis (Ph. D.)--London School of Economics.
Bibliography: p.
Includes index.
1. Corporations--Ireland--Finance. 2. Corporations--Taxation--Ireland. 3. Corporate profits--Ireland--Effect of inflation on. I. Title.
HG4144.S74 1987 658.1'5'09415 87-14908
ISBN 0-566-05441-8

Printed and bound in Great Britain by
Athanaeum Press, Newcastle Upon Tyne

Contents

Tables

Symbols used in this book

A	=	All tax allowances other than export tax relief and accelerated depreciation
C	=	Accounting depreciation calculated according thistorical cost concepts
D	=	Accelerated depreciation allowances for tax purposes
E	=	Value of Exports
F	=	Total external finance
G	=	Capital Grants Received
i	=	Interest payments
J	=	Share issues
K	=	Capital employed using historical cost concepts
L	=	Balance Sheet tax liabilities
O	=	Stock adjustment
S	=	Value of sales
T	=	Cash tax payment

Summary

It has been argued by Feldstein and others that the interaction of inflation, accounting conventions and the fiscal system has resulted in a rise in taxation on real corporate profits in the United States. A similar argument has been applied to the United Kingdom. This rise in tax rates is used by Feldstein to explain both a fall in corporate share values in the United States expressed in terms of constant prices and also a fall in investment as a proportion of G.N.P. It is also widely believed in Ireland and other countries that the interaction of inflation and historical cost accounting has led to a rise in tax rates on corporate profits.

In contrast this book argues that in Ireland tax rates on corporate profits calculated according to historical cost conventions have declined during the period 1964-84. This is explained by the growth and diffusion of tax incentives and, in addition, by the existence of considerable lags between the earning of profits in the corporate sector and the collection of taxes on those profits. Secondly, using concepts of profits which are adjusted for inflation invarious ways, including current cost accounting, it is argued that corporate profits may not be very much below those of historical cost accounting. Thus it is concluded that fiscal incentives, coupled with lags in the collection of corporate tax, have more than compensated for the rise in taxable profits due to inflation and have resulted in a decline in tax rates on real corporate profits in Ireland.

Thirdly, it is argued that fiscal incentives have had an important effect on the form of financing, in particular the increased use of leasing and debt finance. The form of external finance, such as leasing, in turn has considerable implications for the volume and nature of new investment.

The book draws on Irish Government data, O.E.C.D. data and also on the published accounts of non-financial companies operating in Ireland during the period 1964-84. Most of the companies are Irish owned and fluctuate in number between 60 and 140 during the period considered.

I would like to acknowledge the help of the late Professor A.R. Prest of the London School of Economics who supervised the Ph.D thesis on which this book is based. I would also like to acknowledge the invaluable advice and assistance of Peter Connell of the Computer Laboratory, Trinity College, Dublin, and of Steve Satchell of Trinity College, Cambridge. Some of the material contained in chapters 3 and 7 of this book has already been published in 'Corporate Tax - Effective Tax Rates on Profits', Journal of the Statistical and Social Inquiry Society of Ireland vol.XXIV, part III, 1981, and 'Fiscal Incentives and Corporate Finance: A Flow of Funds Analysis', forthcoming, Journal of the Statistical and Social Inquiry Society of Ireland.

1 The corporate fiscal system in Ireland

1.1 Introduction

The purpose of this book is to estimate effective tax rates, as distinct from nominal tax rates on corporate profits in Ireland and secondly to examine the effect of fiscal incentives on corporate financing. The study relates to public companies in Ireland during the period 1964-84. Throughout the book the terms corporation, as in corporation tax, and company are used interchangeably. Chapter 1 describes the Irish fiscal system and attempts to estimate the cost of various fiscal incentives. Chapter 2 describes the study population. Chapter 3 contains some estimates of average effective tax rates on corporate profits and Chapter 4 considers the effect of inflation on corporate profits and tax rates. Chapter 5 examines the distribution of tax rates amongst companies included in the study. Chapter 6 describes alternative tax strategies which firms may pursue and considers some implications for investment. Chapter 7 examines the effect of fiscal incentives in a flow of funds context and Chapter 8 contains a summary of the main findings and considers some implications for tax reform and industrial strategy.

The following section is a brief summary of major developments in the taxation of corporate profits in Ireland from 1922, the foundation of the State, until 1986. Corporation tax is currently assessed in Ireland on profits arising during an accounting period. For taxation purposes corporate profits in Ireland are measured using accounting conventions very similar to those in the United Kingdom, although particular tax allowances are different. Taxable profits are thus an amalgam of accounting conventions and tax law.

Since the formation of the State in 1922 and until 1976 company profits in Ireland were subject to both an income tax and a corporation profits tax, using an imputation system[1], which was largely neutral in relation to the tax rate on retentions versus distributions. During the period 1922-76 there were variations in both tax rates. In addition, while corporation tax was usually allowed as a deduction in computing profits which were subject to income tax, there were periods when this was not the case, for example 1970-71. In 1976 a single corporation tax was introduced at a rate of 50 per cent[2], but in contrast to the United Kingdom there was no advance payment of Corporation Tax (A.C.T.) on payment of dividends. This had been suggested in a white paper on Corporation Tax published in 1972[3], but it was rejected on the grounds that the cash flow of companies distributing dividends would be adversely affected and that the benefit of accelerated depreciation allowances would be reduced. Advance payment of corporation tax was finally introduced in 1983, although important exemptions were granted to manufacturing firms in 1986. From January 1981 the corporate tax rate for non-manufacturing companies was 45 per cent and was raised to 50 per cent in 1982. The various changes in tax regimes for corporations operating in Ireland are summarised in Table 1.1.

The Irish corporate tax system is characterised by an elaborate system of fiscal incentives, the most important of which are:-

(a) Export tax relief.
(b) Depreciation allowances.
(c) From January 1981 a 10 per cent rate of Corporation Tax for manufacturing firms.

Table 1.7 (p. 22) summarises the main fiscal incentives available to the corporate sector for the period 1964-84.

Table 1.1
Main features of the taxation of corporate profits in Ireland 1922-86

1922-75	1976-80	1981-82	1983-85	1986
Corporate Profits were subject to Corporation Profits Tax and an Income Tax	Corporation Tax at a single rate of 50 per cent in 1976 and at 45 per cent for 1977-80.	The Corporate Tax Rate for Manufacturing companies was reduced to 10 per cent and set at 45 per cent for most other companies for 1981 and 50 per cent for 1982	Advance Corporation Tax was introduced in 1983	Dividends from manufacturing companies were subject to a reduced rate of A.C.T.
Special Features:				
Corporation Tax could be deducted in computing profits liable to Income Tax except for 1971-72	No Advance Corporation Tax	No Advance Corporation Tax	Dividends paid abroad exempted from A.C.T.	Dividends paid abroad exempted from A.C.T.

1.2 The diffusion of fiscal incentives

When examining the evolution of the current corporate fiscal system in Ireland it is useful to divide the corporate sector into domestic and international components; the main distinction being that the domestic component, which may be indigenously owned and controlled, trades largely in the domestic economy, while the international component, consisting in this case of subsidiaries of multinational firms, broadly defined[4], trades largely in the international economy. For various reasons multinational firms may react to fiscal incentives in a different way to domestic firms, by for example switching profits from one country to another using transfer pricing[5]. In addition in Ireland there are various fiscal incentives specifically designed to influence the location decision of multinational firms. The most important of these incentives during the period 1964 to 1984 were tax relief on exports, capital grants, and since 1981 a 10 per cent corporate tax rate for manufacturing firms. The level of these incentives is considerably influenced by inter-country competition for international investment.

It is difficult nevertheless to exclude domestic firms from the benefits of fiscal incentives largely designed to attract international enterprises, as there is a marked tendency for a fiscal incentive designed for one particular area or sector to be diffused gradually throughout the economy. Clark Joel has described this proccess of diffusion of fiscal incentives for Central American countries, and also gives some reasons fot its occurrence which appear equally valid for more developed countries[6]. Some of these reasons are 'lobbying by affected interests' and the difficulty of formulating 'meaningful criteria' to limit the scope of tax exemptions. Special interest groups may also campaign for tax concessions unique to themselves, or which arise only in special cases. For example, Siegfried[7] comments that because of lobbying and political pressures by 'special interest groups', in the United States 'many special tax provisions apply only to a single firm or to a small group of firms'.

The reasons for the growth of special interest groups and an analysis of their activities have been examined in some detail by Olson[8]. Olson argues that the emergence of special interest groups is largely a function of the time period that a society has been stable. Smaller groups are also more likely to engage in collective action than larger groups[9]. Pressure groups have little incentive to campaign to make an economy more efficient, since such a campaign may have considerable costs, but members of the group would only get a small part of the benefits. Hence pressure groups will be largely concerned with affecting the allocation of resources, and for this reason Olson refers to them as 'distributional coalitions'. Lobbying increases the complexity of the tax code and, Olson argues, creates an incentive 'to find ways of getting around the regulations or ways of profiting from them in unsuspected ways[10].

It is also difficult to formulate 'meaningful criteria' to limit the scope of tax exemptions and this is not confined only to fiscal incentives. Selective Employment Tax (S.E.T.) in the United Kingdom, while levied on all firms was reimbursed to firms engaged in manufacturing activities, and hence the duration of this tax was characterised by continuing disputes about the classification and liability to tax of various industries and occupations. According to Reddaway[11], soon after the introduction of S.E.T. bread roundsmen were classified as transport workers rather than salesmen, and hence became exempt from S.E.T. on the 'grounds that they follow a pre-determined route and deliver pre-determined orders'. More serious anomalies arose in the case of manufacturers who were also engaged in wholesaling (exempt) compared with wholesalers and distributors (taxed). Such anomalies led to diversification by exempt firms into other non-exempt activities, while retaining overall exemption from S.E.T.[12]

In Ireland, largely as a result of a diffusion process, fiscal incentives which were initially introduced to stimulate exports and to attract foreign direct investment have been extended throughout the manufacturing sector, and, to a reduced extent, the services sector. For example, tax relief on profits from exports was first announced in 1957 in the form of a 50 per cent reduction in tax on profits from exports above a base year, provided the profits from these exports were retained within the firm[13]. Hence as initially conceived export tax relief was a differential profits tax, which was only of benefit to firms that retained their profits from exports. This measure was criticised when introduced for not being generous enough, particularly when compared with incentives to exporters in other countries at that time. Sean Lemass who subsequently became Taoiseach (Prime Minister) stated while in opposition:

> 'It is quite clear that if the Government is hoping through this measure to arouse significant foreign interest in Irish industrial possibilities, they are not going far enough'[14].

A change in Government in 1957 allowed these ideas to be put into effect. The Budget Statements for 1957 and 1958 announced increases in the time period for which exemptions on export profits would apply. For example, the Budget Statement for 1958 states:-

> 'To give added impetus to the expansion of exports and a further encouragement to both home and foreign industrialists to build, extend and equip factories within the next few years to manufacture for export, I propose to lengthen from five years to ten years the maximum period of 100 per cent exemption for new or increased exports'.

It is important to note that tax relief on exports when first introduced, in contrast to the initial proposal, was available whether profits from exports were retained or distributed. Secondly, the period of time for which tax relief was to apply was extended, as well as the size of the tax reliefs granted. Eventually export tax relief was extended until the year 1990. Thirdly, while export tax relief was available to both foreign and Irish owned firms, the main beneficiaries were exporting firms, which were largely foreign owned. It is likely that this result was anticipated, and was facilitated by the partial dismantling of the Control of Manufacturers Acts in 1958, and their repeal in 1964. These Acts were enacted in 1932 and 1934 following the election of a Fianna Fail Government led by DeValera, with the intention of restricting ownership of Irish industry to Irish nationals. These measures were motivated partly by economic nationalism and partly by a desire to stimulate industrial development. At the same time as these Acts were passed, various other measures designed to stimulate industrial development were also introduced, such as tariffs and quotas and the establishment of various State owned industries to develop turf deposits, refine sugar, etc. These enterprises are the main aspect of economic policy of the 1930's to have survived until the present day[15]. When proposing an amendment to the Control of Manufactures Acts, Lemass stated:-

> 'One of the main reasons for preparing and introducing a bill to amend the Control of Manufactures Act is to advertise as widely as possible that foreign investment in industrial development involving export trade is welcomed and will be facilitated'[16].

In addition the Control of Manufactures Acts were not very successful in their aim. Many foreign owned companies were exempted from the provisions of these Acts. It was also relatively easy to avoid the provisions of these Acts by forming a sales company separate from a manufacturing company and controlling the manufacturing company by licenses and contracts.

The Budget Statement in 1956 in response to a recommendation by the Committee of Inquiry into Taxation on Industry[17] announced the introduction of an initial allowance of 20 per cent on capital expenditure on new machinery and plant. The stated intention was to encourage additional investment, and most Budget Statements since then have announced increases in these allowances. The Budget of 1967 was the first to introduce 100 per cent accelerated allowances which were initially limited to the Designated Areas. These were (and still are) certain areas suffering from above average economic and social problems, located largely in the West of Ireland. In 1971 100 per cent accelerated depreciation allowances were extended to the country as a whole. The general reason given for increasing depreciation allowances was to increase investment. For example, the Budget Statement of 1967 states:-

> 'As a specific encouragement, however, to higher investment in manufacturing industries and an improvement in our competitive position in free trade conditions, I propose to raise to 50 per cent the initial allowance of 40 per cent which applies to capital expenditure incurred in the period to 31st March 1968 on new machinery and plant'.

The major part of foreign investment in Ireland consists of subsidiaries of multinational companies and subsidiaries of other firms controlled outside Ireland. Because most output is exported, profits are largely exempt from corporate tax. Hence depreciation allowances may be of no benefit to these firms in reducing corporate tax payments, as long as most output is exported. Companies trading largely in the domestic economy do not benefit to the same extent from export tax relief, and so depreciation allowances may be used to reduce tax payments. In addition, some domestic companies have developed considerable exports[18], and tax exemptions similar to those on exports have been granted to certain companies in the services sector, for example, engineering services connected with engineering contracts in other countries.

The use of leasing has also spread tax savings from accelerated depreciation and other allowances to non-manufacturing companies, such as financial institutions and banks[19]. Restrictions on the use, and value in terms of tax allowances, of leasing were introduced in 1984 and extended in 1986 because of the growth of leasing and consequent loss in tax revenue. Leasing refers to the lease of assets by the owner (lessor) to another party (lessee). The ownership of the assets remains with the lessor, who therefore receives the benefits of depreciation allowances or capital grants associated with the assets. In some cases, where the assets purchased received a sufficiently high capital grant, leasing charges may be minimal or even negative. Leasing assets from others is particularly attractive to companies which pay no tax, for example because of export tax relief or because of losses. Such companies cannot benefit from accelerated depreciation allowances as they have no taxable profits which may be offset against tax allowances. Leasing assets to other companies is also attractive to companies which have low tax allowances and hence high taxable profits, as it provides a means by which taxable profits and tax payments may be reduced by using accelerated depreciation allowances. This is demonstrated in the following example:-

Example

	(1)		(2)
Profits	100	Profits	100
Tax at 50 %	50	Depreciation Allowances	100
	---		---
Profits after Tax	50	Taxable Profits	0
		Tax	0

		Profits after Tax	100

In the above example in case (1) there are no tax allowances, but in case (2) because of the purchase of assets which have been leased there are depreciation allowances of 100 , resulting in taxable profits of zero. In both cases pre-tax profits remain the same both with and without leasing. However profits after tax have increased substantially with leasing (case 2). For companies with taxable profits, the use of leasing is certain to result in lower tax payments for the lessor, and the size of the reduction will depend on the distribution of tax allowances between the lessor and lessee. Leasing may also result in an increase in pre-tax profits for the lessor, depending, for example, on the charges for leased assets. Hence the net effect of leasing on post tax profits will depend on the size of leasing charges and the distribution of tax allowances between lessor and lesee. This point is examined further in Chapter 6.

In Ireland, as in other countries, depreciation allowances may not be carried backwards in order to reclaim tax already paid. A similar situation exists in relation to losses, although under certain circumstances losses may be carried backwards to the immediately preceding accounting period. However surplus depreciation allowances (or losses) do not earn interest if carried forward. Hence it might be expected that, in general, excess depreciation allowances will be sold by leasing capital equipment, because the discounted value of excess tax allowances becomes smaller the further into the future that they are used to reduce tax payments. The use of leasing means that tax allowances need not exceed taxable profits. Thus leasing has effectively led to a market in capital allowances, though an imperfect market, which is dominated by banks operating in an oligopolistic market structure and is likely to be characterised by asymmetries in information. The total volume of leasing is also constrained by the absolute size of taxable profits of lessors or potential lessors, which in Ireland is largely the banking sector[20].

If profits of different activities in the corporate sector are taxed at different rates, for example a 10 per cent tax rate for manufacturing companies, depreciation allowances are more valuable to the higher taxed sector. Hence different rates of corporate tax for different companies could also give rise to leasing. In Ireland most companies faced the same nominal tax rate for the period 1964-80. The growth of leasing in Ireland during this period may be largely explained by surplus depreciation allowances. Since 1981 the introduction of a 10 per cent tax rate to manufacturing companies has given an added incentive to leasing.

A number of lending schemes based on tax savings have also developed. These schemes have generally involved the provision of finance to the manufacturing sector, the returns on which (interest or dividends) are either tax free or taxed at a reduced rate: for example preference share financing and loans known as 'section 84' loans. The development of 'section 84' loans provides a good illustration of the diffusion of fiscal incentives. These loans refer to section 84 (2d) of the Corporation Taxes Act, 1976, which is identical to an anti-tax avoidance provision in an earlier United Kingdom tax act, that is section 233 (2d) of the Income and Corporation Taxes Act, 1970. In the United Kingdom this section was designed to ensure that profits of companies which were distributed as interest payments rather than dividends were treated for tax purposes as distributions of dividends. In Ireland, however, for many companies profits and dividends are exempt from tax because of export tax relief. Hence if interest payments were treated as payments of dividends for these companies, they were also tax free to the recipient. Because of this particular tax status, for a company not liable to Corporation Tax, 'section 84' loans were also a cheaper source of finance to a borrowing company. Subsequently companies paying no corporation tax, or paying corporation tax at a reduced rate because of depreciation allowances, also issued 'section 84' loans. In the U.K. in recent years financial institutions have used section 233 of the Income and Corporation Taxes Act 1970 to issue similar loans, until this was prevented by the 1982 Finance Act. In Ireland in 1984 tax advantages were removed from additional 'section 84' lending and in 1986 the tax advatages on all 'section 84' loans were reduced.

Both preference share financing for an exporting company and 'section 84' loans reduce the cost of capital to the manufacturing sector, because the returns are either tax free or taxed at a reduced rate but they also result in lower tax payments by the provider of finance. It is most unlikely that these fiscal incentives were planned by the State, but more likely represent an unplanned diffusion of fiscal incentives.

Capital grants were first introduced as an incentive to investment in the designated areas' in 1952 at rates of up to 50 per cent of the cost of plant and machinery. The 'designated areas' were certain areas in the West of Ireland which had above average rates of unemployment, emigration, etc. These grants were subsequently extended to the rest of the country in 1956. Since the general introduction of capital grants the proportion of fixed assets financed by grants has tended to increase along with the range of expenditures that are eligible to receive capital grants[21].

The main form of capital grant is for fixed investment in new industry in manufacturing and certain service industries. These grants are referred to as 'New Industry' grants. 'New Industry' capital grants may be paid at a legal maximum rate of 60 per cent of the cost of fixed assets. However usually grants are paid at a rate of 45 per cent of the cost of fixed assets in the non-designated areas, and only at a rate of 60 per cent in the 'designated areas'. Manufacturing firms not eligible for 'New Industry' grants have been generally eligible for grants referred to as 're-equipment' grants. 'Re-equipment' grants are paid at a rate of 25 per cent of fixed assets in the non-designated areas and at a rate of 35 per cent in the 'designated areas'. Depreciation allowances and other tax reliefs may be claimed in addition to all fixed asset grants. Depreciation allowances are allowed on the cost of an asset gross of any grant that may have been paid, in the case of plant and machinery, but net of capital grants in the case of industrial buildings. The same provisions apply to a firm purchasing capital equipment for leasing. However, the Industrial Development Authority in recent years has restricted the amount of equipment which may be leased to 35 per cent of total assets[22]. In 1984 in order to benefit fully from accelerated depreciation allowances, leased assets were required to form part of a grant aided package negotiated with the Industrial Development Authority. Finally in 1986 capital allowances could only be calculated on the value of assets net of any capital grants paid[23].

In 1978 it was announced that a general corporation tax rate of 10 per cent for manufacturing firms would be introduced in 1981. A Government statement issued in connection with the introduction of this tax rate stated that it was designed to replace tax relief on profits from exports:-

> 'The existing Export Sales Relief Scheme has proved to be one of the most effective elements in the IDA`s investment promotion programme. This programme has succeeded in making Ireland an attractive location for overseas investment. However, since this scheme is due to end in 1990 and is therefore, already beginning to lose its attractiveness as an incentive, I have obtained the approval of my colleagues in Government for a new scheme which will guarantee that Ireland remains an attractive location for this type of investment'[24].

An additional factor leading to the introduction of a 10 per cent tax rate may have been criticism of the Export Sales Relief scheme by the Commission of the E.E.C. as being contrary to the Treaty of Rome[25].

Introducing a 10 per cent tax rate for all manufacturing companies was a significant extension of tax incentives. Previously in order to benefit from tax relief firms were required to (a) export, or (b) undertake additional investment, or (c) increase employment. Now, however, firms merely need to engage in activities classified as manufacturing. In addition a 10 per cent tax rate has been extended to certain non-manufacturing companies such as computer service companies and new service industries located at the

Shannon industrial free zone[26]. In general the 10 per cent tax rate for manufacturing firms compared with export tax relief encourages manufacturing activity as a goal in itself. Implicit in such a goal is the belief that increased manufacturing activity will in turn lead to higher economic growth, compared with a uniform tax rate on the corporate sector as a whole. However, the additional groups of firms to benefit from a general 10 per cent tax rate compared with export tax relief are firms engaging in essentially non-tradable activities which may be monopolistic in nature (for example the cement and mineral water sectors) and firms manufacturing for the domestic market.

It is difficult to appreciate why this latter group of firms is favoured compared with many non-manufacturing activities, such as transport or general engineering services. There are a number of arguments, for example those advanced by Kaldor[27], in favour of tax reliefs for manufacturing activities, compared with non-manufacturing activities. Kaldor has argued that tax reliefs aimed at manufacturing activities improve resource allocation by affecting the returns to investment in manufacturingand secondly that there is greater economic growth through growth in manufacturing output. The first point assumes resources will be misallocated in the absence of tax reliefs for manufacturing investment. It is argued in Chapter 6 of this book that this is likely to be true of the Irish economy because of (1) institutional bias in financial institutions; (2) in addition there are likely to be Capital Market imperfections, for example economies of scale in raising funds on the Stock Market; and (3) tax reliefs encourage investment in property, and channel funds towards institutions such as pension funds and life insurance companies. In relation to the argument about economic growth and growth in manufacturing output, Kaldor[28] has recently commented that increasing production in manufacturing is likely to be associated with falling labour demand and rising unemployment so that past relationships between the growth in productive employment and economic growth may no longer hold. There is also a further difficulty in that investment in many non-manfacturing activities (transport, engineering services) could aid growth in the output of manufacturing activities.

The Commission on Taxation[29] has suggested other reasons for fiscal incentives aimed at the 'unsheltered sctor' which the Commission largely defines as manufacturing industry. These are, the infant industry argument, the need to attract foreign direct investment, and to offset shortcomings in other policy areas. These criteria may be criticised. For example there is the problem of defining an infant industry compared with a non-viable industry, but more importantly a general 10 per cent tax rate for all manufacturing firms does not satisfy these criteria. The problem is that more specific targeting is likely to bc incompatible with the Treaty of Rome.

While the lower rate of tax for manufacturing companies was intended to replace export tax relief, companies established before January 1981 could choose either to retain the benefits of export tax relief, or alternatively they could choose to be taxed at a nominal tax rate of 10 per cent. Companies were required to exercise this option before January 1981. It is possible though, for companies established before January 1981 to benefit both from export tax relief and a corporate tax rate of 10 per cent. This may be done by forming a manufacturing company separately from an exporting company. The exporting company would continue to benefit from export tax relief, while the manufacturing company could be taxed at 10 per cent[30].

In addition to these fiscal incentives, tax relief on the increase in the value of stocks was introduced in 1975 and finally terminated in 1986. This tax relief was introduced largely in response to a high rate of inflation and increasing nominal values of stocks. This in turn placed considerable pressures on liquidity in the corporate sector. Stock relief was limited to manufacturing companies, construction companies, the farming sector, and companies selling goods to these three categories. When introduced the whole increase in the value of stocks, less 20 per cent of taxable trading income, was allowed as a tax relief. In 1978 the relief was limited to 75 per cent of the increase in the value of stock, less 20 per cent of taxable income from trading. Stock relief was essentially a partial inflation adjustment which ignores other effects of inflation on corporate profits, for example the effects of gearing. Some of these other effects are examined in Chapter 4.

Finally, to conclude this section the Commission on Taxation in Ireland in its first report made a number of recommendations which if implemented would have considerable implications for current fiscal incentives. One of these proposals has already been implemented, that is that a form of advance corporation tax should be introduced. Other proposals are that :-

(1) Interest would be no longer tax deductible;

(2) Capital allowances would be computed on the original cost of an asset indexed in line with the Consumer Price Index. In addition depreciation on buildings would only be allowed for tax purposes when the building was disposed of;

(3) Losses and capital allowances carried forward would also be indexed in line with the Consumer Price Index;

(4) The rate of imputation would be increased to 100 per cent in line with the underlying rate of corporation tax.

The Commission deal in a second report with issues such as '.... the level of incentives that should be provided, whether these should be through the tax system, and if so, in what form'[31]. Some of the implications of the second report of the Commission on Taxation are discussed in Chapter 8.

1.3 Some specific aspects of the fiscal system for corporations in Ireland

The previous section has described the evolution of the corporate system in Ireland, as a process of continual diffusion of fiscal incentives. The purpose of this section is to describe in more detail some of the specific aspects of the corporate tax system in Ireland which are directly relevant to particular arguments in this book.

The current Irish system of corporation tax is an imputation system[32] in that all profits are charged to corporation tax, but dividends are given a tax credit, which may be offset against personal taxation, or if the recipient of the dividend is not liable to tax, the tax credit may be repaid. As the rate of imputation was limited to 3/7 of the net distribution, up to April 1983, and 30/65 of the net distribution thereafter, and the corporation tax rate was 50 per cent, the Irish system of corporation tax might be more accurately described as a partial imputation system.

Double taxation treaties entered into between Ireland and other countries in general provide that foreign shareholders will receive a credit for all Irish corporate tax paid in assessing their liability to tax in their own country. In some cases dividends received may be exempted from further tax. In the case of the double taxation treaty between Ireland and the U.K. where less than 10 per cent of the equity is owned by a resident of the U.K. and the shareholder is not liable to tax, the tax credit may be reclaimed subject to a withholding tax (= 15 per cent of the sum of the dividend plus the tax credit). In cases where more than 10 per cent of the equity is owned by a U.K. shareholder, the shareholder is not entitled to reclaim the tax credit, but all Irish Corporation Tax paid may be used as a credit against tax payable in the U.K.

If an income tax rate of 35 per cent is assumed for the period 1964-76, Table 1.2 shows nominal tax rates on corporate profits for the period 1964-84.

Table 1.2
Nominal tax rates on company profits 1964-84[a]
per cent

	1964-66	1967-70	1970-71	1972-74	1975-76	1977	1978-80	1981	1982-84
Company Rate	47	50	58	50	50	45	45	50	50
Growing[b] Firm						25	25		
Capital[c] Gains Tax					26	26	30	30	40

Notes to Table 1.2

(a) For most years tax changes were introduced from 5th April. So, for example, the tax rate of 58 per cent was in force from 5th April 1970 until 5th April 1972

(b) In order to qualify sales and employment must have increased by 5 per cent and 3 per cent respectively during the year in which relief is claimed over the previous year. For

1978-80 the qualification for a 25 per cent rate of corporate tax was changed to one of an increase in employment only. This relief was ended in 1980 and in 1982 a new tax relief was introduced, consisting of a deduction against taxable profits of £10 per week for each new employee above the preceeding twelve month period.

(c) From April 1978 capital gains may be adjusted for inflation before capital gains tax is applied. The taxation of capital gains is discussed later in this chapter.

Source:- Budget Statements presented to Dail Eireann, and Annual Reports of the Revenue Commissioners 1964-84.

Table 1.2 shows that a reduced rate of corporation tax was introduced in 1977 for manufacturing companies which increased their employment and sales volume by 5 per cent and 3 per cent per annum. In 1978 the qualification for a lower rate of corporation tax was reduced to one of increasing employment only. This relief was ended in 1980 and tax allowances for additional employment were introduced in 1982. There are also lower corporate tax rates for small firms. For the period 1964-65 and 1966-75 , with the exception of 1970-71,the first £2,500 of profits were taxed at rates of 38 per cent and 40 per cent respectively. For 1970-71 the tax rate was 48 per cent. From 1976 to 1981 profits up to £25,000 were taxed at 35 percent, from £25,000 to £35,000 the tax rate varied from 35 per cent to 45 per cent, and profits greater than £35,000 were taxed in toto at 45 per cent[33]. From January 1982 the standard rate of corporation tax was set at a rate of 50 per cent.

As already discussed, from January 1981 corporation tax on manufacturing firms has been at a reduced rate of 10 per cent. However dividends paid to non-corporate resident shareholders are subject to income tax, and dividends will carry a reduced tax credit, but at a higher rate of imputation of the underlying corporate tax. The tax credit is equal to one half the amount of corporation tax paid multiplied by the proportion of post tax profits paid out in dividends. This sum is equal to 5/90 (1/18) of the distribution[34].

Example

Profits	100
Corporation Tax	10

Dividends	90
Tax Credit	5

Taxable Income	95

Income tax is then calculated as follows :-

Income Tax at 50 per cent	47.5
Less tax credit	5.0

Income Tax Payable	42.5

Capital gains tax was first introduced at a rate of 26 per cent in 1974. In

1978 the capital gains tax rate was increased to 30 per cent, but capital gains could be adjusted for the rise in the Consumer Price Index. If capital gains on certain fixed assets (machinery and equipment) are reinvested in other fixed assets capital gains tax may be deferred. This provision is known as 'roll-over' relief. From 1978 the rate of capital gains tax was made a function of the period of ownership of the asset, so that the rate of capital gains fell to zero if an asset were held for 21 years. This latter provision did not apply to companies, but only to persons resident within Ireland. It is possible that a company could pay capital gains tax on disposal of assets, and in addition a shareholder could also pay capital gains tax on disposal of shares in the same company. From April 1982 capital gains tax became rather more progressive. If an asset is sold within one year of ownership the tax rate became 60 per cent, from one to three years 50 per cent and beyond three years 40 per cent. Tapering relief was also abolished. Not surprisingly, in view of the list of exemptions, the total amount raised by capital gains tax has been small. The following sums were raised by this tax in the ten years 1975 to 1984 (all amounts are in £IR million):- 0.04, 0.426, 1.47, 3.16, 4.07, 5.98, 6.17, 8.21, 8.68, and 9.43.The following are a number of more specific features of the corporate tax system in Ireland:-

(1) There are considerable lags in the collection of corporate tax in Ireland[35]. Until the year 1981 taxes on corporate income were paid in two portions. The first part was paid nine months after the accounting year end, and the second portion was usually paid on January 1st following the date of payment of the first portion of corporation tax. Thus the final payment of corporation tax was generally paid between 12 months and 21 months after the accounting year end date. These lags resulted from the payment of Corporation Tax in two parts corresponding to the dates of payment of Corporation Profits Tax and Income Tax prior to 1976. Corporation Profits Tax was generally paid nine months after the accounting year end date, and income tax was payable on January 1st following this date. In 1981 the statutory lag in the final payment of corporation tax was reduced by three months, and a further reduction of three months took place in 1982. In 1985 a single date for payment of all corporation tax was introduced six months after the end of the accounting period. In addition if Corporation Tax due is not paid on the statutory dates, an interest charge may be imposed on overdue tax payments.

(2) The corporate tax system is progressive at low rates of tax. At current rates of tax the average tax rate on profits below £25,000 is 40 per cent and gradually rises to 50 per cent on profits greater than £35,000. For profits between £25,000 and £35,000 the marginal rate of tax is greater than the average rate of tax, and above £35,000 the marginal rate of tax is equal to the average rate of tax.

(3) In general, interest is allowed as a tax deduction against taxable profits. However, there are a number of instances where interest is not allowed as a tax deduction. As in the case of other tax allowances the tax deductibility of interest payments has been gradually extended[36].

(4) Under the Irish corporate tax system in force until 9th February 1983, the firm effectively collects tax due on dividends on behalf of the Exchequèr, and, in the general case, after a time lag this tax is paid to the Exchequer. If

a firm paid no tax because, for example, of accelerated depreciation allowances, dividends paid had a tax credit attached and effectively tax appeared to have been paid on behalf of the shareholder to the Exchequer. However this tax was not paid to the Exchequer because of various tax allowances. The firm had thus increased its cash flow and was in a position to pay a higher net dividend or interest payment. The shareholder who receives a dividend, or debt owner who receives interest in the case of `section 84' loans, may have been liable to additional tax above the rate of tax credit.

(5) There is an alternative to leasing as a means of avoiding surplus depreciation allowances, and that is diversification by firms into activities in which profits are taxed at different tax rates. Surplus depreciation allowances could then be transferred within a group of companies. That is, the market for depreciation allowances could be internalised within the firm. In Ireland, a company is defined as a member of a group if 75 per cent of its shares are owned by another company[37]. It is also possible to transfer tax allowances between companies in the case of a consortium consisting of five or fewer companies which together own all the shares of a trading company[38].

(6) Export tax relief is granted as a proportion of exports to total sales. Dividends from companies with exports are also exempt from personal income tax in proportion to the export/sales ratio. For this reason some companies whose profits are exempt from tax because of export sales relief have issued preference shares to certain employees. These shares are also referred to as 'executive shares'. One company in the study (I.C.P.) paid IR£ 0.46 million on 1000 shares issued at IR£1 each in the period 1982-84.

(7) Particular problems may arise with double taxation agreements for subsidiaries of multinational companies operating in Ireland. Double taxation agreements are used to ensure that income such as dividends, which are transferred from one fiscal system to another, are not taxed twice. This is done by providing a tax credit for tax already paid, which may be offset against tax due in the country to which income is remitted. Double taxation treaties may complicate the use of fiscal incentives by subsidiaries of multinational companies (M.N.C.s). For example, if the fiscal system of the country to which dividends are distributed by the subsidiary to the parent does not grant a tax credit for tax foregone in the country where the subsidiary operates, effective tax rates will be raised. Hence a subsidiary will only benefit from those fiscal incentives which do not result in additional tax payments equal in value to the fiscal incentives granted. For this reason, where there are a number of different fiscal incentives, as in Ireland, subsidiaries will only avail of those tax reliefs which result in a credit being granted. The problem of whether a credit is granted or not generally only arises if income is distributed. Hence companies in this position may retain all profits, while transferring funds using some other means, such as an intersubsidiary loan. Most countries with which Ireland has double taxation agreements grant a credit, even if tax has not been paid, but two important exceptions are the United States and the United Kingdom.

Survey evidence in Ireland relating to the location decisions of firms[39] has revealed general satisfaction with the operation of fiscal incentives, and this may indicate that problems with double taxation treaties have not arisen. This evidence is in contrast to some survey evidence from other countries[40]. However surveys of parent companies of subsidiaries operating in Ireland might reveal some problems with double taxation treaties.

1.4 The cost of fiscal incentives

Table 1.3 shows some estimates of the cost to the Exchequer for the years 1974 to 1980 of leasing and tax based lending. These costs were estimated by cumulating deferred tax and treating the total as an interest free loan. Table 1.3 shows that both forms of fiscal incentive have increased substantially in cost in recent years. If the cost of leasing were estimated on the basis of the amount of deferred tax, rather than treating deferred tax as an interest free loan, the costs shown in Table 1.3 would be likely to be substantially higher. This latter procedure assumes that deferred tax is treated as being equivalent to an equal sum paid as a non-returnable grant, rather than as an interest free loan.

Table 1.3
The cost of tax based lending
IR£ million (Constant 1980 prices)

	1974	1975	1976	1977	1978	1979	1980
Leasing[a]	1	2	4	8	14	21	25
Section 84 Loans[b] and Preference Share Financing		11	2	6	11	22	24
	---	---	--	---	---	---	---
	1	13	6	14	25	43	49

Notes to Table 1.3

(a) On p. 439 of the Telesis Report the cost of leasing is estimated as '... if it were lending to banks the amount of deferred tax - free of interest'. A different time profile of cost would be obtained if tax deferred was written off, which is largely the procedure followed in published company accounts. If the stock of leased assets remained constant or declined slowly, the former measure would lead to higher costs than the latter measure. If, as is more likely in Ireland, the stock of leased assets is growing rapidly the latter measure would lead to higher costs than the former measure. Johansen[41] examines depreciation allowances in terms of the present value of tax payments, and concludes that depreciation allowances are of greatest value to an expanding firm.

(b) In the case of `section 84' loans the cost is estimated by multiplying the amount involved by the interest rate adjusted by the tax rate. So that, if x is the amount of finance provided, r the interest rate, and t the tax rate, then the cost = $x.r(1 - t)$.

Source:- Telesis, A Review of Industrial Policy, National Economic and Social Council, Dublin, 1982.

Table 1.4 shows an estimate of the cost to the Exchequer of various tax reliefs based on revenue foregone. However first a word of warning, the published source for this data states :- 'many of the estimates supplied are very tentative and are subject to a wide margin of error'.

Table 1.4 shows the cost of capital allowances on leased and non-leased assets, as well as the cost of `section 84' loans, and a reduced rate of corporation tax for profits below £35,000. All these costs are based on tax foregone, which should not be taken to imply that abolishing these reliefs would result in an equivalent amount of revenue being raised. This is because abolishing these tax reliefs would be likely to lead to various adjustments in the corporate sector, for example changed methods of financing, or disinvestment by multinational companies, or relocation of Irish firms to other countries[42]. In addition there is an argument that the net cost of tax expenditures on the budget deficit is less than the gross amount because of increased economic activity thereby generated[43].

Table 1.4
The cost of various tax reliefs 1978 to 1984
IR£ million

	1978	1979	1980	1981	1982	1983	1984
Capital Allowances[a] on Leased Assets	20.0	39.0	34.5	38.5	92.0	72.0	72.5
Capital Allowances[a] on Other Equipment	17.0	18.0	31.0	35.5	97.0	146.2	171.5
`Section 84' Loans and[b] preference share financing	1.3	1.7	5.3	12.7	63.0	73.0	86.0
Reduced rate of Corporation[c] Tax on profits below £35,000	4.5	5.0	5.5	7.0	8.0	7.5	7.3
Total	42.8	63.7	76.3	93.7	260.0	298.7	337.3

Notes to Table 1.4

(a) Relates to the period ending 5th April of the following year. Source:- This information was given in response to a Parliamentary Question 14 June 1983, 7 December, 1983, and 18 January, 1984.

(b) Source: Parliamentary Question 18th January 1984 and 22nd October 1986. Separate figures for the cost of preference share financing and 'section 84 loans are not available. This data also includes tax relief on foreign currency borrowing.

(c) Source:- Parliamentary Question 14th June 1983 and 22nd October, 1986.

However such an argument applies equally to all Government expenditures, for example road building. Given the complexity of the tax structure, the existence of tax exhausted companies, and financial intermediation in tax allowances, the net effect of tax allowances on Government revenues as distinct from any other form of Government expenditure is likely to be extremely difficult to quantify. As expected the costs shown in Table 1.4 are substantially higher than those estimated by the Telesis report. If the cost of leasing shown in Table 1.4 were expressed in constant (1980) pounds, the difference would be even greater. It is interesting to note from this table that the cost of allowances on leased assets is higher than the cost on non-leased assets for the period 1978-81 and that the cost of leased assets reached a peak in 1981 and then fell. A second point of interest is the growth in the cost of `section 84' loans, which grew from a cost of IR£ 1.7 million in 1979 to IR£ 63.0 million in 1982 and to IR£ 86 million in 1984. 'Section 84' loans amounted to 7.8 per cent of total private sector lending by December 1982, and reached a peak of 9.9 per cent in May 1984 and remained around 9.1 per cent despite restrictions introduced in 1984[44]. For more recent years the cost of preference share financing is thought to be relatively unimportant[45].

The total cost of 'section 84' loans, preference share financing, and accelerated capital allowances has been estimated at IR£ 252.0 million for 1982 compared with IR£ 86.7 million in 1981. Part of this increase is due to reducing the lags in the payment of corporation tax[46] so that companies were assessed on two years' profits in 1982, and were also able to claim allowances for two years. The cost of these allowances continued to increase in subsequent years but not at the same rate.

Table 1.5 shows expenditure on leased assets by the two major banks in Ireland, which are thought to account for approximately 80 per cent of all leasing activity. For the year 1980, for example, net of capital grants and of any leased assets which may have been sold by the banks, the two banks spent an extra IR £79 million on leased assets. Assuming an average tax rate of 45 per cent, the cost in terms of deferred tax amounted to IR£ 36 million. If it is assumed that all leased assets attracted an average grant of 25 per cent, the total amount spent on leased assets amounted to IR£ 105 million in 1980, and resulted in deferred tax of IR£ 47 million. The same calculations and assuming a tax rate of 50 per cent for the year 1983 results in estimates of deferred tax of IR£ 40.0 million and IR£ 53 million (assuming a grant rate of 25 per cent). For the year 1980 the Telesis estimate of the cost of capital allowances on leased assets amounted to IR£ 25 million, the cost provided in response to a Parliamentary Question was IR£ 34.5 million, and the cost estimated for the two major banks in Ireland was in the region of IR£ 36 to IR£ 47 million.

Table 1.5

Expenditure on fixed assets leased 1974-83[a]

IR£ million

	1974	1975	1976	1977	1978	1979	1980	1981	1982	1983	1984[d]
Balance[b] Sheet Total	38.9	53.8	82.2	117.7	211.4	274.4	353.2	423.6	494.2	573.8	300.9
Annual Increase	14.9	28.4	35.5	93.7	63.0	78.8	70.4	70.6	79.6	41.3	
Balance[c] Sheet Total Grossed up by 25 per cent	51.9	71.7	109.6	156.9	281.9	365.9	470.9	564.8	658.9	765.1	401.2
Annual Increase	19.8	37.9	47.3	125.0	84.0	105.0	93.9	94.1	106.2	55.1	

Notes to Table 1.5

(a) Expenditure on assets leased by the two major banks in Ireland (Allied Irish Banks and Bank of Ireland). The data relate to the period ending March 31st of the following year.

(b) Gross of depreciation.

(c) This assumes that all assets attracted an average grant of 25 per cent, although it is possible that some assets may attract a grant rate of up to 60 per cent, which is the legal maximum for new industry grants. The data has been rounded to one decimal place.

(d) Relates to Bank of Ireland only. Allied Irish Banks was omitted due to changes in accounting practice

Source:- Annual Report and Accounts of Allied Irish Banks, and Bank of Ireland for March 1975 to March 1985.

The estimate of cost in terms of tax foregone of IR£ 47 million in 1980 assumed total grants paid on leased assets amounted to IR£ 26 million, compared with a published figure of IR£ 16.4 million. This suggests that the average grant paid on leased assets is not as high as 25 per cent but is somewhere in the region of 15 per cent to 20 per cent. This may be explained by the purchase and lease by banks of non-grant aided assets such as cars, transport equipment, and amusement machines. In addition it is likely that the data for grants paid on leased assets does not include capital grants from E.E.C. sources such as F.E.O.G.A. grants.

From Table 1.4 and Table 1.5 it can be seen that the large increase in costs of leased assets in 1982 is not reflected in increased expenditures by the two main banks. Even though the cost of leased assets in the year 1982 has been artificially increased it is likely that expenditures by the two main banks account for a diminishing proportion of the cost of leased assets since 1982.

Table 1.6 shows the amount paid under the more important capital grant schemes for the period 1974-84, and also shows tax foregone due to export sales relief for 1978-84. Table 1.6 shows that the single most important category of grant aid is on projects classified as `new industry'. Table 1.6 also shows that the cost of export sales relief is far larger than the 10 per cent tax rate for manufacturing companies. Numerous other grants and tax concessions also apply to the corporate sector, however the ones discussed in this section are the most important[47]. The most important incentives omitted from this discussion are training grants and exchange rate guarantees on loans to the corporate sector first introduced in 1978. The Industrial Development Authority spent IR£ 9.97 million on training grants in 1980, IR£ 15.0 in 1981, IR£ 20.1 in 1982, IR£ 23.0 in 1983, and IR£ 27.3 in 1984. Other Government agencies also provide training grants, for example, An Chomhairle Oiliuna. Loans to the corporate sector with exchange rate guarantees were first introduced in 1978. The interest rate on these loans is lower than that prevailing in Ireland. These loans originate from E.E.C. bodies such as the European Investment Bank, and are administered in Ireland by a State owned bank (The Industrial Credit Company). Assuming these loans were repaid at exchange rates prevailing in October 1983, the total cost of these loans to the State amounted to approximately IR£15.4 million from the commencement of the scheme in

June 1978 up to December 1981, IR £8.5 million for the year 1982, and IR £16.7 million for the period January to October 1983[48]. Table 1.8 appendix shows total grants, tax concessions, and some other expenditures by the State of direct benefit to the corporate sector in Ireland, in so far as these have been identified. This table also shows lending by Government agencies to the corporate sector, in order to make comparisons with the level of State aid to the corporate sector in other countries. Excluding lending by State agencies to the corporate sector, State aid amounted to approximately IR£ 871.6 million in 1984, or 6.0 per cent of G.N.P., compared with IR£ 178.8 million in 1978, or 2.74 per cent of G.N.P. In recent years the main growth has been in tax exemptions and labour subsidies, while capital grants have remained at approximately the same nominal level. For 1984 the total cost of capital grants and tax exemptions amounted to IR£ 832.6 million, 19.8 per cent consisted of grant payments, 28.2 per cent consisted of export tax relief, and 29.3 per cent consisted of capital allowances. Chapter 5 examines these costs in relation to total Goverment revenues.

In summary, the corporate sector in Ireland may currently avail itself of two main types of fiscal incentive. The first is that which is of most benefit to foreign direct investment, although domestic firms are not excluded: that is, exemption from corporation tax on any profits earned from exports and grants for capital expenditure on `new industry'. From January 1981 corporation tax on manufacturing firms (both domestic and foreign owned) is at a reduced rate of 10 per cent. This lower rate of tax for manufacturing companies was intended to replace export tax relief. However, companies established before January 1981 had the option of choosing to retain the benefits of export tax relief, or of being taxed at a nominal rate of 10 per cent.

Table 1.6
The cost of export sales relief and capital grants paid 1974-84
IR£ million

	1974	1975	1976	1977	1978	1979	1980	1981	1982	1983	1984
New Industry[a] Grants	8.4	19.8	27.9	24.6	33.1	38.4	65.8	76.2	77.5	87.1	66.5
Re-Equipment[a] Grants	0.2	1.1	4.1	9.6	9.0	7.9	12.8	14.2	8.4	8.3	6.0
Grants Paid[a] on Leased Assets	3.7	8.6	9.4	7.1	6.8	18.1	16.4	20.2	19.1	15.9	16.0
FEOGA[b] Grants	2.6	2.2	2.9	1.8	1.4	1.6	3.8	3.2	5.5	5.9	6.8
Total	14.9	31.7	44.3	43.1	50.3	66.0	98.8	113.8	110.5	117.2	95.3
Export Sales[c] Tax Relief					58.0	94.0	103.0	116.0	106.5	323.4	234.6
Reduced Rate of Tax on manufacturing profits								29.0	40.0	90.1	95.8

Notes to Table 1.6

(a) For nine months.

(b) These are E.E.C. grants for capital investment to improve Agricultural Processing and Marketing, and are administered by the Industrial Development Authority. Source: Annual Report of the Minister for Agriculture, for the years 1982-84, and Department of Agriculture for the years 1975-81.

(c) Relates to the period ending 31st March of the following year, and estimated as tax foregone because of this tax concession. This figure also includes export tax relief arising from the Shannon Industrial Estate, except for the year 1982.

Sources:- The data on capital grants is published in the Annual Reports of the Industrial Development Authority, Dublin. Data on the cost of Export Sales Tax Relief was published as an answer to a Parliamentary Question on 14th June 1983, 23rd June 1983, 7 December 1983, and 22nd October, 1986. The cost of a reduced rate of tax on manufacturing profits was published in the Commission on Taxation, p. 156 for 1981, the Annual Report of the Revenue Commissioners for 1982, and in a Parliamentary Question of 22nd October 1986 for the years 1983-84. In some cases the data has been rounded to one decimal place.

The second main type of fiscal incentive is that which is of most benefit to domestic companies, consisting of various depreciation allowances, including accelerated depreciation[49], and capital grants for 're-equipment'. In addition, most of the recently established 'small industry' grants have been paid to domestically owned firms. Table 1.7 summarises some of the more important fiscal incentives and grants available to the corporate sector in the period 1964-84.

Table 1.7

Summary of the main fiscal incentives available for 1964-84[a]

(number indicates percentage which is tax deductible)

Depreciation	1964-66	1967	1968	1969-70	1971	1972-74	1975-77	1978	1979	1980	1981-84
Plant and Machinery:-[b]											
Initial Allowances	40	50	60	60	60	100	100	100	100	100	100
or											
Free Depreciation					100	100	100	100	100	100	100
Buildings:-											
Initial Allowances	10	10	10	10	10	10	50	100	100	100	100
Annual Depreciation	2	2	2	2	2	2	4	4	4	4	4
Export Tax Relief	100	100	100	100	100	100	100	100	100	100	100
Interest Relief[c]	100	100	100	100	100	100	100	100	100	100	100
Tax Relief on[d] Stock Profits	100	100	100	100	100	100	100	100	75	75	75
Capital Grants											
New Industry	33	33	35	35	35	35	35	35	35	35	45
Re-equipment	25	25	25	25	25	25	25	25	25	25	25
Small Industry[e]				45	45	45	45	45	45	45	45
Research and[f] Development					35	35	35	35	35	45	45

Notes to Table 1.7

(a) The data relates to firms operating outside certain designated areas, largely in the West of Ireland, and the Dublin area. Grants of up to 60 per cent of the cost of fixed assets may be paid in the designated areas to manufacturing firms, and since 1971 an additional 20 per cent investment allowance may be claimed. Lower grants and depreciation allowances applied in the Dublin area until 1977, but those lower rates have only applied to depreciation allowanace since then.

(b) Either free depreciation or initial allowances may be claimed. Wear and tear allowances may also be claimed instead of free depreciation allowances, and in addition to investment allowances.

(c) During the period 1964-84 most forms of interest payment were deductible for tax purposes

(d) Stock relief was limited to 75 per cent of the increase in the value of stocks from 1979 and in 1983 was limited to price increases only.

(e) Firms employing less than 50 people.

(f) In 1982 the grant per project was set at a maximum of IR£ 150,000. Grants are also available for running costs.

Since 1975 firms may receive grants of up to IR£ 20 a week per employee for new employment for a limited time span (under one year). From 1978 to 1980 firms in the clothing, footwear, and textile industries received a grant of IR £5 per employee per week.

Sources:- Budget Statements presented to Dail Eireann 1963-84, Annual Reports of An Foras Tionscal, 1963-69, and Annual Reports of the Industrial Development Authority, 1970-84.

Appendix 1

Total State aid to the corporate sector in Ireland

This appendix quantifies the total amount of direct State aid to the corporate sector in Ireland, and secondly compares this total amount with State aid in five other countries :- West Germany, United Kingdom, Norway, Sweden and Italy. The cost of State aid in these latter countries has been recently estimated by Carlsson[50].

There are considerable difficulties in making inter-country comparisons of State-aid to the corporate sector. Carlsson comments (p. 6) 'Data on government subsidies is one type of information which most Governments are not eager to divulge, or whose diffusion they sometimes actually prevent'. Hence there are few inter-country comparisons of State aid to the corporate sector. In addition the corporate sector may be defined differently in different countries, for example including or excluding State owned industries. There may also be difficulties in identifying and classifying different subsidy schemes, for example State aid to the aerospace industry could be classified as sectoral aid, or as aid for Research and Development[51]. Governments may also actively attempt to hide or disguise certain forms of State aid because they contravene international treaties such as has occurred recently in the U.K. in relation to subsidised loans relating to exports to E.E.C. countries[52]. There may also be difficulties in costing aid. Most of the costs listed in Table 1.8 appendix consist of either cash grants or tax expenditures.

An exception is the amount shown as 'Direct Cost of Training Operations'. From discussions with AnCO it appears that benefits to the corporate sector lie somewhere between 10 per cent and 60 per cent of total expenditure, as approximately 40 per cent of expenditure consists of direct payments to trainees, and 10 per cent of expenditure relates to training of apprentices already in employment. It has been arbitrarily assumed that 25 per cent of the expenditure on training undertaken by the Industrial Training Company (AnCO) accrues to the corporate sector, for example, where a firm avoids the necessity of training employees, because they have already been trained. Another exception relates to expenditure on the Work Experience Programme. The amounts shown are State payments to participants in this Programme, which are similar in amount to unemployment benefit. It is likely that the value of the Work Experience Programme to firms is greater than the amounts shown in Table 1.8.

Finally grants paid by the E.E.C. to firms in agriculture and food processing (F.E.O.G.A. Grants) have also been included in Table 1.8. In addition some of the expenditure on training may be recouped from the E.E.C.

Table 1.8
The cost of State aids to the corporate sector in Ireland 1978-84
IR£ million

Labour Subsidies[a]	1978	1979	1980	1981	1982	1983	1984
Employment Incentive Scheme	7.0	4.0	4.1	2.0	2.6	2.3	1.5
Employment Maintainance Scheme	5.0	8.0	3.5	0.0	0.0	0.0	0.0
Work Experience Programme	0.6	2.8	2.1	2.1	5.0	7.0	5.6
Total	12.6	14.8	9.7	4.1	7.6	9.3	7.1
AnCO[b]							
Direct Costs of[c] Training Operations	3.9	5.4	6.2	8.3	12.7	18.1	21.2
Grants Paid	0.8	1.6	2.8	2.9	3.3	7.5	9.2
Technical Assistance Grants	0.5	0.6	0.9	1.0	1.1	1.3	1.4
Total	5.2	7.6	9.9	12.2	17.1	26.9	31.9
Capital Grants							
Industrial Development[d] Authority	55.4	79.7	110.9	135.8	141.3	156.0	147.1
Shannon Free Airport[e] Development Company	0.4	1.4	3.5	3.3	4.4	4.7	1.8
Udaras na[e] Gaeltachta	2.3	3.7	3.7	4.6	7.1	5.5	5.0
F.E.O.G.A.[f]	1.4	1.6	3.8	3.2	5.7	5.9	6.8
Exchange Rate Guarantees[g]	0.7	0.8	0.1	0.7	1.2	2.8	4.2
Total	60.2	87.2	122.0	146.9	159.7	174.9	164.9
Total Tax Expenditures[h]	100.8	157.7	179.3	238.7	398.5	711.9	667.7
Net Lending by State Agencies[i]							
Industrial Credit Company	18.5	41.9	45.2	58.6	99.6	52.2	33.9
Foir Teoranta (State Lending Agency)	0.4	1.4	8.0	2.5	12.6	21.4	14.9
Total	18.9	43.3	53.2	61.1	112.2	73.6	48.8

Notes to Table 1.8 Appendix

(a) Source:- Estimates for the Public Service for the years 1977-85, Stationery Office, Dublin.

(b) Source:- Annual Report and Accounts of An Chomhairle Oiliuna (AnCO - National Training Authority) for the years 1977-84.

(c) Benefits accruing to the corporate sector are estimated at 25 per cent of the total cost of direct training operations.

(d) Source:- Annual Reports and Accounts of the Industrial Development Authority, 1978-84. Most, but not all of this expenditure consists of capital grants for expenditure on fixed assets.

(e) Source:- Estimates for the Public Service, for the years 1977-85, Stationery Office, Dublin.

(f) Press Release, Department of Agriculture, Dublin.

(g) This figure excludes unrealised exchange rate losses. For the period up to 31st December 1981 realised and unrealised exchange rate losses on lending to the corporate sector are estimated at IR £12.4 million, for 1982 IR£ 8.5 million and for the ten months to 31st October 1983 are estimated at IR£ 16.7 million. Source:- Parliamentary Question 7th December 1983 and 22nd October 1986.

(h) Source: Table 1.4 and Table 1.6.

(i) Source:- Annual Reports and Accounts of Industrial Credit Company, 1978-84, and Annual Report and Accounts of Foir Teoranta 1978-84.

Carlsson includes all loans by State agencies as State aid, rather than attempt to work out the subsidy element in each loan. In addition Carlsson does not include tax exemptions, except in the case of West Germany.

Table 1.8 appendix quantifies the cost of various forms of State aid to the corporate sector in Ireland for the period 1978-84. The Review of Industrial Performance for 1986 also estimates the costs of State aid to the corporate sector which differ from the estimates in this appendix[53]. The Review divides State aid into two components : (a) drect State aid which is estimated to vary between IR£ 370 million and IR£ 400 million for the period 1983-86; (b) the cost of tax incentives which is estimated to vary between IR£ 220-250 million for the same period. Direct State aid is higher than the estimate included in this appendix because of the inclusion of the costs of administration and services of IR£117-150 million, largely consisting of the pay of an estimated 3500 public servants involved in the provision of services, etc. The cost of tax foregone is lower than the estimates in this paper because tax reliefs thought to largely benefit foreign owned firms was excluded on the basis that foreign owned firms would not locate in Ireland if various tax reliefs were not granted. Finally this appendix also includes loans by State agencies.

Table 1.9 Appendix expresses the costs in Table 1.8 Appendix as a percentage of G.N.P. Total costs as a percentage of G.N.P. show a rising trend from 3.02 per cent in 1978 to 7.4 per cent in 1983 and then down to 6.3 per cent in 1984. Excluding tax exemptions, State aid as a percentage of G.N.P. was 1.47 per cent in 1978, reaching a peak of 2.38 per cent in 1982 and then falling to 1.72 per cent in 1984. From Table (1) of Carlsson, it appears that State subsidies to the corporate sector in Ireland (omitting tax exemptions) are similar to those in Italy for 1978 (3.02 per cent in Ireland compared with 2.6 per cent in Italy) but below those for Sweden at 3.5 per cent. Sweden appeared to have the highest level of State subsidies of all the countries examined. West Germany and the United Kingdom had the lowest level of State aid at 1.6 per cent and 1 per cent of G.N.P. respectively. The high level for Sweden is largely accounted for by specific aid directed towards the ship building and steel sectors. Tax exemptions are likely to be considerably more important in Ireland than in other countries, while loans are likely to be less important. According to Carlsson most export subsidies are given in the form of subsidised interest rates on loans, whereas in Ireland export subsidies consist largely of tax exemptions.

Chapter 5 compares capital grant payments to the corporate sector in Ireland with payments in the U.K. and other O.E.C.D. countries.

Table 1.9
State aid to the corporate sector in Ireland as a percentage of G.N.P.

	1978	1979	1980	1981	1982	1983	1984
Total	197.0	309.8	374.0	463.0	693.9	993.8	916.2
Per cent of G.N.P.	3.02	4.06	4.15	4.27	5.60	7.44	6.34
Total less[a] Tax Exemptions	96.2	152.1	194.7	224.3	295.8	281.9	248.5
Per cent of G.N.P.	1.47	1.99	2.16	2.07	2.45	2.11	1.72
Total less[b] lending by the State	178.8	267.3	320.9	402.6	582.9	923.0	871.6
Per cent of G.N.P.	2.74	3.11	3.56	3.71	4.70	6.80	6.03

Notes to Table 1.9 Appendix

(a) Excluding cost of Exchange Rate Guarantees
(b) Including cost of Exchange Rate Guarantees

Notes

[1] See Department of Finance, *Company Taxation in Ireland*, Prl. 2628, 1972, Stationery Office, Dublin, ch. 3, or *Commission on Taxation*, Direct Taxation, Stationery Office, Dublin, 1982, especially Appendix 17.

[2] Revenue Commissioners, *Guide to the Corporation Tax*, Revenue Commissioners, Dublin, 1976.

[3] See Department of Finance, 1972, op. cit. p. 150, and Department of Finance, *Proposals for Corporation Tax*, Stationery Office, Dublin, Prl. 3713, 1974, pp. 11-12.

[4] United Nations, *Multinational Corporations in World Development*, Praeger Publishers, London, 1974, p. 3.

[5] For a summary of empirical evidence relating to transfer pricing see S. Lall, 'Transfer Pricing by Multinational Firms', *Oxford Bulletin of Economics and Statistics*, vol. 35, no. 3, 1973, pp. 173-195, United Nations Conference on Trade and Development, *Dominant Positions of Market Power of Transnational Corporations* TD/B/C2/167, 1978 or J.C. Stewart, 'Multinational Companies and Transfer Pricing', *Journal of Business Finance and Accounting*, vol. 4, 1977, pp. 353-371. For a discussion of empirical evidence relating to the use of transfer pricing in Ireland see J.C. Stewart, 'Some Aspects of the Financial Behaviour of Multinational Companies Operating in Ireland', in J.H. Kelly and J. Fitzpatrick (eds.), *Perspectives of Irish Industry*, Irish Management Institute, Dublin, 1985.

[6] Clark Joel, 'Tax Incentives in Central American Development', *Economic Development and Cultural Change*, vol. 19, no. 2, pp. 229-252.

[7] J. Siegfried, 'Effective Average U.S. Corporation Income Tax Rates', *National Tax Journal*, vol. XXVII, 1974 pp. 245-259.

[8] See M. Olson, *The Rise and Decline of Nations*, London: Yale University Press, 1982, and M. Olson, *The Logic of Collective Action*, Harvard University Press, Harvard, 1965.

[9] M. Olson, ibid, 1982, p. 31.

[10] M. Olson, ibid, 1982, p. 70.

[11] W.B. Reddaway, *Effects of the Selective Employment Tax*, First Report, H.M.S.O., London, 1970, p. 185. See also M.T. Sumner, The Reform of *Corporation Tax: A Review of the Green Paper*, Salford Papers on Economics, 1982, p. 5, for some Canadian examples of arbitrary definitions of manufacturing. Similar problems have also arisen in Ireland, particularly since the introduction of a ten per cent tax rate for, manufacturing firms. See *Irish Press*, November 18th 1985.

[12] W.B. Reddaway, *Effects of the Selective Employment Tax*, Final Report, Cambridge University Press, 1973, Cambridge, p. 134.

[13] Dail Debates, vol. 160, p. 1614.

[14] Dail Debates, vol. 160, p. 1628.

[15] See F.S.L. Lyons, *Ireland Since the Rising*, Collins and Fontana, Glasgow, 1973, pp. 610-620.

[16] Dail Debates, vol. 165. p. 534.
[17] Department of Finance, *Committee of Inquiry into Taxation on Industry*, Pr. 3512, Stationary office, Dublin, 1956.
[18] Some companies have been reported as exporting in order to gain tax relief and have an Irish distributor reimport the goods, *Irish Times*, 22th December, 1978.
[19] A similar transfer of depreciation allowances has also taken place in the United Kingdom and more recently in the United States.
[20] These points are developed further in Chapter 6.
[21] A description of grants available to the corporate sector in Ireland is contained in Telesis, *A Review of Industrial Policy*, National Economic and Social Council, Pl. 409, Stationery Office, Dublin, 1982, pp. 157-161, or in the annual reports of the Industrial Development Authority, Dublin.
[22] Telesis, op. cit. p. 191.
[23] This change had also been announced in the Budget Statement of 1979 but was not implemented in the following finance bill.
[24] Contained in a statement issued by the Minister for Industry, Commerce, and Energy, Mr. D. O'Malley in Brussels, on 20th December 1978.
[25] J. McGrath, 'New Tax Relief Aims to Spur Re-Investment', *Irish Times*, June 10th 1980. See also Commission on Taxation, *Direct Taxation The Role of Incentives*, appendix (4), and p. 184, Pl 1755, Stationery Office, Dublin, 1984.
[26] One of the main companies to benefit from these changes at the Shannon Free Airport zone was Guiness Peat Aviation. See *Irish Times* 30th June, 1981 and *Irish Times* 14th April, 1984.
[27] N. Kaldor, 'Economics of the Selective Employment Tax', pp. 224-225 in *Reports on Taxation* vol. I, Duckworth, London, 1980.
[28] N. Kaldor, ibid, p. 229.
[29] Commission on Taxation, Second Report,1984, op. cit. p. 51
[30] A market has also developed for the purchase and sale of companies entitled to claim export tax relief.
[31] Commission on Taxation, First Report, 1982 , op. cit. p. 387.
[32] Commission on Taxation, ibid., p. 333.
[33] ibid., p. 332.
[34] ibid., p. 550.
[35] Revenue Commissioners, op. cit. p. 15.
[36] Commission on Taxation, First Report, 1982, op.cit. p. 332.
[37] ibid. , pp. 333-334.
[38] A good example of this arrangement was the joint ownership of Fieldcrest Ltd., a company which manufactured towels in Ireland, and is now in liquidation, by the Bank of Ireland, Carroll Industries - a cigarette manufacturer, and Fieldcrest Mills Inc., a United States based textile company.
[39] Allied Irish Banks, *Report on Attitudes of Overseas Companies Towards Investment in Ireland*, Dublin: Allied Irish Banks, 1981, and Industrial Development Authority, *Survey of Grant Aided Industry*, Stationery Office, Dublin, 1967.

[40] Y. Aharoni, *The Foreign Investment Decision Process*, Harvard Graduate School of Business, Boston, 1966, and Clark Joel, op. cit. 1971.
[41] L. Johansen, *Public Economics*, North-Holland, London, 1971, pp. 240-256.
[42] For this reason the *Review of Industrial Performance 1986*, Dublin, Stationery Office, 1987, gives some estimates of the cost of tax relief for what is defined as 'an Irish resident tax unit' (p. 91) and excludes 'general profit relief applying to income that generally flows abroad'. These costs are referrred to as 'minimum estimates'. However it may be the case that while not all tax expenditures represent a net cost to the State, they may represent the value of the subsidy required to ensure the establishment or location in Ireland of particular economic activities.
[43] National Planning Board, *Proposals for Plan 1984-87*, prl. 2309, Stationery Office, Dublin, 1984, pp. 213-215.
[44] Central Bank of Ireland, *Quarterly Bulletin*, September 1983, *Quarterly Bulletin*, Summer 1984, and *Annual Report* 1985, Table C3.
[45] Parliamentary Question of 18 January, 1984.
[46] ibid.
[47] See Commission on Taxation, *Second Report*, 1984, pp.164-169; National Economic and Social Council, *Regional Policy in Ireland: A Review*, Report no. 4, Prl. 4147, Stationery Office, Dublin, 1975, Appendix 1, Table A1, and Department of Finance, 1972, op. cit. p. 24. Some of the additional tax reliefs listed in these publications are:- (1) Tax relief on dividends and interest on certain stocks and shares of companies operating within the State. This tax relief was ended in February 1983; (2) Up to half the capital cost of providing electricity to manufacturing companies may be paid by the State to the Electricity Supply Board; (3) Grants may also be paidfor factory rents; (4) Local Authorities may grant rates remission on industrial premises; (5) Tax Relief on export sales was also granted to certain service companies operating from the Shannon Industrial Estate. A 10 per cent rate of tax also applies to these service companies.
[48] Parliamentary Question, December 7, 1983.
[49] See Department of Finance, 1972, op. cit. for a further discussion of the availability of accelerated depreciation allowances, especially, pp. 22-25.
[50] B. Carlsson, 'Industrial Subsidies in Sweden: Macro-Economic Effects and an International Comparison', *Journal of Industrial Economics*, vol. XXXII, 1983, pp. 1-24.
[51] These problems are further discussed in A.R. Prest, *How Much Subsidy ?*, IEA Research Monograph, no. 32, Institute of Economic Affairs, London, 1974.
[52] In this example exports to certain E.E.C. countries were routed through Switzerland in order to qualify for loans with a subsidised rate of interest, *The Guardian*, December 16th 1986.
[53] See *Review of Industrial Performance 1986*, op. cit. pp.32-38.

2 The selection of firms in the study

All firms in the private sector in Ireland may be classified as public or private. The most common distinction between a public and a private company is that a private company cannot have more than fifty shareholders. The 1963 Companies Act in Ireland, which is almost identical to the 1948 Companies Act in the United Kingdom , requires all public companies to file a Balance Sheet and a Profit and Loss Account for each accounting period with the Registrar of Companies. These documents are then made available for public inspection. During the period 1964-84 the number of public companies fell from 396 to 341[1].

2.1 The study population

The total population of public companies was used as a data source for this study, but the following categories were excluded:- (i) non trading companies; (ii) financial and investment companies; (iii) State - owned companies; (iv) subsidiaries of other public companies included in the study[2]; and (v) small companies, that is companies with an annual turnover of less than IR£ 1 million, or the sum of fixed plus net current assets plus short term borrowing less than IR£ 0.5 million in 1980. Lower cut off points were used for earlier years. Two other companies (Alliance and Dublin Gas Company and the Cork Gas Company) were also included from the year 1975 on, when their accounts were standardised with those of public companies. One company was omitted for the period 1976-84 (Smurfit Ltd.) and one for the period 1973-84 (R.T.D. Group). In the case of Smurfit Ltd. sales within Ireland amounted to less than one third of total sales and production within Ireland amounted to one-third of total production in the period 1976-84. Most of the production and sales of the R.T.D. Group were in the United Kingdom in the period 1973-84. Hence tax payments for these two companies are largely determined by factors other than the Irish fiscal system.

For purposes of calculating tax rates in Chapter 3 of this thesis, the study population was divided into two groups: (i) Irish or partly Irish owned companies, and (ii) wholly owned subsidiaries of multinational companies. This was done for two main reasons: first, the possibility of the artificial manipulation of profits by M.N.C.s. This might occur through the use of transfer pricing, which would in turn affect tax rates. Secondly, certain anomalies arose in relation to tax payments by subsidiaries of two oil companies included in the study (Irish Shell and Esso)[3].

By far the largest group of companies included in the study consisted of Irish or partially Irish owned companies. This is because very few wholly owned subsidiaries of M.N.C.s operating in Ireland are public companies, and are thus not obliged to publish any financial information. Those M.N.C. subsidiaries that are public companies, and hence included in this study, are all long established (pre 1964) and are public companies for a variety of reasons. For example some of those established before the repeal of the Control of Manufactures Acts in 1958 may have been obliged to sell a majority of ordinary shares to persons resident in Ireland[4]. Subsequent to the repeal of the Control of Manufactures Acts in 1958 some of these shares may have been repurchased in order to obtain majority control. Other M.N.C. subsidiaries as well as Irish owned companies issued securities which were traded on the Dublin Stock Exchange in order to benefit from a lower rate of tax on dividends or interest payments. This relief was first introduced in 1936 and was ended in 1983.

The study population thus consists of non-financial, Irish or partly Irish owned companies in the private sector, and a small group of non-financial wholly owned subsidiaries of multinational companies operating in Ireland. Most of the M.N.C.s included in the study, in contrast to other M.N.C.s which are located in Ireland, trade largely in the domestic economy. There was no instance where output was totally exported or supplied to an affiliate, but there were some examples of companies purchasing inputs from affiliates, such as the oil distribution companies. All the companies included in this study are listed in the appendix to this chapter.

Data was obtained from the published accounts of these companies for the period 1964-84 inclusive. The year 1964 was the first year of operation of the Companies Act (1963). Ireland operates on an April to April fiscal year and companies may choose their own accounting year end date, although the most common year end date was December 31st followed by March 31st. There are also some sector specific year end dates for company accounts, for example January 31st for retail stores, and October 31st for companies involved in milling and the storage of grain. The following rule of thumb was used in allocating company accounts to different year end dates. A company whose accounting year ended between January 1st and June 30th was attributed to the preceding calendar year, and a company whose accounting year ends between July 1st and December 31st was attributed to the current calendar year[5]. For more recent years approximately half of all companies included ended their accounting year on December 31st, although in general these companies accounted for more than half of the total pre-tax profits of the study group as a whole. Table 2.1 shows the percentage of companies ending their accounting year on December 31st, and the percentage of pre-tax profits accounted for by these companies for the seven years 1978-84.

Table 2.1
The proportion of companies ending their accounting year on December 31st for the years 1978-84

Year	1978	1979	1980	1981	1982	1983	1984
Percentage of Companies	46.5	45.8	47.9	49.4	50.0	52.8	50.0
Percentage of Pre tax Profit	56.5	61.3	62.9	56.3	52.8	46.2	49.7

2.2 Profits and employment of the study group compared with aggregate profits and employment

Table 2.2 shows net earnings (profits after tax) of the study group compared with net earnings of U.K. and U.S. companies direct investment in Ireland for the period 1973-84. The year 1973 was the first year for which data relating to the profits of U.S. firms in Ireland was published. Table 2.2 shows that net earnings of the study group approximately doubled over the period 1973-79 to IR£ 93.48 million, and then fell in the period 1980-83 before recovering slightly in 1984. The profits of U.K. owned firms increased approximately three times in the period 1973-79 to IR£ 96.4 million, reached a peak in 1981 of IR£ 129.8 million and have fallen since then, but the profits of U.S. direct investment increased approximately six times in the period 1973-79 to IR£ 191.1 million and amounted to IR£ 969.2 million in 1984. Another point of interest is that aggregate profits of the study group have fluctuated to a greater extent than aggregate profits of U.S. or U.K. firms operating in Ireland. Between 58 per cent and 75 per cent of the net earnings of U.K. companies arose from manufacturing activities. The Food, Drink, and Tobacco sector accounted for between 31 per cent and 47 per cent of net earnings, of which the largest single component is likely to be the profits of Guinness (Ireland). In contrast manufacturing accounts for almost all of the earnings of U.S. firms in Ireland. The Chemical and Allied Products sector accounted for between 62 per cent and 76 per cent of net earnings of U.S. firms in the period 1973-82 , 50 percent for 1983 and 47 per cent for 1984.

Table 2.2
Net earnings of companies in the study compared with net earnings of U.S and U.K. direct investment in Ireland 1973-84
IR£ million[a]

Year	1973	1974	1975	1976	1977	1978	1979	1980	1981	1982	1983	1984
Irish[a] or Partly Irish owned	50.49	28.88	26.58	48.03	55.97	74.45	94.57	56.86	68.92	46.79	44.52	63.21
Foreign[b] owned companies	1.65	3.43	3.90	2.05	16.42	14.48	15.03	15.67	-2.34	4.83	11.42	7.20
Study Group Total	52.14	32.31	30.48	50.08	72.39	88.93	109.60	72.53	66.58	51.62	55.94	70.41
U.K[c] Direct Investment	34.1	33.7	48.7	59.0	64.6	86.0	96.4	101.2	129.8	110.7	72.2	76.7
U.S.[d] Direct Investment	33.2	42.1	71.2	106.9	157.0	149.0	191.1	209.0	330.2	443.9	668.7	969.2

Notes to Table 2.2

(a) Both Sterling and the U.S. dollar were converted into Irish Pounds at the average market rate in December of each year.

(b) Defined as pre-tax profits minus cash tax payments, minus the share of associated company profits.

(c) Excluding oil companies up to 1983. Defined as U.K. companies share of overseas subsidiaries and associated net profits, plus interest received plus net profits of branches overseas, and after deducting depreciation and overseas tax on dividends.

(d) Defined as the U.S. parent firm's equity in the net income (after foreign income tax) of their foreign affiliates plus net interest received on intracompany accounts, less withholding taxes on dividends and interest.

Sources:- Business Monitor MA4, London: H.M.S.O.; Survey of Current Business, various issues Department of Commerce of the United States, Washington.

Most of the firms included in this study were engaged in manufacturing activities, and there was a general trend over the period 1964-84 for the non-manufacturing firms to diversify into manufacturing activities. For the year 1984, out of 66 companies included, only 12 companies (18 per cent) appeared not to engage in some manufacturing activity. This compares with 33 companies out of 132 (25 per cent) in 1964. Four of the 12 companies were involved in hotels and travel, three companies in property, two in hardware merchandise, one company in oil distribution, one in leasing/hiring office equipment and one in auctioneering. The largest single grouping of firms was in food, drink and agriculture related industries with 18 firms. Many firms during the study period diversified into other manufacturing sectors, and in some cases from manufacturing into distribution, for example Waterford Glass. Similarly, some firms engaged in non-manufacturing activities diversified into manufacturing activites, for example Arnotts, a department store.

The population of non-financial public companies on which this study is based has also changed considerably during the period 1964-84 as a result of new public companies, mergers, takeovers and liquidations. During the period 1964-84, 70 of the companies included in the study either merged with, or were taken over by other companies[6]. Of these 70 companies, 37 companies were taken over or merged with existing public companies. Twenty-nine companies went into liquidation or had receivers appointed, of which nine were textile companies. There were 24 new public quoted companies. As a result of these changes there has been a considerable reduction in the number of public companies, and, as can be seen from Table 2.3, a reduction in the number of companies included in the study population from 116 in 1973 to 66 in 1984. During the period 1964-72 the number of companies included rose from 133 in 1964 to 144 in 1967 and then fell to 116 in 1973.

Table 2.3 shows that the study group accounts for a diminishing proportion of total corporate trading profits in Ireland. Trading profits are defined in Table 2.3 as pre-tax profits plus interest payments. Trading profits of the study group fell from approximately 26 per cent of aggregate trading profits in 1973 to 5.8 per cent in 1984, although with some fluctuation from year to year. As not all companies in the study disclose interest payments, trading profits for the study group are underestimated particularly for the earlier years (1973 and 1974). In addition some companies in the study group have subsidiaries operating in other countries, and hence trading profits of the study group include profits of subsidiaries operating abroad, whereas aggregate Irish data excludes profits of subsidiaries operating abroad. These errors may be compounded by another error, as aggregate trading profits are estimated using depreciation for tax purposes, rather than historic cost depreciation. Depreciation for tax purposes includes accelerated depreciation, and is likely to be considerably greater than depreciation calculated according to historic cost conventions. However recent revisions to trading profits in the National Accounts for the period 1975-82 may have corrected for this and other factors.

For the year 1964 pre-tax profits of the study group (excluding interest payments) amounted to approximately 25 per cent of total trading profits in Ireland, (the highest proportion for any of the years 1964 to 1984). Hence it is likely that trading profits of the study group (pre-tax profits plus interest payments) as a proportion of total trading profits in Ireland was at its highest point at the beginning of the period 1964-84 and gradually declined throughout the period.

Table 2.3
Trading profits of companies in the study compared with aggregate trading profits in Ireland 1973-84

IR£ million

Year	1973	1974	1975	1976	1977	1978	1979	1980	1981	1982	1983	1984
Trading[a] Profits of Study Group	73.7	70.1	62.2	78.0	104.1	123.8	165.3	143.0	137.3	120.6	114.8	123.3
Number of Companies Included	116	117	113	109	103	99	96	94	85	78	72	66
Trading[b] Profits of all Companies in Ireland	278.4	325.8	375.6	537.1	721.7	865.8	1008.2	973.6	1369.5	1511.2	1784.6	2107.0
Trading Profits of Study Group as a Percentage of Total Trading Profits	26.5	21.5	16.6	14.5	14.4	14.3	16.4	14.7	10.0	9.1	6.4	5.8

Notes to Table 2.3

(a) Defined as pre-tax profits plus interest payments. Pre-tax profits have been arrived at by deducting depreciation calculated according to historic cost conventions.

(b) Defined as pre-tax profits plus interest payments. Pre-tax profits have been arrived at by deducting depreciation allowances calculated for tax purposes. This figure also excludes overseas earnings of Irish subsidiaries operating abroad.

Sources:- National Income and Expenditure 1979 and 1985, Stationery Office, Dublin, 1981 and 1986, Table A.1.

Finally to conclude this description of the study population, Table 2.4 shows the numbers employed by firms in the study group for the three years 1978-84, and the total numbers at work in Ireland for comparative purposes.

Table 2.4
Numbers employed by the study group and percentage of aggregate employment
'000

Year	1978	1979	1980	1981	1982	1983	1984
Numbers Employed by wholly owned M.N.C.s in the study	5.7	5.8	5.2	4.7	4.6	4.3	3.6
Total Numbers Employed by the Study Group	69.4	66.8	62.9	55.5	52.6	47.4	42.9
Percentage of Aggregate Employment	6.2	5.8	5.4	4.8	4.6	4.2	3.9

Sources:- Numbers employed by firms in the study group was obtained from the Annual Reports of Companies, and also from Irish Business, January 1979-85, Irish Financial Publications Ltd. Dublin, Data on aggregate employment were obtained from Department of Finance, Economic Review and Outlook for 1983, and 1986, Stationery Office, Dublin, 1983 and 1986.

Table 2.4 shows that companies in the study accounted for approximately 3.9 per cent of the total employment for 1984[7]. Over the seven years 1978-84 the percentage of total employment and the total numbers employed by firms in the study has fallen. Although employment data are not available for all firms for all years, the study group appears to account for a falling share of total employment also in the years 1964-77.

Table 2.5 shows employment for 20 firms in the study which were in continuous existence for the period 1964-84. In addition a further seven firms which were taken over or merged with these firms are also included. Table 2.5 shows that employment rose in the years 1965-70, fell from 1970-75, rose again from 1975-80 and then fell in the year 1980-84. However the rise in employment between 1965 and 1970 is partly accounted for by takeovers of existing firms, rather than new investment, while the rise in employment between 1975 and 1980 is partly accounted for by firms in this sub group investing outside Ireland (for example Cement Roadstone). It is also of interest to note that these 20 firms received IR£ 52.4 million in grants for investment in fixed assets in the period to 1984.

Table 2.5
Employment for 20 firms in the study for 1965-84

Year	1965[a]	1970	1975[b]	1980[c]	1984
Employment	25581	33877	31231	33768	27190
Accumulated Grants (£ million)	1.219	6.493	15.044	31.483	52.418

Notes to Table 2.5
(a) Includes data for one firm for 1966
(b) Includes data for one firm for 1976
(c) Includes data for one firm for 1981
Source:- Annual Reports of Companies and the Annual Survey of Public Companies, published by the Irish Times.

In conclusion there has been a considerable change in the population of non-financial public companies over the period 1964-84. The three main features of this change are:- (1) Diversification mostly through merger and takeover of other companies, but in some cases by investing abroad; (2) the closure of firms operating in the traditional sectors such as textiles, and in other sectors formerly protected by tariffs, such as car assembly; (3) a reduction in the relative importance of non-financial public companies, whether expressed in terms of profits or employment.

The next chapter examines further the definition of profits and the trend in tax rates over the period under examination.

Notes

[1] Sources:- *Companies General Annual Report for 1964* and 1984, Department of Industry and Commerce, Stationery Office, Dublin.

[2] In two cases subsidiaries of other public companies were included and the parent excluded. In one case (Thwaites), this was due to extensive operations in the U.K. by the parent (E. & J. Bourke) and in the other (Associated Properties) due to the absense of consolidated accounts with the parent company (Estates Development) until 1975, at which point the parent was included. One company was omittted entirely, because statutory requirements in relation to disclosure of certain data required for this study, were not complied with (South of Ireland Asphalt Company).

[3] The possible use of transfer pricing and other aspects of the financial behaviour of M.N.C.s included in this study are examined in J. Stewart, 'Some Aspects of the Financial Behaviour of Multinational Companies in Ireland' in J. Kelly and J. FitzPatrick (eds.) *Perspectives on Irish Industry*, Irish Management Institute, Dublin, 1986, and in J. Stewart, 'A Study of the Financing of Multinational Companies in Ireland 1964-1980', *Irish Business and Administrative Research*, vol. 4, no. 2, 1982, pp. 72-86.

[4] It was also possible to obtain an exemption from the Control of Manufacturers Acts. A more detailed discussion of why these companies are public companies is contained in J. Stewart, ibid, p. 73.

[5] Adopting the Department of Industry convention for U.K. companies would result in almost the same allocation of firms to different calendar years. See M.A. King, *Public Policy and the Corporation*, Chapman and Hall, London, 1975 p. 278 for a description of this convention, or A. Singh and G. Whittington, *Growth, Profitability and Valuation*, Cambridge University Press, Cambridge, 1968, appendix A.

[6] A takeover was defined as a change in ownership, rather than the purchase by an existing majority shareholder of the remainder of the ordinary shares.

[7] This figure is a slight over-estimate as a number of firms have subsidiaries operating outside the Republic.

Appendix 1

Firms included in the study and the years for which they are included

(a) *Irish or partly Irish owned*

	Years Included	Sector
Abbey	1972-84	Construction
Abbey Clothing	1965-76	Clothing Manufacturer
Alliance and Dublin Gas	1973-84	Town Gas Supply
Arklow Pottery	1964-77	Manufacture of Pottery
Arnott	1963-82	Retailing
Ashtown Tinbox (Ireland)	1968-75	Tin Box Manufacture
Associated Properties	1964-74	Property Company
Autozero	1969	Cold Storage
Bacon Company of Ireland	1964-84	Bacon Processing
Barrow Milling Ltd.	1964-82	Flour Milling
Batchelors	1963-69	Food Processing
Bellville Holdings	1966-81	Manufacture of Fertilizers
Bolands	1963-75	Flour Milling
Booth Pool	1964-68	Car Assembly & Distribution
J. & G. Boyd	1964-84	Hardware Merchandise
Braids	1964-84	Joinery Manufacturer
Brittain	1971-74	Car Assembly
Brooks Watson	1963-82	Builders Provider
Brown Thomas	1964-82	Retailing
Browne & Nolan	1964-68	Printing & Publishing
P.C. Cahill	1963-71	Wholesale Chemists
Cannock & Co.	1963-81	Retailing
Carrigaline Pottery Co.	1963-77	Manufacture of Pottery
Carroll Industries	1963-84	Cigarette Manufacturer
Castle Brand	1965-82	Manufacture of Kitchen Utensils
Castlebar Bacon Co.	1963-84	Bacon Processing
Castle Guard Textiles	1964	Cotton Spinning
Cement Roadstone	1964-84	Construction Materials
Chipboard	1963-78	Manufacture of Wood Products
Clarence Hotels	1963-84	Hotels
Clondalkin paper	1964-84	Packaging Materials Manufacturer
Concrete Products of Ireland	1966-84	Builders Providers
Convoy Woollen Co.	1963-84	Manufacture of Woollen Goods
Cork Gas Company	1976-84	Town Gas Supply
James Crean	1964-84	Wholesale Distributor
Creation Group	1968-72	Printing & Publishing

Crowe Wilson	1965-71	Wholesale Drapery Distribution
John Daly & Co.	1963-71	Mineral Water Manufacturers
Dinan Dowdall	1963-67	Builders Providers
Dock Milling Group	1965-84	Flour Milling
Thomas Dockrell	1963-71	Builders Providers
J. Donohoe	1965-80	Mineral Water Manufacturers
Doreen Holdings	1968-82	Manufacture of Clothing
W. Drummond and Sons	1963-72	Seed Merchant
Dublin Artisans Dwellings	1964-82	Property Company
Dublin & Central Properties	1963-76	Property Company
Dubtex Clothing	1964-78	Clothing Manufacturer
Dunloe House Group	1965-84	Clothing Manufacturer
Dungarvan Leathers	1963-72	Manufacture of Leather
Dwyer	1964-84	Property Company (formerly clothing manufacturer)
Edenderry Shoe Company	1964-84	Manufacture of Footwear
Elan	1979-84	Drug development
Erin Peat Products	1963-75	Manufacturers of Garden Products
Estates Development	1975-84	Property Company
Ever Ready	1963-76	Distributor of Car Parts
Ferrier Pollock	1964-78	Wholesale Drapers
Findlater	1963-67	Food & Drink Retailing
Fine Wool Fabrics	1963-70	Clothing Manufacturer
Fitzwilton	1964-84	Investment Holding Company
Flogas	1979-84	Distribution of Bottled Gas
Freedex	1964-71	Manufacture of Handbags
Fruit Importers of Ireland	1977-84	Fruit Importer
Gibson Guy & Smallridge	1965-67	Manufacture of Packaging
Glen Abbey	1964-84	Clothing Manufacturer
R. & J. Goff	1974-84	Bloodstock Auctioneering
J. & L.F. Goodbody	1964-81	Manufacture of Plastic Bags
Graves & Company	1964-70	Builders Providers
Green Group	1965-77	Cinema & Property Company
Green Property Company	1978-84	Property Company
Greenmount & Boyne	1965-74	Manufacture of Linen Goods
Gresham Hotel	1964-74	Hotel
R. & H. Hall	1963-84	Cereal Storage and Transport
John Halliday	1964-70	Manufacture of Footwear
Hammond Holdings	1964-76	Scrap Metal
Harcourt Irish Holdings	1963-80	Manufacture of Metal Springs
Harringtons & Goodlass Wall	1963-76	Paint Manufacturer
Hayes, Cunningham & Robinson	1963-71	Retailer Chemists
Heiton Holdings	1965-84	Builders Providers

Hely Group	1964-69	Printing and Packaging
I.C.P.	1979-84	Drug Testing
I.W.P.M. Holdings	1964-80	Wallpaper Manufacturer
Independent Newspapers	1964-84	Newspaper Publishers
Irish Distillers	1963-84	Distilling
Irish Dunlop	1963-70	Manufacture of Tyres
Irish Glass Bottle Co.	1964-84	Manufacture of Glass Containers
Irish International Trading Co.	1964-84	Hardware Merchandise
Irish Leathers	1964-82	Manufacturers of Leather
Irish Oil & Cake Mills	1963-82	Margarine Manufacturers
Irish Pharmaceuticals	1966-79	Manufacture of Pharmaceuticals
Irish Press	1965-84	Newspaper Publishing
Irish Ropes	1964-84	Manufacture of Carpets
Irish Tanners	1964-68	Manufacture of Leather
Irish Times	1963-72	Newspaper Publisher
Irish Wire Products	1964-84	Manufacture of Nails & Screws
Irish Worsted Mills	1963-70	Manufacturers of Cloth
W. & R. Jacob	1964-84	Manufacture of Biscuits
Jameson Ltd.	1965	Distilling
Janelle Ltd.	1973-80	Clothes Manufacturer
Jones Group	1973-84	Shipping and Engineering
Jurys Hotel Group	1981-84	Hotels
Kilkenny Engineering	1967-71	Manufacture of Farm Equipment
Edward Lee & Co.	1975-77	Retailing
Leethems (Ireland)	1964-72	Clothing Manufacturer
Lyons Irish Holdings	1963-84	Wholesale Tea & Cake Manufacturer
McBirney	1963-73	Retailing
McCairns	1964-82	Vehicle Distribution
McFerran & Guilford	1963-64	Builders Providers
McInerny	1971-82	Construction
Maguire & Paterson	1963-79	Manufacture of Matches
T. & C. Martin	1963-66	Builders Providers
Martin Mahony	1963-73	Clothing Manufacturer
Massers Waterford Iron Founders	1963-74	Iron founders
May Roberts	1963-69	Wholesale Chemists
Mayco	1965-76	Toy Manufacturer
Memory Computers	1978-84	Computer System Design
Merchants Warehousing	1964-84	Cold Storage & Warehousing
Metal Products (Cork)	1963-81	Manufacture of Fasteners
Milford (Donegal)	1964-84	Flour Milling
A.Millar & Co.	1965-80	Tea, Wine & Spirit Merchants
Minch Norton	1963-84	Mallsters & Grain Merchants

Monsell Mitchell	1964-69	Builders Providers
Mooney	1965-77	Public Houses
Moore Holdings	1964-73	Manufacture of Clothing
Murdochs	1963-69	Hardwear Merchandise
J.J. Murphy	1976-80	Brewery
Navan Carpets	1968-71	Manufacture of Carpets
Newbridge Holdings	1963-71	Manufacture of Cutlery
Norish	1980-84	Cold Storage
John C. Parkes	1963-77	Hardware Merchandise
Peterson Tennant	1964-81	Food Distributor
Pye (Ireland)	1963-81	Distributor of Electrical goods
R.T.D. Group	1971-72	Distribution of Car Parts
Ranks (Ireland)	1964-82	Flour Milling
Rawson	1964-66	Manufacture of Footwear
Readymix	1967-84	Construction Materials Manufacturer
Roadstone	1964-69	Quarrying & Road Construction
Rohan Group	1971-84	Construction
Salts	1964	Worsted Spinners
Seafield Gentex	1965-84	Textiles manufacturer
Shannon Meats	1964-84	Meat Processing
Smith & Pearson	1964-76	Structural Steelwork
Smith Group	1963-73	Car Distributor
Smurfit	1964-75	Packaging Materials
Smyth & Company	1963-78	Clothing Manufacturer
Solus Teoranta	1963-80	Manufacture of Light Bulbs
Sunbeam Wolsey	1963-84	Knitwear Manufacturer
Swan Ryan International	1965-84	Hotels and Tourism
Swift Brook Paper Mills	1964-68	Manufacture of Paper
Switzer	1964-70	Department Stores
T.M.G.	1963-82	Iron Foundry
Temple Press	1964-66	Printing
Thwaites	1965-67	Mineral Water Manufacturer
Torc Manufacturing	1964-72	Manufacture of Office Equipment
Trimproof	1967-69	Manufacture of Clothing
Unidare	1964-84	Manufacture of Cables
United Drug & Chemical Company	1963-72	Pharmaceutical Manufacturer
Wardell, Roberts (formerly Baker Wardell)	1965-84	Tea Merchants
Waterford Glass	1968-84	Crystal Glass Manufacturer
Joshua Watson	1964-71	Malting

Williams & Woods	1964-75	Manufacturers of Food Products
Williams (H.)	1964-80	Supermarket Chain
Woodchester Investments	1979-84	Leasing & Rental of Office goods
J.H. Woodington	1963-84	Manufacture of Footwear
Youghal Carpets	1964-84	Carpet Manufacturer

(b) *Wholly owned subsidiaries included*

A.C.E.C.	1963- 84	Manufacture of Electrical goods
Batchelors	1970-79	Food Processing
Beamish & Crawford	1963-84	Brewery
Bovril	1963-80	Wholesale Food Distributor
Butlins	1963-84	Tourism
Cadbury (Ireland)	1963-84	Chocolate Manufacturer
Esso	1963-83	Oil Distributor
Fullers	1963-71	Caterers & Confectioners
Gypsum Industries	1963-84	Building Materials Manufacturer
H.B. Chocolates	1973-75	Manufacture of Chocolate
Irish Board Mills	1963-76	Timber Products
Irish Refining Company	1963-81	Refining
Irish Shell	1963-84	Oil Distribution
Jeyes (Ireland)	1963-71	Cleaning Products Manufacturer
Millar & Beatty	1975-77	Retailing
Mining Company of Ireland & Strachan Brothers	1965-80	Import & Sale of Lead Products
Nicholas Laboratories	1964-80	Wholesale Chemists
Odeon (Ireland)	1963-75	Cinemas
Rowntree-MacKintosh	1964-84	Manufacture of Chocolate Products

3 Effective direct tax rates on profits

Considerable controversy surrounds the measurement of profit in company accounts. Continuous inflation has underlined some of the problems involved. Current accounting practice in the United Kingdom and Ireland, also obscures the amount of direct tax that companies pay. Kay and King comment:- 'that the fact that many companies pay little or no tax is often not evident from their published company accounts. Some companies show substantial tax charges in their accounts when in fact they are paying little or no tax at all'[1]. A similar comment applies to Irish companies as accounting standards in Ireland closely follow those in the United Kingdom. In addition many features of United Kingdom Finance Acts are incorporated in to subsequent Irish Finance Acts. A combination of differing or controversial measures of profit and obscure reporting of tax paid makes the calculation of tax rates on profits for the corporate sector a difficult if not arbitrary process.

This chapter attempts to estimate effective direct tax rates, calculated from the published accounts of Irish companies, during the period 1964-84. In the following discussion the expression 'effective tax rates' is used to contrast with nominal tax rates. Before discussing the measurement of effective tax rates the problem of the incidence of a tax should be noted. An estimate of direct tax payments by companies may not be the same as an estimate of the incidence of direct tax on companies. This is because companies may be able to shift the burden of tax through higher prices on their products, so that consumers of these products ultimately end up paying the tax. In other words the formal incidence of a tax may not be the same as the effective incidence. Indeed many economists would agree with Kay and King[2] that in the long run the formal incidence of a tax is irrelevant to its effective incidence. This may not be true in the short run. The traditional argument, as stated for example by Kaldor[3], was that to the extent that firms maximise profits, the formal incidence of a tax is equal to the effective incidence. Others have argued that oligopolistic behaviour rather than competitive behaviour is more normal in a modern economy. Hence the introduction of a profits tax may result in a general rise in prices. King[4] argues that the incidence of corporate tax in an economy dominated by oligopolies depends on a number of complex factors, such as the determinants of corporate investment, and is difficult to estimate. The difficulty of estimating the incidence of a tax is also emphasised by Atkinson and Stiglitz[5].

There have been a number of empirical investigations of the extent of short run shifting of corporation tax, not all of which are in agreement as to the extent to which short-run shifting takes place. For example, Dusansky[6] concludes that there is 100 per cent corporate tax shifting in the U.S.A. In contrast Oakland[7] found no evidence of short-run shifting of corporation taxes in the U.S.A. Both studies relate to similar time periods and use similar data. A study by Davis[8] found no evidence of short-run shifting of corporate taxes in the United Kingdom. Prest and Barr[9] conclude that the opportunites for short-run shifting are much less in a relatively open economy such as the United Kingdom, than in the United States. A similar argument can be applied to the Irish economy. Irrespective of the degree of shifting which may occur, the formal incidence of a tax is still useful in examining various aspects of the corporate sector, for example, the absolute amount of corporate retentions, and hence corporate saving rates. The formal incidence of a tax becomes even more useful in an analysis of the effects of taxation, if there is little or no shifting of corporate taxes.

Before describing how tax rates are measured in this chapter, some differing approaches to measuring tax rates are first discussed.

3.1 Alternative approaches to measuring effective tax rates

A recent study of effective tax rates comments that 'there are several different concepts of effective tax rate'[10]. Fullerton[11] categorises studies of effective tax rates into four basic types. The first two types identified by Fullerton are average tax rates on (a) corporate income and (b) total capital income. The other two types are marginal tax rates on (a) corporate income and (b) income from capital. Auerbach[12] uses a similar classification, namely into (a) those based on cost of capital studies which are used to estimate marginal tax rates and (b) those based on historic flows of taxes, profits, etc. A study by King, Fullerton and others[13] describes the average approach as backward looking whereas the marginal approach is forward looking. Both approaches have their uses. Fullerton, for example, says that average effective tax rates may be used to estimate 'the reduction in taxes associated with accelerated depreciation and the investment tax credit'. However both Auerbach and Fullerton[14] argue that the average approach may not provide a good indication of the incentive to undertake new investment, whereas the marginal approach may do so. There may also be no necessary correlation between marginal and average tax rates. For example a firm with low investment in the past would have higher average tax rates than a firm with recent high net investment, but the marginal tax rate on new investment could be the same. A study by Henderson and Fullerton[15] found that average and marginal tax rates calculated for eighteen industries in the U.S. for the period 1973-76 had almost zero correlation. Fullerton also cites a study by Hulten and Robertson of aggregate marginal and average corporate tax rates in the U.S., for the period 1950-85, which found that the graph of average and marginal tax rates frequently crosses[16]. However more recently Gravelle argues that marginal tax rates are always below average tax rates for the same period, and furthermore that marginal tax rates for recent years have been zero[17].

There are a number of difficulties involved in estimating marginal effective tax rates, for example the margin needs to be carefully defined. Different definitions will produce different tax rates, for such as, a marginal change in the rate of return, or the interest rate. In a four country study by King, Fullerton and others[18] discussed later in this chapter the margin is defined as 'a small increase in the level of real investment in the domestic nonfinancial corporate sector, financed by an increase in the savings of domestic households'. Effective tax rates were then calculated assuming a fixed rate of return on investment and alternative tax rates were calculated assuming a fixed real interest rate.

It is also likely that the marginal tax rate on an identical investment for two firms is different, depending, for example, on the existence of accumulated tax allowances, the gearing ratio, and in the U.K. and Ireland, the location of the investment. Indeed Auerbach comments[19] that effective marginal tax rates may differ across investments. Hence each firm may face a different marginal effective tax rate. Under these circumstances calculating an industry, or asset specific, marginal tax rate may also be an inaccurate predictor of marginal tax rates on new investment. The estimated average marginal tax rate may be such that no new investment is predicted to take place, yet particular circumstances for individual firms may result in net new investment.

Finally studies of marginal effective tax rates by, for example, King, Fullerton and others depend on the existing distribution of type of asset, type of finance, and the source of finance. To the extent that these change, the estimated average marginal tax rate will also change. King and Fullerton[20] say 'the associated mean tax rate may not be the actual future tax rates to be expected in a country which is changing the pattern of its capital stock'. Their study also assumes that all relevant tax allowances are claimed[21].

Apart from predicting the marginal tax rates on new investment, calculating average effective tax rates has other useful functions, for example estimating corporate retentions, or examining flows of funds in the corporate sector, as is done in Chapter 7 of this book. Average tax rates and aggregate tax payments are also useful in examining Government tax

...RSITY COLLEGE Library

revenues, and the cost of various fiscal incentives. In this latter context calculating average effective tax rates and hence aggregate tax payments, using historical cost data, may be more useful than marginal tax rates. The approach adopted in this chapter is based on historical profits and tax payments, which are used to calculate average effective tax rates across all firms, and in Chapter 5 the distribution of tax rates for firms in the study.

Within this general approach there are two main alternatives in estimating effective tax rates for the corporate sector:-

(1) The aggregate or macro level approach using aggregate data to estimate both the tax base and tax payments;

(2) The company or micro level approach which attempts to estimate tax rates for individual companies. This is the approach adopted in this chapter.

Within these two approaches there are a number of variations, and the following summary will attempt to highlight these differences. There are four studies reviewed here which use the aggregate approach, that is those by Rosenberg, Siegfried, Feldstein and Summers, and Feldstein, Dicks-Mireaux and Poterba[22].

Rosenberg calculates tax rates on income from capital for the non-financial sector of the United States for the years 1953-59. Rosenberg argues that the most meaningful definition of income to use as the tax base would be 'the maximum that could be consumed in a given period consistent with the maintenance of wealth or of income potential'. Taxable income, that is the tax base, is defined to include income attributable to equity shareholders plus net interest received plus net rent and capital gains realised. Aggregate tax payments are then estimated from a variety of published sources in order to calculate tax rates (T/P) for various sectors. The average tax rate for all sectors was found to be 37.27 per cent for the period 1953-59, but there was considerable intersectoral variation in tax rates. Within the corporate sector, the two sectors petroleum and coal products and lumber and wood products had the lowest tax rates at 25.43 per cent and 28.69 per cent respectively[23].

Siegfried performed a similar study for the United States for 1963 for the mining and manufacturing sectors. Rather than compute one tax ratio (T/P) for all sectors and for each individual sector, Siegfried calculated six different tax rates in which various adjustments were made to both the tax base, P and taxes paid, T. These various definitions of the tax base P were obtained by adding to 'true accounting profits' the 'reduction in taxable income arising from special tax provisions'[24]. Again considerable intersectoral variation in tax rates was found. The coal mining and petroleum sectors were found to have the lowest tax rates for various definitions of T and P. Siegfried concludes by suggesting a number of applications of the tax rates developed, for example, to indicate the effect of various subsidies.

Feldstein and Summers focus particularly on the effects of inflation in estimating aggregate tax payments, and tax rates (T/P), for the non-financial corporate sector in the United States for 1974. In addition tax rates (T/P) are estimated for a more limited group of 327 large manufacturing companies for 1976. Feldstein and Summers differ from the previous two studies discussed in (a) emphasising the effects of inflation by, for example, making adjustments for depreciation and inventory profits; and (b) emphasising that all taxes on corporate sector income should be included. They state[25] that 'it is important to look through the corporation to the individuals and institutions that provide the equity and debt capital' and hence tax paid by the owners of corporate securities and corporate debt, and capital gains paid by equity owners is included in the tax base P. Rosenberg included tax on interest receipts and tax on capital gains in T, Feldstein and Summers allow for different tax rates amongst owners of equity capital, for example financial institutions, and also for an effective reduction in capital gains tax, due to the taxation of realised capital gains rather than accrued capital gains. Feldstein and Summers conclude that the effect of inflation was to raise the effective tax rate in the non-financial corporate sector from 43 per cent to 66 per cent in 1977, and that this increase in tax rates was likely to have reduced the rate of capital formation. These results are discussed further in Chapter 4 which deals with inflation adjustments.

In a more recent study of U.S. non-financial corporations, Feldstein, Dicks-Mireaux and Poterba estimate effective tax rates for the period 1953-79. This study in contrast to previous studies includes property tax[26]. The tax rates estimated include tax paid by corporations, and as in the previous study by Feldstein and Summers, tax payments by their shareholders and creditors other than the Government. Total income is defined as the sum of corporate interest payments, corporate profits adjusted for capital depreciation and stock appreciation. Total effective tax rates varied between 65 per cent and 75 per cent for the period 1953-61, varied between 53 and 64 per cent in the period 1962-68, and varied between 66 and 84 per cent in the period 1969-79. In general the highest tax rates were found to be associated with periods of peak inflation.

Although the study by King, Fullerton and others is a study of marginal effective tax rates on saving and investing, they also calculate average effective tax rates for U.S. non-financial corporations for the period 1978-80. The study by King, Fullerton and others also stresses the need to consider the taxation of interest and the interactions between personal taxation and corporate taxation. However they estimate the average effective tax rate at 58.5 per cent compared with 69.4 per cent for Feldstein, Dicks-Mireaux and Poterba for 1979. The difference is partly explained by improved data[27] and also by some differences in methodology, for example services from banks are treated as tax-free income to bank depositors and capital gains tax on nominal capital gains is treated differently. The study by King, Fullerton and others found marginal tax rates varying from 37 per cent to 50 per cent for the U.S. depending on the chosen assumptions; for example, the rate of return on assets. Finally the King and Fullerton study found considerable variation in marginal effective tax rates for the four countries examined. If a fixed rate of return on investment of 10 per cent were assumed, marginal effective tax rates were found to be 3.7 per cent for the U.K., 37.2 per cent for the U.S., 35.6 per cent in Sweden, and 48.1 per cent in W. Germany[28].

A second approach to measuring average effective tax rates in the corporate sector is to attempt to measure tax rates for each individual firm. One method of doing this has been described by Mayer and Morris[29] for the United Kingdom tax system. Mayer and Morris have developed a model of the United Kingdom tax system incorporating rates of tax, depreciation allowances and other relevant variables. When used in conjunction with published accounting information, the model may be used to estimate current tax liabilities, and hence tax payments. Mayer argues that a model of the tax system is neccessary to estimate tax payments because of the difficulty of extracting information from company accounts. Mayer says:-

> 'It may be surprising to those readers unfamiliar with company accounts to be told that a model of the tax system is required to determine the distribution of tax payments across companies. For those who have tried to extract information of tax liabilities from company statements little justification will be required for effectively ignoring published data in establishing distributions'[30].

Using this approach, aggregate tax payments for the corporate sector in time period t may be estimated by summing tax payments, and taxable profits across all firms $\sum_{i=1}^{n} T_{it} / \sum_{i=1}^{n} P_{it}$, where n is the number of firms.

The method of measuring tax payments proposed by Mayer and Morris may be regarded as an alternative to that developed in this chapter, and hence it is worth examining some possible benefits and problems that may arise from this approach.

(1) The first problem is that Mayer and Morris focus only on Mainstream Corporation Tax. Advance Corporation Tax is treated as a tax on the personal sector only. That is, no attempt is made to look through the corporation to estimate the tax liabilities of the providers of capital to the corporate sector. The accounting treatment of tax liabilities in company accounts does not in general distinguish between Mainstream Corporation Tax and Advance Corporation Tax. Hence if it is thought desirable to estimate Mainstream Corporation Tax liabilities only, a model of some sort is required. However if the focus of interest is total corporate tax payments on corporate profits paid by the company, that is including both Mainstream Corporation Tax and Advance Corporation Tax, corporate tax liabilities as published in company accounts may be used to estimate tax payments. This assumes companies disclose all tax liabilities whether deferred or not;

(2) The model developed by Mayer and Morris may provide only a crude estimate of cash tax payments (tax paid in cash by the firm) as the timing of tax payments is not considered. It may be assumed of course that all tax payments are made on the statutory dates. Further problems may arise if taxable profits and hence tax payments are subject to subsequent revisions due for example to changes in inventory valuations. This may result in unexplained changes in Balance Sheet tax liabilities; that is Balance Sheet tax liabilities reported in time period t may differ from those reported in time

period t + 1 for period t;
(3) For these reasons the Mayer and Morris approach may not be very useful in estimating the effect of tax payments on corporate cash flows and corporate financing. This is particularly true of fiscal systems such as in Ireland up to 1983, where tax is deducted from dividends by corporations (= Advance Corporation Tax), but may not be paid to the Exchequer due to various allowances.

The Mayer and Morris approach also has certain advantages. For example:-
(1) Tax payments by a firm may be split into a number of different portions. The split between Mainstream Corporation Tax and Advance Corporation Tax has already been mentioned. Tax payments may also be split into those paid domestically as well as taxes paid abroad. This latter point may be particularly important in an economy with considerable investments abroad such as the United Kingdom;
(2) Tax Liabilities arising from various fiscal provisions may also be estimated. Hence the total value of various tax concessions may be estimated for each firm, or expressed in another way - the total tax foregone.

3.2 Measuring effective direct tax rates

This section describes firstly how tax payments are measured in this book. Secondly some differing concepts of profit are described, and finally estimates of effective direct tax rates are presented. Tax payments are estimated on a cash paid basis and are called 'cash tax payments' to differentiate them from the tax charge in the Profit and Loss Account. The tax charge in the Profit and Loss Account includes tax deferred due to accelerated depreciation, stock relief, etc. and also makes no allowance for lags in the collection of tax. Accelerated depreciation results in a portion of the tax charge, equal to the allowance for accelerated depreciation, to be deferred until some future period, thus resulting in a considerable divergence between the tax charge in the Profit and Loss Account and 'cash tax payments'. Recent accounting changes have reduced this discrepancy to a considerable extent for depreciation allowances, but not for other timing differences[31].

Since 1976 all companies include with their accounts a statement of Sources and Applications of funds[32] and some companies did so before 1976. 'Cash tax payments' are generally shown in such a statement. Where the figure was not shown in a Statement of Sources and Application of Funds, the amount was estimated according to the following procedure. An increase in Balance Sheet tax liabilities (deferred, future and current tax) was deducted, and a decrease in Balance Sheet tax liabilities was added, for each accounting period to the tax charge shown in the Profit and Loss Account. Stated more formally let T_t be the tax charge in the Profit and Loss Account in time period t, L_t total current Balance Sheet tax liabilities, and L_{t-1} Balance Sheet tax liabilities in the previous period. Then $(L_t - L_{t-1})$ = change in Balance Sheet tax liabilities, where the expression in brackets may be positive or negative. Tax payments in period t will then be = T_t - (L_t - L_{t-1}). Two further adjustments were also made:-

(1) An increase in future tax arising from revaluations was excluded from the calculation, as profits and tax liabilities arising from revaluations are generally excluded from profits and tax charges in company Profit and Loss Accounts;

(2) Tax charges attributable to associated companies were also excluded from the calculation, as such payments involve no cash outflow by the parent company.

The following example using the Accounts of the Clondalkin Mills Paper Group for 1977, illustrates the divergence between taxation as shown in the Profit and Loss Account and 'cash tax paid' and the procedure for estimating 'cash tax paid'. The 1977 Profit and Loss Account for Clondalkin Paper Mills showed the following amounts for profits before tax and tax due:-

	1977
Profits before taxation	£2,836,903
Taxation	£1,093,705

Profits after taxation	£1,743,198

Tax liabilities were shown in the Balance Sheet for 1977 and 1976 as follows:-

	1977	1976
Current Tax Liabilities	£1,422,469	£721,043
Deferred Taxation	£1,289,625	£1,298,800
	-------------	-------------
	£2,712,094	£2,019,843

Thus there was an increase in total tax liabilities of £692,251. This increase in tax liabilities (tax owing but not yet paid) was deducted from the tax charge in the Profit and Loss Account resulting in 'cash tax paid' of £401,454. This was the amount shown in the statement of Sources and Applications of Funds, of tax paid, for 1977.

Usually a 'cash tax payment' which is lower than the tax charge in the Profit and Loss Account results in an increase in Balance Sheet tax liabilities, and a 'cash tax payment' which is greater than the tax charge in the Profit and Loss Account is reflected in a reduction in Balance Sheet tax liabilities. However in a few cases changes in Balance Sheet tax liabilities will not be reflected in tax charges in the Profit and Loss Account, for example, where firms merged or took over another firm, or where subsidiaries were sold off, and so these firms were omitted for that year.

All tax payable by the company on behalf of shareholders is included. As such the 'cash tax payment' is a combination of company tax payments, and personal tax payments collected by the company on behalf of shareholders. Total tax payments on corporate profits may be higher than this amount depending on the proportion of shareolders who have marginal tax rates higher than the tax collected on their behalf by the firm, and lower depending on the number of shareholders who have marginal tax rates lower than this amount, for example pension funds and charitable trusts. Combining company tax payments and personal tax payments may be justified by the difficulty of identifying which portion of tax paid is due to precisely which tax provision, and because a division between the corporation and its shareholders may be of great legal significance, but is not necessarily of great significance in understanding corporate financial behaviour. As mentioned earlier Feldstein and Summers[33] also stress the importance of 'looking through' the corporation to suppliers of finance. They include tax payments by shareholders (on dividends and capital gains) and tax payments by lenders of finance when estimating the effects of inflation on corporate tax payments for the United States. Lawson and Clark[34] also focus on what is termed an 'entity' concept of profitability (including interest payments) as distinct from an 'equity' concept of profitability, that is profits attributable to shareholders, which is the concept used in this chapter[35].

Capital gains tax paid by a company is included in 'cash tax payments' as shown in the flow of funds account, but because the total amount raised by capital gains tax in Ireland is small, and as companies in this study constitute a small proportion of total assets liable to this tax, the amount attributable to companies in this study is likely to be negligible. Hence including this tax is unlikely to have much effect on the estimates of tax paid on profits[36].

'Cash tax payments' are however defined to include tax paid by both the shareholder and the company and because the returns to shareholders may take the form of either distributions or capital gains via retentions, capital gains paid by both the company and shareholders should be included. There are no published estimates of receipts from capital gains on company securities, but, as for tax on capital gains by companies in the study, the amount involved is likely to be low or negligible because of :- (1) loss offset provisions; (2) share prices in Ireland during the period 1964-84, as in other countries, have not kept pace with inflation[37]; (3) since 1978 inflation as measured by the consumer price index may be offset against this tax.

Four different definitions of profits are used in calculating tax rates on profits. All four definitions are measured ex post, that is based on historical events. Hicks[38] argues such profit measures are of limited usefulness unless windfall gains or losses are excluded. To the extent that these profit figures include such windfall gains or losses, the profit figures may be of greater interest, as Hicks comments, to economic historians than to theoretical economists. The first concept of profits used in this chapter is termed taxable profits (P). Taxable profits are profits before any allowances are deducted. As such they represent the maximum amount of profit that may be taxed if a firm is not in a position to claim any allowances, for example, a non-exporting firm, with no capital expenditure which qualifies for tax allowances, and which is unable to claim stock relief. Taxable profits were measured as profits before tax plus the provision for depreciation, both as they appear in the Profit and Loss Account, because depreciation charged in company accounts, in contrast to accelerated depreciation, is not a tax allowable expense[39]. The profits or losses attributable to associated companies were deducted for consistency with the measure of 'cash tax payments'. For more recent years a portion of capital grants received may be added to reported profits, and such amounts were also deducted in calculating taxable profits.

Investment income was included in the measure of taxable profits. Most companies had no investment income, and where some was reported it was generally of small amounts; however, investment income is shown net of tax in company accounts, and as a result taxable profits are slightly underestimated.

Taxable profits as defined in this chapter depart in several respects from an ideal concept of taxable income as described for example by Kaldor[40]. Taxable profits may overstate real profits because of inflation, and because no allowance has been made for depreciation, that is the principle of maintaining capital intact has been ignored. If true economic depreciation is deducted from taxable profits, that is depreciation required to maintain the capital stock intact, an estimate of 'pure profits' plus the return to share capital is obtained[41]. This second measure of profits is termed share capital profits (pre-tax profits - accounting depreciation). Deducting depreciation would be consistent with the notion of maintaining capital intact as described by Hicks[42]. More recently the Meade Committee[43] also recognised this principle as being an essential aspect of any practical definition of income for tax purposes.

Depreciation as it appears in company accounts is used as an approximate measure of true economic depreciation in calculating share capital profits in this chapter. However depreciation as shown in the Profit and Loss Account is likely to understate true economic depreciation on plant and machinery, because real assets are likely to have increased in value when expressed in current money terms due to inflation. Hence accounting depreciation is an inaccurate measure of true economic depreciation. Apart from the problems posed by inflation, there are other difficulties in measuring true economic depreciation; for example the problem of estimating future capital values. For these reasons Hayek[44] suggested that all capital expenditure should be deducted in calculating profit, a procedure which is now widely used in calculating profits which may be assessed for tax, due to the widespread use of 100 per cent initial allowances.

A third definition of profits used in this chapter is obtained by adding capital grants to taxable profits (P + G). This measure is termed gross available profits, and is the maximum cash flow which may be allocated by the firm without recourse to external financing, or the sale of fixed assets. The final measure of profits is obtained by adding capital grants to share capital profits (P - C + G), as suggested by Burgess and Webb[45], and which is implicit in the Hicksian concept of income. This measure is termed net available profits.

Using these four definitions of profits, four definitions of tax rates were calculated as follows, where n is the number of firms:

For the Firm		For the Corporate Sector
(1) The ratio of 'cash tax payments to taxable profits in time period t.	T_{it}/P_{it},	$\sum_{i=1}^{n} T_{it} / \sum_{i=1}^{n} P_{it}$, t = 1964, 1965.......
(2) The ratio of 'cash tax payments' to share capital profits in time period t.	$T_{it}/(P_{it} - C_{it})$,	$\sum_{i=1}^{n} T_{it} / \sum_{i=1}^{n} (P_{it} - C_{it})$, t = 1964, 1965....
(3) The ratio of 'cash tax payments to gross available profits in time period t.	$T_{it}/(P_{it} + G_{it})$	$\sum_{i=1}^{n} T_{it} / \sum_{i=1}^{n} (P_{it} + G_{it})$, t = 1964, 1965....
(4) The ratio of 'cash tax payments to net available profits in time period t.	$T_{it}/(P_{it} - C_{it} + G_{it})$,	$\sum_{i=1}^{n} T_{it} /(P_{it} - C_{it} + G_{it})$, t = 1964,1965...

Table 3.1 shows 'cash tax payments', taxable profits, and the ratio of current 'cash tax payments' to current taxable profits for Irish or partly Irish owned firms in the study group. Table 3.2 shows the same information for wholly owned subsidiaries of multinational companies in the study. The tax ratio shown in Table 3.1 can be seen to vary considerably from year to year, but has fallen from approximately 27 per cent in the earlier years to 9-12 per cent for more recent years. While this ratio is not an estimate of the rate of tax on 'pure profit' or on the returns to share capital, it is nevertheless important in examining the effects of tax concessions and likely changes in tax rates and tax concessions. For example, the reasons causing this ratio to be low or zero for individual firms, resulting in tax exhausted companies, are also likely to make marginal tax rates low or zero, and additional fiscal incentives or increases in tax concessions may have little effect.

Table 3.2 shows a similar downward trend in tax rates for wholly owned subsidiaries of multinational comapnies included in the study, except that tax rates fell to approximately 4 per cent in 1977 and rose substantially in the period 1979-82. This is almost entirely accounted for by higher reported profits and hence higher tax payments by the two oil companies in the study. The subsidiaries of Irish Shell and Esso paid IR£ 6.373 million in corporate tax in 1979, IR£ 3.682 million in 1980, IR£ 3.973 million in 1982, and IR£ 2.453 million in 1982 compared with an estimated IR£ 2.37 million in the entire period 1964-78[46].

Table 3.1
Tax paid, the ratio of 'cash tax payments' to taxable profits, and capital grants received for Irish or partly Irish owned companies in the study 1964-84
IR£ `000

Year	No. of Firms	Cash Tax Payments (T)	Taxable Profits (P)	T/P (per cent)	Annual Capital Grants Received (G)	Net Government Receipts (T - G)
1964	118	5227	19338	27.03	920	4307
1965	122	5122	20849	24.57	1383	3739
1966	128	6017	21805	27.59	1430	4587
1967	129	7047	24167	29.16	2145	4902
1968	126	7220	30370	23.77	1342	5878
1969	123	6609	31903	20.72	3351	3258
1970	114	7278	29134	24.98	2714	4564
1971	114	7341	34510	21.27	2783	4558
1972	108	8447	52733	16.02	3663	4784
1973	100	8211	73871	11.12	3248	4963
1974	100	11944	59794	19.98	3534	8410
1975	96	7910	52987	14.93	5688	2222
1976	94	8098	75158	10.77	4985	3113
1977	88	13135	89828	14.62	3866	9269
1978	84	13266	114860	11.55	4891	8375
1979	81	14027	141619	9.90	3608	10419
1980	80	17394	113057	15.39	6452	10942
1981	75	15080	129044	11.69	11144	3936
1982	70	13583	111395	12.19	6349	7234
1983	64	12598	111337	11.32	4294	8304
1984	59	11492	125642	9.15	4389	7103

Source:- Annual Reports of Companies in the Study

Table 3.2
Tax paid, the ratio of 'cash tax payments' to taxable profits, and capital grants received for wholly owned M.N.C. subsidiaries 1964-84

IR £'000

Year	No. of Firms	Cash Tax Payments (T)	Taxable Profits (P)	T/P (per cent)	Annual Capital Grants Received (G)	Net Government Receipts (T - G)
1964	15	861	4702	18.31	126	735
1965	16	1290	4178	30.88	240	1050
1966	16	954	3652	26.12	362	592
1967	15	772	3199	24.13	104	668
1968	16	669	4486	14.91	69	600
1969	15	557	3948	14.11	42	515
1970	17	818	4668	17.52	179	639
1971	17	1084	5877	18.44	286	798
1972	15	1192	7190	16.58	190	1002
1973	16	956	5872	16.28	315	641
1974	16	712	7937	8.97	250	462
1975	17	227	7956	2.85	250	-23
1976	15	568	5880	9.66	117	451
1977	14	791	20848	3.79	33	758
1978	13	1169	19680	5.94	156	1013
1979	13	7273	26842	27.10	289	6984
1980	12	4311	24786	17.39	934	3377
1981	9	4178	7712	54.18	875	3303
1982	8	3416	14607	23.39	1533	1883
1983	8	1274	19138	6.66	830	444
1984	7	868	13323	6.52	1410	-542

Source:- Annual Reports of Companies in the Study

Calculating an effective tax rate as distinct from the ratio of current 'cash tax payments' to current taxable profits is made more difficult because tax paid in period t may be largely a function of profits earned in years t - 1 and/or preceding years, and by the possibility that firms may carry losses forward which may be offset against taxable profits in future years. Overcoming these problems would require a breakdown of the proportion of each year's 'cash tax payments' which related to preceding year's profits, or alternatively the tax rate could be calculated over the entire life cycle of the firm. The true rate of tax would be the discounted sum of future tax payments arising from current profits, to current profits, in the former case, and the ratio of the discounted sum of total tax payments to the discounted sum of total profits in the latter case. That is, in the first case where

$T_{i\cdot} = \sum_{j=i}^{mi} T^*_{ij}(i + r)^{-j}$, where T^* is the tax payment attributable to the current

years trading, r is the discount rate, and m is the number of periods in which tax payments relating to current years profits are paid. In the second case

$T_{i\cdot} = \sum_{j=1}^{mi} T^*_{ij}(1 + r)^{-j}$ and $P_{i\cdot} = \sum_{j=1}^{mi} P^*_{ij}(1 + r)^{-j}$, where T^* = annual 'cash tax

payment', P^* = annual profit or tax base, m is the number of years for which the firm survives, and r is the discount rate.

In an attempt to take account of these factors an average of 'cash tax payments' over varying definitions of current profits lagged one year was calculated for the periods shown in Table 3.3. For example column (1) shows the ratio of current 'cash tax payments' to taxable profits for three year periods, where for each individual firm i, 'cash tax payments' = T_{it} $+T_{it+1}$ $+T_{it+2}$, and profits are defined as $P_{it-1} + P_{it} + P_{it+1}$.

Column (1) Table 3.3 shows that the rate of taxable profits paid in 'cash tax payments' declined considerably over the period 1964-83. The difference between the statutory rate of tax (Appendix 1 to Chapter 1) and these estimates of the tax rate indicate the amount of tax foregone as a result of various allowances.

If true economic depreciation is deducted from taxable profits, that is depreciation required to maintain the capital stock intact, the estimated tax rates would be higher. It may be the case, though, that other adjustments resulting from inflation would approximately counter balance this effect. Some of the effects of inflation on effective tax rates are examined in the following chapter. If depreciation as it appears in company accounts is used as a measure of true economic depreciation, column (2), Table 3.3, shows the estimated tax rate, using share capital profits (P - C) as the base. Column (2) illustrates the same trend of declining tax rates as column (1), although tax rates increased slightly in the period 1981-83 compared with 1979-81.

Table 3.3
Estimated tax rates for Irish/partly Irish owned companies 1964-83

	(1)	(2)	(3)	(4)
	$\sum_{i=1}^{n} T_{it} / \sum_{i=1}^{n} P_{it}$	$\sum_{i=1}^{n} T_{it} / \sum_{i=1}^{n} (P-C)_{it}$	$\sum_{i=1}^{n} T_{it} / (P+G)_{it}$	$\sum_{i=1}^{n} T_{it} / (P-C+G)_{it}$
t= 1965-67 / 1964-66	29.34	40.33	27.67	37.25
t= 1968-70 / 1967-69	24.42	33.66	22.63	30.35
t= 1971-73 / 1970-72	20.62	27.83	19.12	25.16
t= 1974-76 / 1973-75	14.98	20.81	14.04	19.05
t= 1977-79 / 1976-78	14.45	19.02	13.77	17.86
t= 1980-82 / 1979-81	12.00	17.35	11.37	16.06
t= 1982-84 / 1981-83	10.71	18.71	10.08	16.89

T = 'cash tax payment'
P = taxable profits
n = number of firms
D = accounting depreciation
G = annual capital grant received
t = aggregate data for three years divided by aggregate data for three years lagged one period

Column (3), Table 3.3 shows the estimated tax rate if gross available profits (P + G) is used as the tax base. Finally column (4) shows the effect of using net available profits (P - C + G) as the tax base. These latter two measures are similar to those obtained using taxable profits, and share capital profits as the tax base, because capital grants are a small proportion of internal cash flows. All four measures of the tax rate illustrate a decline in tax rates over the entire period considered, although for two of the measures there is an increase in tax rates for the period 1981-83 compared with 1979-81.

Table 3.4 shows tax rates calculated for wholly owned M.N.C. subsidiaries included in the study. All four measures show declining tax rates until the period 1973-75, followed by a considerable rise in tax rates and then a fall for the most recent period. As has already been explained in relation to Table 3.2, this rise in tax rates is due to higher reported profits, and tax rates, by two oil companies included in the study.

Table 3.4
Estimated tax rates for wholly owned M.N.C. subsidiaries in the study 1964-83

	(1)	(2)	(3)	(4)
	$\sum_{i=1}^{n} T_{it} / \sum_{i=1}^{n} P_{it}$	$\sum_{i=1}^{n} T_{it} / \sum_{i=1}^{n} (P-C)_{it}$	$\sum_{i=1}^{n} T_{it} / (P+G)_{it}$	$\sum_{i=1}^{n} T_{it} / (P-C+G)_{it}$
t= 1965-67 / 1964-66	24.07	43.68	22.75	39.51
t= 1968-70 / 1967-69	17.57	36.03	17.25	34.71
t= 1971-73 / 1970-72	18.22	32.77	17.57	30.73
t= 1974-76 / 1973-75	6.92	13.85	6.67	12.88
t= 1977-79 / 1976-78	19.90	26.03	19.76	25.80
t= 1980-82 / 1979-81	20.06	26.98	19.38	25.76
t= 1982-84 / 1981-83	13.41	24.41	12.44	21.37

T = 'cash tax payments
P = taxable profits
n = number of firms
C = accounting depreciation
G = annual capital grant received
t = aggregate data for three years divided by aggregate data for three years lagged one period

Another way of looking at capital grants in relation to tax payments would be to subtract them from tax payments, thus showing the net effect on Government revenues. Table 3.1 showed that this amount for Irish/partly Irish owned companies remained fairly stable in the period 1964-73 at IR£ 3 to IR£ 5 million, and fluctuated between IR£ 2 and IR£ 11 million in the period 1974-84, thus showing a substantial fall in real terms over the entire period. The main feature of Table 3.2 which shows the same data for M.N.C. subsidiaries included, is the considerable increase in net tax receipts in the period 1979-82. As not all tax revenue accrues to the Irish Exchequer, because some companies have subsidiaries operating in other countries, this measure is an overestimate of Irish Government net tax receipts. Net receipts are further reduced by other forms of State support to the corporate sector, such as training grants and employment grants[47].

If tax rates (T/P) for firms with no manufacturing activities in 1980-84 are considered, and excluding the two oil distribution companies, estimated tax rates are higher, but a downward trend is still evident. For example the ratio of 'cash tax payments' to taxable profits for the periods shown in Tables 3.2 and 3.3 were (per cent): 34.83, 35.97, 36.33, 32.67, 19.96, and 24.35, and 24.70.

A final point of interest from Table 3.1 relates to the effect of lags on payment of taxes. Corporate profits tax is collected in arrears, and hence a fall in reported profits, such as in 1979-80 or in 1973-74, had the effect of increasing the overall level of tax rates, thus adding to liquidity problems resulting from the fall in reported profits. Overall Balance Sheet tax liabilities may also be reduced for reasons other than a fall in profitability, for example a decline in investment, and hence accelerated depreciation allowances, which would also increase effective tax rates.

Tax payments may be deferred by using accelerated depreciation allowances, or because of lags in the collection of tax, and so deferred tax allowances are an important source of finance to the corporate sector, in the form of an interest free loan. The same phenomenon also occurs in other countries, for example, as a result of these accrued tax liabilities (probably arising from a combination of rising profits and lags in the collection of tax). Lintner[48] found that the overall ratio of internal to external financing had shown little change over the period 1900-55 for U.S. non-financial companies, despite a decline in security issues.

The next chapter considers the effect of inflation on profits based on historical cost accounting, and also considers the effects of inflation adjustments on the various estimates of tax rates discussed in this chapter.

Notes

[1] J.A. Kay and M.A. King, *The British Tax System*, 3rd edition, Oxford University Press, Oxford, 1983, p. 183.

[2] J.A. Kay and M.A. King, 1983, ibid. p. 9.

[3] N. Kaldor, *An Expenditure Tax*, George Allen and Unwin, London, 1956, p. 14.

[4] M.A. King, *Public Policy and the Corporation*, Chapman and Hall, London, 1977, p. 248.

[5] A.B. Atkinson and J.E. Stiglitz, *Lectures on Public Economics*, McGraw-Hill, 1980, London, p. 160.

[6] R. Dusansky, 'The Short - Run Shifting of the Corporation Income Tax in the United States', *Oxford Economic Papers*, vol. 24, pp. 357-371.

[7] W.H. Oakland, 'Corporate Earnings and Tax Shifting in U.S. Manufacturing', *Review of Economics and Statistics*, August, 1972, pp. 235-244.

[8] J.M. Davis, 'An Aggregate Time Series Analysis of the Short - Run Shifting of Company Taxation in the United Kingdom', *Oxford Economic Papers*, 1972, vol. 24, pp. 357-371.

[9] A.R. Prest and N. Barr, *Public Finance*, Weidenfeld and Nicolson, London, 1979, p. 448.

[10] M.A. King and D. Fullerton (eds.), *The Taxation of Income from Capital*, University of Chicago Press and National Bureau of Economic Research, Chicago, 1984, p. 304.

[11] D. Fullerton, 'Which Effective Tax Rate?', *National Tax Journal*, vol. XXXVII, no. 1, 1983, pp. 23-41, especially p. 25.

[12] A.J. Auerbach, 'Taxation, Corporate Financial Policy and the Cost of Capital', *Journal of Economic Literature*, vol. XXI, 1983, pp. 905-940.

[13] M.A. King and D. Fullerton [eds.) op. cit. p. 74.

[14] A.J. Auerbach, op.cit. p. 930; D. Fullerton, 1983, op. cit. pp. 23-24.

[15] D. Fullerton and Y.K. Henderson, *Long Run Effects of the Accelerated Cost Recovery System*, National Bureau of Economic Research, working paper no. 828, National Bureau of Economic Research, 1981, New York, p. 23.

[16] Fullerton, 1983, op. cit. p. 29.

[17] J.G. Gravelle, 'Which Effective Tax Rate? A Comment and Extension', *National Tax Journal*, vol. XXXVIII, 1986, pp. 103-110.

[18] M.A. King and D. Fullerton (eds.), op. cit. p. 8

[19] A.J. Auerbach, op.cit. p. 929.

[20] M.A. King and D. Fullerton, (eds.) op. cit. p. 309. See also D.F. Bradford and D. Fullerton, 'Pitfalls in the Construction and Use of Effective Tax Rates', in C.R. Hulten (ed.), *Depreciation, Inflation, and the Taxation of Income from Capital*, The Urban Institute Press, Washington, D.C., 1981, for a discussion of some difficulties in measuring effective tax rates using a cost of capital approach.

[21] M.A. King and D. Fullerton (eds.), ibid., p. 27

[22] L.G. Rosenberg, 'Taxation of Income From Capital by Industry

Group', in A.C. Harberger and M.J. Bailey (eds.), *The Taxation of Income from Capital,* The Brookings Institution, Washington, 1969, pp. 123-184; J.J. Siegfried, 'Effective Average U.S. Corporation Income Tax Rates', *National Tax Journal*, vol. XXVII, 1974, pp. 245-259; M. Feldstein and L. Summers, 'Inflation and the Taxation of Capital Income in the Corporate Sector', *National Tax Journal*, vol. XXXII, 1979, pp. 445-470; M. Feldstein, L. Dicks-Mireaux and J. Poterba, 'The Effective Tax Rate and the Pretax Rate of Return' *Journal of Public Economics*, vol. 21, 1983, pp. 129-158.

[23] These low tax rates can be explained by tax concessions which only apply to these sectors.

[24] Siegfried (1974), op. cit. p. 245.

[25] M. Feldstein and L. Summers (1979), op. cit. p. 448.

[26] M. Feldstein, L. Dicks-Mireaux, and J. Poterba (1983), op. cit. p. 130.

[27] M.A. King and D. Fullerton (eds.) op. cit. pp. 265-267.

[28] M.A. King and D. Fullerton (eds.) ibid. p. 269.

[29] C.P. Mayer and C.N. Morris, *A Disaggregated Model of U.K. Corporation Tax*, Institute for Fiscal Studies, London, Working Paper, no. 33, 1982.

[30] C.P. Mayer, 'The Structure of Corporation Tax in the U.K.', *Fiscal Studies*, vol. 3, 1982, pp. 121-141

[31] See Institute of Chartered Accountants in Ireland, *Accounting for Depreciation*, Statement of Standard Accounting Practice, no. 12, 1977.

[32] See Institute of Chartered Accountants in Ireland, *Statements of Sources and Applications of Funds*, Statement of Standard Accounting Practice, no. 10, 1974.

[33] M. Feldstein and L. Summers, op. cit. p. 448.

[34] G.H. Lawson and A.W. Stark, 'Equity Values and Inflation: Dividends and Debt Financing', *Lloyds Bank Review*, January, 1981, p. 41-59.

[35] There are important differences between these two concepts. For example, unanticipated inflation causes a real transfer of wealth from lender to borrower. Inflation even if anticipated may also result in a real wealth transfer, in cases of contractual saving, or where financial intermediaries operate in oligopolistic markets. That is the 'Fisher Effect' - nominal interest rates adjusting to reflect the rate of inflation plus the rate of interest - may not hold. The 'Fisher effect' has recently been referred to as 'modified Fisher's law' if taxes are considered, and as 'strict Fisher's law' if taxes are ignored, M.A. King and D. Fullerton (eds.), op. cit. p. 292. See also P. Cagan and R.E. Lipsey, *The Financial Effects of Inflation*, Ballinger Publishing Company, for the National Bureau of Economic Research, 1978, Cambridge, Mass., pp. 34-48.

[36] See Chapter 1 pp. 13-14.

[37] Although there are subperiods within the period 1964-84 where this is not true. For example, from December 1975 to December 1980 the All Share Index rose 1.96 times and the Consumer Price Index 1.22 times. Over the entire period 1964-84 the All Share Index as compiled

by the Central Statistics Office rose by 3.55 times and the Consumer Price Index 8.68 times. Sources:- *Irish Statistical Bulletin*, Various issues, and Economic Series, various issues, published by the Central Statistics Office, Dublin.

[38] J.R. Hicks, *Value and Capital*, Oxford University Press, Oxford, 1941, p. 179.

[39] M.F. Morley, *The Fiscal Implications of Inflation Accounting*, The Institute for Fiscal Studies and the Institute of Chartered Accountants in England and Wales, London, 1974, p. 5, and Inflation Accounting Committee, *Inflation Accounting*, Cmnd. 6225, H.M.S.O. London, 1975, p. 199.

[40] N. Kaldor, *An Expenditure Tax*, George Allen and Unwin, London, 1956, pp. 69-70.

[41] J.A. Kay and M.A. King 1983, op. cit. pp. 165-168.

[42] J.R. Hicks, 'Maintaining Capital Intact: A Further Suggestion"' *Economica*, vol. IX, 1942, pp. 276-280.

[43] J.E. Meade, *The Structure and Reform of Direct Taxation* , Institute for Fiscal Studies, London, p. 31, definition A.

[44] F.A. Hayek, 'The Maintainance of Capital', *Economica* , vol. 11, 1935, pp. 241-276.

[45] G. Burgess and A. Webb, 'Rates of Return and Profit Shares in the United Kingdom', *Lloyds Bank Review*, April, no. 112, 1974, pp. 1-9.

[46] The effect of changes in profit margins and hence tax rates is discussed in the context of 'profit switching transfer pricing', for both the oil companies, and other subsidiaries of M.N.C.s included in the study in a paper entitled 'Some Aspects of the Financial Behaviour of Multinational Companies Operating in Ireland', by J.C. Stewart in J.H. Kelly and J. FitzPatrick (eds.) Perspectives on Irish Industry, Irish Management Institute, Dublin, 1985.

[47] Employment Maintainance Subsidies were first introduced in April 1978 and ended in 1982. In 1978 16 firms included in the study received such subsidies. Fourteen of these 16 firms disclosed the amount received, and this came to IR£ 1.949 million. In 1979 15 firms received IR£ 2.849 million, in 1980 12 firms received IR £1.92 million, in 1981 12 firms received IR£ 1.44 million, and in 1982 8 firms received IR£ 0.459 million.

[48] J. Lintner, 'The Financing of Corporations' in E.S. Mason (ed.) *The Corporation in Modern Society*, Harvard University Press, Cambridge, 1959, pp. 166-201.

4 The effects of inflation on corporate profits and tax rates

Preceding chapters have alluded to some of the distortions in company accounts resulting from inflation. This chapter discusses the effects of inflation on profits as conventionally measured, and hence the implications of adjustments for inflation on the estimates of the rate of tax on company profits (T/P) estimated in Chapter 3. Secondly the effects of inflation on company savings and liquidity are examined.

According to Cagan and Lipsey the standard theory of the effects of inflation emphasises that yields on financial assets rise in order to compensate for inflation. Hence the owners of financial assets suffer capital losses on financial assets whose yield is fixed in nominal terms[1]. Money balances also decline in real terms and this decline could be viewed as a form of taxation. A rise in the yield of financial assets is fully reflected in corporate profits, estimated in the conventional way, in terms of higher interest charges. The standard theory also recognised that a rise in interest rates may have other effects on corporate profits, for example companies owning financial securities will suffer a fall in their nominal value which may not be shown in conventionally prepared company accounts.

Fisher[2] argued that nominal interest rates tend to rise with the rate of inflation, so that in equilibrium with perfect foresight and in the absence of taxes, real rates of interest are unchanged. This is known as the 'Fisher effect'. Inflation thus causes a fall in the price of fixed interest securities because of the rise in interest rates, and if inflation is unanticipated a capital loss to the owners. Conversely a fall in inflation will result in a fall in interest rates, and a rise in the price of fixed interest securities, and a capital gain to the owners. Fisher[3] argues that a rise in the market value of securities due to a fall in interest rates is not part of income. Fisher states '... income in any year is radically different from the ups and downs of one's capital value in that year - whether this is caused by saving or the opposite, or by changes in the rate of interest or by so-called chance'. In contrast Prest and Barr conclude that a portion of such capital gain may be regarded as income but not all of it, depending on the preferences of asset owners for combinations of income and capital.

This chapter does not attempt to adjust profits of owners of fixed interest securities for capital gains or losses due to interest rate changes. However because ownership of fixed interest debt is unusual for companies in this study population (non-financial companies), omitting this adjustment will not have much effect on the overall results.

4.1 Some effects of inflation on company accounts

More recent discussion of the effects of inflation on corporate profits, has had a much broader context. It has been recognised that inflation affects all aspects of company accounts but to different degrees and in different directions[5]. The effects of inflation as currently published in company accounts may for convenience be grouped into three areas:-

(1) Inflation affects the reported profits by understating certain costs, that is, depreciation and materials used. Depreciation is understated because the nominal value of all real assets of the firm has increased, but conventional accounting depreciation is calculated on the purchase price of assets. The cost of materials used is understated because they are valued at their purchase price (First In First Out), not their current value or their replacement cost. The tax system in Ireland and the United Kingdom in contrast to that in the United States does not allow inventories to be valued on a Last In First Out basis. If it did so, some of the effects of inflation on corporate profits would be reduced. In 1975 companies in Ireland were allowed to offset against taxable profits the increase in the nominal value of stocks. This was subsequently reduced to 75 per cent of the increase in the value of stocks. Reported profits might also be adjusted for the change (+ or -) in the finance required for the monetary working capital of the business (trade debtors and trade creditors)[6]. These changes may result in gains or losses from inflation depending on whether trade debtors are greater than trade creditors or vice versa.

(2) Inflation affects the Balance Sheet by increasing the values of all real assets and reducing the real value of monetary liabilities. This results is what has become known as a holding gain. It may also be the case that holding gains are larger than the general rise in prices, and thus may result in real capital gains. Historically this has occurred in the case of land and buildings. Holding gains may also be smaller than the general rise in prices, resulting in real capital losses.

(3) Because of (2) shareholders as residual owners of the firms's assets make capital gains, generally referred to as monetary gains, at the expense of the owners of monetary liabilities, for example owners of long term debt, and various creditors such as the Government.

For more recent years a number of companies included in the study have published profit figures adjusted for inflation[7]. The basis for these adjustments is the Sandilands Report[8], which recommended a system of inflation adjustments known as Current Cost Accounting. The Sandilands Report argued that the most appropriate concept of profit is a slight adaptation of that provided by Hicks[9]. That is :-

> 'A company's profit for the year is the maximum value which the company can distribute during the year and still expect to be as well off at the end of the year as it was at the beginning'.

It is important to realise that this is a subjective concept in the sense that it relies on predictions or expectations. The Meade Committee[10] concluded that a definition of income based on expectations was not practical for tax purposes. The difficulties are compounded when inflation is uncertain. Secondly there is considerable ambiguity relating to the concept of 'welloffness'. Whittington[11] has identified three differing concepts of 'welloffness' used by Hicks. That is; (a) Maintaining intact the capital value of prospective receipts; (b) Maintaining purchasing power; (c) Maintaining purchasing power in real terms.

The Sandilands Report notes that the concept of maintaining capital value intact is a central problem with their definition. In economic terms the Report defines income as:-

> 'The discounted value of all future net cash flows at the end of the year, less the discounted net present value of the future net cash flows at the beginning of the year, plus the net cash flow arising within the year after making adjustments for the introduction of new capital during the year'[12].

The Sandilands report recommended[13] that a Balance Sheet should show the 'value' to a business of a company's assets, and that depreciation should be calculated on this value. It is also recommended that a stock adjustment should be made, so that stock appreciation is not included in profits. In spite of acknowledging the Hicksian concept of income the Sandilands Report[14] recommends excluding all 'holding gains', that is capital gains resulting from inflation[15]. The Sandilands Report concludes that an adjustment for depreciation and stock prices is all that is necessary to adjust the Profit and Loss Account for inflation[16].

The Sandilands proposals for inflation adjusted accounts were examined here because they form the basis for inflation adjusted profits as currently published[17] known as current cost accounts (C.C.A.). The main difference is that an allowance is also made for monetary assets (negative adjustment) and monetary liabilities (positive adjustment) and also what is termed a gearing adjustment[18]. The gearing adjustment is obtained by multiplying the increase in the cost of sales adjustment (depreciation adjustment + stock adjustment + monetary working capital adjustment) by the gearing ratio (ratio of debt to debt + equity). This amount, if positive, is added to profits, and if negative, subtracted from profits.

4.2 Empirical studies of inflation adjustments

For 34 companies included in this study which published inflation adjusted accounts in 1981, total pre-tax profits as conventionally measured using historic cost concepts amounted to IR£ 78.178 million, and fell to IR£ 23.233 million using published inflation adjusted account based on S.S.A.P. 16. This would appear to indicate that inflation adjusted profits are substantially lower than those using historic cost accounting. However there are various methods of adjusting company accounts for inflation, for example the value of assets may be estimated in different ways, such as value to the business as a going concern or market value. Further problems arise in estimating market value. Frequently as in Ireland a general price index may be used (the Consumer Price Index), whereas as argued in the Sandilands Report and elsewhere specific price indices may be more desirable. The following sections describe various possible adjustments for inflation to company accounts prepared using historic cost concepts. These various adjustments have considerable effects on estimated profits and hence on tax rates. The following sections argue that profits fully adjusted for inflation would be much closer to historic cost profits than the inflation adjusted profits currently published.

Inflation adjusted profits as currently published in the U.K. and Ireland include only part of the monetary gain accruing to shareholders as income. It is likely that inflation adjusted profits, which included as income the total monetary gain resulting from monetary liabilities being reduced in real terms, would result in higher profit figures than the inflation adjusted accounts currently published. It would also be consistent with the Hicksian concept of income or profit to include in inflation adjusted profits the excess of holding gains attributable to ordinary shareholders, over the general rise in prices[19], that is to include any real capital gains resulting from changes in relative prices.

Moore[20] shows the effects on the profits of non-financial companies in the United Kingdom for 1961-77 of various adjustments for inflation[21] and estimates three different inflation adjusted profits. Post-tax profits attributable to equity shareholders which were fully adjusted for inflation were found to be 10-15 per cent below post-tax profits as conventionally measured. The inflation adjustments estimated by Moore deducted additional costs resulting from inflation, and included the full monetary gain and real holding gains or losses arising from differential rates of inflation for various assets. For three of the years 1970-77 fully adjusted profits were greater than reported profits. Modigliani and Cohn[22] also argue that the real profits of non-financial corporations in the United States, for the period 1950-77, expressed as a fraction of value added, have not fallen when fully adjusted for inflation but are best described as trendless. What Modigliani and Cohn refer to as the conventional view of a falling profits trend results from treating interest payments as an expense, rather than partly an expense and partly a repayment of debt. This is because inflation reduces the real value of debt, and so with inflation interest payments may be split into two components, part repayment of debt and part payment of interest. This is another way of stating that real capital gains arising from debt financing are not included in profits as measured by historic cost conventions.

Davidson and Weil[23] estimated the effect of proposals for inflation adjusted accounts by the Financial Accounting Standards Board in the United States[24]. These proposals were termed 'general price level adjusted accounting', and involve adjusting revenues and expenses for inflation, as well as items appearing in the Balance Sheet, and including in profits the gain or loss on monetary items. For 1974, for the 30 companies that constitute the Dow Jones Industral Average index, excluding monetary gains, inflation adjustments resulted in income amounting to 67.7 per cent of historical cost income. Including the monetary gain inflation adjusted profits amounted to 99.4 per cent of historical cost profits. For 24 utility companies inflation adjusted profits including the full monetary gain were 225.5 per cent of historical cost profits, due to the higher than average proportion of debt in the capital structure.

More recently Bulow and Shoven[25], using previously unpublished flows of funds Balance Sheet data for U.S. non-financial corporations, estimated aggregate inflation adjusted profits for the period 1946-79. Bulow and Shoven concentrate on adjusting Balance Sheet items for inflation with income as a residual. Bulow and Shoven calculate nine different definitions of income, including for comparative purposes those based on historic cost accounts and National Income Accounts. In general profits fully adjusted for inflation were found to be more volatile than partially adjusted profit figures, or historic cost profits and National Income profits. For seven of the years 1946-79 profits fully adjusted for inflation were higher than historic cost profits (1950, 1966-67, 1969, 1974, 1978-79). This is particularly true of periods of high inflation (1974, 1978-79). Conversely in years of low inflation, fully adjusted profit figures were considerably below historic cost profits, for example the years 1975-76.

In a study relating to 230 U.K. non-financial companies for the period 1966-81 by Kay and Mayer, inflation adjusted profits were found to be lower than historic cost profits, but inflation adjusted profits were also found to be quite sensitive to particular inflation adjustments[26]. Kay and Mayer examined the effect on historic cost profits and rates of return of current cost adjustments (C.C.A.), constant purchasing power adjustments (C.P.P.) and what they term 'hybrid' adjustments. Constant purchasing power adjustments differ in a number of ways from C.C.A. adjustments, for example the use of a general price index to revalue assets, and to calculate stock appreciation and monetary loss, compared with the use of specific price indices in C.C.A. adjustments. In addition gains on borrowing are addded to profits. The 'hybrid' adjustments calculated by Kay and Meyer involved the use of a consumer price index to revalue stocks and net monetary assets whereas fixed assets are revalued at replacement cost in order to estimate depreciation[27]. In general, constant purchasing power adjustments were found to result in higher profits and rates of return than current cost accounts adjustments, but the 'hybrid' adjustments produced the highest profits and rates of return, although these were still below historic cost profits and rates of return[28].

These studies support the argument that fully inflation adjusted accounts result in higher profit figures than partially adjusted accounts, and in some instances fully inflation adjusted profits may be larger than historic cost profits. However some argue, for example Tideman and Tucker[29], that while inflation adjusted profits may be greater than historical cost profits in the initial period of an inflation, in the long run inflation adjusted profits will be lower than historical cost profits. This is because the monetary gain applies only with continuing inflation. However the extra depreciation adjustments resulting from inflation will last for the length of the life of the capital equipment, and will continue to increase while inflation remains constant or falls. The monetary gain may be greatest relative to additional cost such as depreciation in the initial period of an inflation. Tideman and Tucker conclude[30]:-

> 'For these reasons it is not possible to determine the general effects of inflation on most firms' income by examining their inflation-corrected incomes for only one or two individual years'.

Tideman and Tucker argue that inflation increases tax rates on the true income of a firm, but it does so by reducing real tax rates in the first year of inflation, and increasing tax rates in subsequent years. Hence a switch to inflation adjusted income for tax purposes would result in lower tax payments, although tax payments would be higher in the early years of an inflation.

The argument presented by Tideman and Tucker depends on the level of gearing and the increase in the value of real assets, which determines the size of the monetary gain, and also on the length of life of assets and the rate of inflation, which determines the adjustment required in future years. Tideman and Tucker ignore real capital gains[31] which, for example, Moore found in some years for the United Kingdom to be greater than stock appreciation, for example the years 1974 and 1976. Finally different results are likely if it is assumed that tax on corporate profits is paid in arrears, as is the case in the United Kingdom and Ireland, rather than in the current year as in the United States. This is because tax paid in arrears increases gearing and results in monetary gains to the firm as for any other monetary liability. In conclusion, whether inflation adjusted profits are lower than historical cost profits requires empirical investigation over a number of years.

Table 4.1 shows, for Irish companies that publish inflation adjusted accounts, the increase in the value of real assets, adjusted for inflation as well as inflation adjusted profits as published (column 2). Table 4.1 shows that published inflation adjusted profits are considerably below those prepared according to historic cost conventions. Table 4.1 also shows an estimate of inflation adjusted profits which is higher than published inflation adjusted profits (column 7). Inflation adjusted profits shown in Table 4.1 column (7) are defined as historic cost profits (column 3) plus the full monetary gain (column 6). It can be seen that the inflation adjusted profits shown in column (7) are closer to pre-tax profits using historic cost conventions (column 1), than the inflation adjusted profits currently published (column 2). The correspondence is particularly close for the period 1976-79. The reason for the difference between inflation adjusted profits as published (column 2) and inflation adjusted profits as shown in column (7) is that the former, while deducting in full additional costs, includes only part of the monetary gain accruing to ordinary shareholders. This partial monetary gain is calculated by multiplying additional costs (column 3) by the gearing ratio (debt/debt + shareholder funds) shown in column (5). This sum is then added to pre-tax profits (column 1) minus additional costs (column 3). In contrast the full monetary gain (column 6) is calculated by multiplying the increase in the value of assets (column 4) by the gearing ratio (column 5).

A number of problems arise in making these adjustments for inflation, for example the increase in the value of assets as shown in published current cost accounts is often shown net of revaluations. So the increase in the aggregate value of assets shown in Table 4.1, column (4) is understated. More fundamentally, as has already been discussed, and as Hicks points out:-

> '...the capital value of assets, which are not currently being sold is a matter of judgment, or of opinion'[32].

Table 4.1
Some effects of inflation on company accounts
IR£ million

Year	N[a]	Pre-Tax[b] Profits	Profits[c] Adjusted for Inflation	Addit-[d] ional Costs	Increase[e] in Value of Assets	Average[f] Gearing Ratio	Monetary[g] Gain	Inflation Adjusted Profit Including Monetary Gain	Annual[h] Rate of Inflation
		(1)	(2)	(3)	(4)	(5) %	(6) (4x5)	(7) (1-3+6)	
1976	1	6.657	5.198	2.687	4.715	45.71	2.155	6.125	18.0
1977	1	4.733	3.210	2.401	3.365	36.61	1.232	3.564	13.6
1978	2	5.692	4.718	1.433	3.751	31.64	1.187	5.446	7.6
1979	5	19.453	11.496	8.535	19.866	32.29	6.414	17.332	13.2
1980	19	68.221	31.857	46.124	81.898	20.46	16.758	38.845	18.2
1981	34	78.178	23.233	68.980	121.116	23.44	28.392	37.590	20.4
1982	28	63.778	24.502	54.624	57.442	24.97	14.341	23.495	17.2
1983	10	25.879	15.510	12.324	20.490	18.22	3.734	17.289	10.5
1984	3	10.341	6.272	4.255	3.598	3.58	0.129	6.215	8.6

Notes to Table 4.1

(a) N is the number of firms.

(b) Defined as historical cost profits as reported, less profit of associated companies and capital grants credited to income.

(c) Defined as profits adjusted for inflation using S.S.A.P. no 1 less profits of associated companies and capital grants credited to income.

(d) Largely consisting of additional depreciation charges and additional costs of materials used. An allowance for the change in the monetary working capital (trade debtors - trade creditors) due to inflation is also included. This amount may vary from positive to negative for each firm. A positive amount results if monetary liabilities are greater than monetary assets, resulting in a real gain to the firm. Moore found that the aggregate monetary working capital adjustment for U.K. firms was positive for 1975-77 and negative for 1961-74[33].

(e) Defined as the increase in the Capital Maintenance Reserve, or the Current Cost Reserve in Accounts adjusted for inflation, plus the gearing adjustment.

(f) The ratio of debt to (debt + shareholder funds). Because of differences in accounting treatment of deferred tax this ratio may not be strictly comparable between firms. Deferred tax allowances for any one year are also subject to revision.

(g) Defined as the increase in the value of assets multiplied by the gearing ratio.

(h) Calculated from November of each year.

The gain from inflation Table 4.1, column (6) is also influenced by the gearing ratio (column 5). The gearing ratio is also subjective, in that a portion of it - the proportion of deferred tax which is considered by company accountants as likely to be paid in the future and hence a current liability - is also subjective. Any real gains accruing to equity shareholders have also been ignored. Finally it is also important to note that if assets fall in value, the monetary gain is negative and reduces profits.

4.3 The effects of inflation adjustments on tax rates

Adjusting profits as measured using historic cost concepts raises various issues in relation to taxation. Modigliani and Cohn[34] argue that while corporations are taxed on reported profits and not real profits, they are allowed to deduct total interest payments on taxable profits, even though part of these interest payments are really repayment of debt. This means that corporations are not taxed on monetary capital gains. On average, it is claimed, these two effects largely cancel out for the corporate sector as a whole, although this may not be true of individual firms.

A similar argument applies to taxation on reported profits as compared with taxation on inflation-adjusted profits. In the absence of accelerated depreciation allowances and stock relief, reported profits are over-stated and so effective tax rates are higher. However, monetary gains or real holding gains which accrue to shareholders are not included as part of taxable income. Such gains, for the corporate sector as a whole, are likely to result in real profits over a number of years being of similar magnitude to profits defined using historic cost concepts, although there may be considerable divergences form year to year. As Modigliani and Cohn[35] say 'the tax system in effect taxes what should not be taxed and does not tax what should be taxed'.

The Sandilands Report[36] envisaged tax being charged eventually on current cost profits as defined in the Report, and because current cost profits are almost always lower than historic cost profits, this would result in lower tax payments from the corporate sector. However the Sandilands Report also considered that such a 'fundamental change' should not be introduced without a comprehensive review of taxation as a whole extending beyond the corporate sector. It is interesting to note that the United

Kingdom Green Paper on Corporation Tax[37] estimated that if Corporation Tax had been paid on inflation-adjusted profits using S.S.A.P. 16, for the period 1976 to 1980, the rate of corporation tax would not have been very different from the present rate, although there would have been a substantial redistribution between sectors. The manufacturing and distribution sectors would have paid Stg.£ 150 million more over the whole period, and the financial and other sectors would have paid Stg.£ 150 million less in Corporate Tax.

Table 4.2 shows tax rates for a small number of firms included in this study, using the various definitions of profits shown in Table 4.1. Table 4.2 shows that tax rates using published inflation adjusted profits as the tax base are higher than those using historic cost profits as the tax base. However including the full monetary gain in the tax base reduces tax rates, with the exception of 1984, although tax rates are still above those using historic cost profits. It is likely that if further adjustments were made, for example including real capital gains attributable to equity shareholders, tax rates would fall further. In conclusion tax rates using fully inflation adjusted profits as the tax base are likely to be similar to those using historic cost profits as the tax base.

Table 4.2
Tax rates on historic cost profits compared with inflation adjusted profits (per cent)

	N[a]	T/(P - C)[b]	T/(P - C + G)[c]
Historical Cost Profits as the Tax Base[d]			
1979	4	15.78	14.94
1980	17	15.22	14.57
1981	32	14.27	12.66
1982	26	16.94	15.46
1983	8	26.52	25.77
1984	3	13.35	13.31
Inflation adjusted profits as published in company accounts as the tax base[e]			
1979	4	20.13	18.78
1980	17	26.84	24.87
1981	32	31.41	24.53
1982	26	34.29	28.70
1983	8	39.96	38.30
1984	3	22.02	21.91
Inflation adjusted profits including the full monetary gain as the tax base[f]			
1979	4	18.85	17.66
1980	17	24.04	22.45
1981	32	24.64	18.33
1982	26	36.32	30.11
1983	8	38.61	37.05
1984	3	22.22	22.11

Notes to Table 4.2

(a) N is the number of companies. The two oil companies have been omitted because of the large increase in tax payments by these two companies in 1978.

(b) Defined as Cash Tax Payments/(Profits - Accounting Depreciation)

(c) Defined as Cash Tax Payments/(Profits - Accounting Depreciation + Capital Grants Received).

(d) Defined as historical cost profits as reported in company accounts, less profits of associated companies and capital grants credited to income.

(e) Defined as profits adjusted for inflation as published in company accounts using Statement of Standard Accounting Practice no. 16.

(f) Defined as for column (7) Table 4.1, that is, inflation adjusted profits plus the full monetary gain.

As was previously discussed, Tideman and Tucker argue that the effects of inflation on corporate profits are likely to be quite different for a single period compared with a number of years. Hence it is desirable to examine the effects of inflation on corporate profits over a long time period. Only one company in the study group examined has published inflation adjusted accounts for more than a four year period. Table 4.3 shows tax rates calculated for this company for various definitions of the tax base for the period 1976-84. For one year (1978) tax rates using inflation adjusted accounts, including the full monetary gain, as the tax base are almost the same as tax rates using historic cost profits as the tax base. For the period 1976-80 inflation adjusted profits including the full monetary gain varied between 75 - 99 per cent of historic cost profits (averaging 91 per cent). This is a period when inflation rose and then fell. For the next four years inflation adjusted profits including the full monetary gain varied between 66 and 76 per cent of historic cost profits (averaging 72 per cent). This period was characterised by continuously falling prices. It is also interesting to note that the gearing ratio declined continuously for this company. A fall in the gearing ratio and inflation rate has the effect of lowering inflation adjusted profits compared with historic cost profits. The effects of inflation adjustments on company profits for a single period cannot be extrapolated to the corporate sector as a whole. This is because while in the aggregate inflation adjusted profits may be similar to historic cost profits, there is likely to be a considerable dispersion around individual companies historic cost profits. Nevertheless the results shown in Tables 4.2 and 4.3 are suggestive of the likely effects of inflation adjustments on tax rates for the corporate sector as a whole.

Table 4.3

Tax rates on historical cost profits compared with inflation adjusted profits for Carroll Industries 1976-84*

Year	Historical Cost Profits	Published Inflation Adjusted Profits	Inflation Adjusted Profits Including Full Monetary Gain	Gearing Ratio	Annual Rate of Inflation
			Per cent		
1976	13.52	17.31	14.69	45.7	18.0
1977	34.90	51.46	46.35	36.6	13.6
1978	42.00	50.71	42.61	31.1	7.6
1979	17.36	19.92	18.20	23.1	13.2
1980	37.54	42.95	40.27	14.9	18.2
1981	16.05	23.50	22.84	10.7	20.4
1982	17.08	24.04	22.80	11.1	17.2
1983	15.79	20.84	20.75	7.5	10.5
1984	13.07	19.96	19.96	0.0	8.6

Note to Table 4.3

(*) This is the only company for which a full set of inflation adjusted accounts are available for the period 1976-84. Profits are defined as for Table 4.2. This company is mostly involved in the manufacture of tobacco products, but is also involved in the manufacture of pharmaceutical products and printing and packaging.

In contrast Feldstein and Summers[38] have argued that inflation in the United States has resulted in a higher effective rate of tax on corporate income (including tax paid by providers of debt), largely because of (a) historic cost depreciation and the taxation of artificial inventory profits, but also because of (b) a tax on nominal capital gains rather than real capital gains. Feldstein and Summers argue that while corporations deduct nominal rather than real interest payments, lenders are obliged to pay tax on nominal interest receipts, so that the two effects largely cancel out. Feldstein and Summers conclude that for the year 1977 for the United States non-financial corporate sector, inflation raised the effective tax rate from 43 per cent to 66 per cent.

In contrast to Feldstein and Summers, King, Fullerton, and others[39] argue that effective average tax rates have increased only slightly with inflation in the U.S.. Feldstein and Summers argue that the tax rate at which corporations deduct interest is similar to the rate at which individuals pay tax on interest receipts, 40.4 per cent compared with 42 per cent, hence there is no gain from the use of debt finance. King, Fullerton and others calculate these tax rates at 49.5 per cent for corporations compared with 23.6 per cent for individuals. As mentioned in Chapter 3 (p.47) the difference in estimated tax rates arises from the assumption that bank depositors receive part of their income in the form of tax free services[40]. Hence they conclude that there are considerable benefits to debt finance under conditions of inflation in the United States. In addition, Moore has argued that for the United Kingdom the effects of historic cost accounting are compenstated for by the non-taxation of holding gains and real capital gains, and this is also likely to be true for companies operating in Ireland. Thirdly, tax payments as defined in this study[41] include tax on capital gains paid by companies, and as argued in Chapter 1 capital gains tax paid by equity shareholders is likely to be negligible. Fourthly, providers of debt and owners of equity shares may be quite different groups. Feldstein and Summers acknowledge in a footnote that 'since lenders and borrowers are not the same individuals, inflation does cause a redistribution of income amongst individuals and institutions'[42]. Tax paid on interest income may only affect corporate income depending on the ability of lenders to secure higher interest payments to compensate for higher tax rates.

Table 4.4 shows selected borrowing and lending rates in Ireland for the period 1972-84. The table shows the Associated Banks' (the four largest banks in Ireland) lending rates on short term loans (< 1 years) to low risk corporate borrowers. Loans of longer duration and higher risk would be charged higher interest rates. It is likely that most firms in the corporate sector would have some borrowings at this rate of interest during the period examined. Table 4.4 also shows rates of interest paid to depositors of small sums (<£5000) and larger amounts (>£25000). These deposit rates are representative, in that similar rates of interest are paid by other financial institutions. Higher rates may be paid but at greater risk to depositors (from smaller financial institutions) or for a minimum period of deposit (> 6 months). Table 4.4 shows that while nominal interest rates have risen in Ireland in conjunction with the inflation rate, real interest rates charged to borrowers fell in the period of peak inflation, (from +1.13 in 1973 to -9.61 in 1975 and from +5.37 in 1978 to -3.45 in 1981), while real interest rates paid to depositors with financial institutions are negative for the entire period, except for large deposits for four years 1973, (+0.63 per cent); 1978 (+2.37 per cent); 1979, (+0.28 per cent); and 1984, (+3.36 per cent).

Inflation results in large transfers of real wealth between different economic units[43]. It is generally accepted that the corporate sector should take account of these real wealth transfers in measuring profits. It is less widely accepted that these real wealth transfers should be taxed.

Table 4.4
Selected borrowing and lending rates in Ireland 1972-84

Year	1972	1973	1974	1975	1976	1977	1978	1979	1980	1981	1982	1983	1984
Annual* Change in Consumer Price Index	8.7	11.4	17.0	20.9	18.0	13.6	7.6	13.2	18.2	20.5	17.2	10.5	8.6
Associated Banks Lending Rate	7.5	12.5	11.75	11.25	13.25	7.5	13.0	15.5	14.0	17.0	14.0	12.75	14.75
Associated Banks Deposit Rate on amounts <£5000	4.0	8.0	8.0	7.25	8.5	3.0	8.5	10.0	7.5	10.0	8.5	7.0	8.0
Associated Banks Deposit Rate on amounts >£25000	5.25	12.0	10.5	8.0	10.5	4.5	10.0	13.5	12.75	15.75	11.75	9.75	12.0

Note to Table 4.4
(*) Percentage change in the consumer price index from November to November
Source:- Annual Reports of the Central Bank of Ireland. All interest rates relate to those prevailing in December of each year.

4.4 The effects of inflation on corporate savings and liquidity

Fully inflation adjusted profits may not be all that different from profits as conventionally defined, but inflation has other effects on the corporate sector. Tideman and Tucker argue[44] that inflation may lead to increased risk of bankruptcy because firms become too highly geared if interest rates fail to rise with inflation. Tideman and Tucker also argue that because inflation distorts profits using historic cost conventions, it increases the required rate of return on investments. Carlton argues that inflation reduces the efficiency of an economic system by increasing uncertainty. This in turn leads to greater market liquidity and more homogeneous goods, compared with less liquid markets and more heterogeneous goods in the absence of inflation[45]. Cagan and Lipsey[46] also argue that inflation has led to much greater uncertainty about profit rates. Cagan and Lipsey focus on the effects of inflation adjustments on the non-financial corporate sector in the United States for the period 1954-77, as well as on other effects of inflation. They conclude that inflation has reduced the real profit rate on owner's equity (P_e/K_e), although there have been considerable fluctuations in profit rates. Cagan and Lipsey did not consider the effects of inflation on tax rates (T/P).

The effect of inflation on corporate liquidity has received considerable attention, and led to the introduction of stock relief, that is tax allowances relating to the increase in the value of stocks during an accounting period, in the U.K. and Ireland. Kay and King comment[47] that the effect of this relief, with other tax allowances 'was to eliminate almost all of the corporation tax liability of U.K. manufacturing industry'. A similar result has largely followed in Ireland, and hence it is worth examining the conditions which gave rise to a reduction in corporate liquidity, and the subsequent granting of stock relief.

Table 4.5, column (5) shows an estimate of the profits available for distribution, or 'free profits' for all firms in the study, that is including wholly owned subsidiaries and Irish/partly Irish owned companies for the period 1964-84. Distributable profits or 'free profits' were estimated by substracting accounting depreciation (D), Cash Tax Paid (T), and a stock adjustment (O)[48], from taxable profits (P). As taxable profits (P) are almost identical to gross internal cash flows[49], this measure is termed distributable profits, that is profits available for distribution to shareholders, or for repayment of liabilities, investment in new assets, etc.

The main feature of Table 4.5 is that distributable profits fell substantially in the periods 1974-75 and 1980-81 (column 5), coinciding with a period of high inflation[50]. The non-financial corporate sector thus faced a considerable reduction in liquidity, and one of the responses was to reduce corporate tax payments by granting stock relief to manufacturing firms. It is important to note that real profits, which include real holding gains attributable to equity shareholders, and monetary gains, may not have fallen, or may have fallen by a small amount.

Alternative responses to relieve this liquidity crisis were possible, and may have been used by some firms; for example realising capital gains. This may not always be possible in the short run, particularly as high inflation coincided with a period of recession. Modigliani and Cohn[51] argue that an alternative approach is that firms could have increased their borrowing. They argue that because the corporate sector has in real terms repaid debt, or reduced gearing in periods of inflation, dividends have fallen in real terms, as internal funds were required to finance increased values of stocks and for asset replacement. It is likely that companies in this study also reduced gearing in real terms. Table 4.3 shows an example of this for one firm in the study group. Thus it is likely that internal funds were pre-empted to finance increased values of stocks and for asset replacement.

If distributable profits (Table 4.5, column 5) are compared with capital grants received (Table 3.1, Chapter 3), it can be seen that capital grants are a much higher proportion of internally generated funds for net investment, etc. than they are of gross internal cash flows. These points are further explored in Chapter 7.

Table 4.5
Distributable profits adjusted for the increase in the value of stocks due to inflation

IR£ Million

Year	N*	Taxable Profits	Accounting Depreciation	Cash Tax Payment	Stock Adjustment	Distributable Profits
		P	C	T	O	(P -C -T -O)
1964	123	23.536	6.401	5.947	2.562	8.626
1965	138	25.027	7.409	6.412	1.931	9.275
1966	144	25.457	8.603	6.971	1.116	8.767
1967	143	27.196	9.050	7.779	1.634	8.733
1968	143	33.776	10.069	7.770	3.798	12.139
1969	138	35.851	10.424	7.166	5.180	13.081
1970	130	33.660	10.445	7.955	3.972	11.288
1971	130	40.246	11.952	8.408	4.724	15.162
1972	121	55.910	14.727	9.329	9.677	22.177
1973	116	79.743	18.436	9.167	22.151	29.989
1974	116	67.731	22.483	12.656	24.712	7.880
1975	112	60.747	22.238	8.137	42.449	-12.077
1976	108	80.398	22.189	8.547	39.460	10.202
1977	102	110.676	24.568	13.926	42.346	29.836
1978	95	134.479	31.318	14.434	27.134	61.592
1979	93	168.461	37.962	21.300	43.323	65.876
1980	91	137.843	44.386	21.705	44.640	27.112
1981	82	134.669	50.649	19.153	73.052	-8.185
1982	77	126.081	57.224	16.887	51.864	0.106
1983	72	130.475	60.663	13.872	29.362	26.578
1984	66	138.965	56.192	12.360	34.103	36.310

Note to Table 4.5

(*) N is the number of firms

In conclusion, this chapter has argued that using fully inflation adjusted profits as the tax base does not change the general conclusion of Chapter 3, that is, the average tax rate on corporate profits has fallen over the period 1964-84, although some individual firms' tax rate may have risen. There is also more uncertainty as to the precise magnitude of the fall in tax rates. Inflation may also increase uncertainty within an economic system, which may have adverse consequences for corporate liquidity. Inflation also has other effects on corporate financing, such as increasing the proportion of capital gains in profits, and the consequent need for external financing. The next chapter examines the distribution of tax rates amongst firms in the study group.

Notes

[1] P. Cagan and R.E. Lipsey, *The Financial Effects of Inflation*, National Bureau of Economic Research, General Series, no. 103, Ballinger Publishing Co., Cambridge, Mass., 1978, ch. 1.

[2] I. Fisher, *The Theory of Interest*, MacMillan, London, 1930, pp. 43-44. An inflation adjusted rate of interest that took account of the fall in the real capital value of debt would be equal to :- $i(1 + \Delta P) + \Delta P$, where i is the pre-inflation interest rate and ΔP is the rate of inflation. See A.R. Prest and N. A. Barr, *Public Finance*, Weidenfeld and Nicolson, London, 1979, p. 429.

[3] I. Fisher, ibid. p. 27.

[4] A.R. Prest and N.A. Barr, op. cit. pp. 334-338; See also J. Whalley, 'Capital Gains Taxation and Interest Rate Changes: An Extension of Paish's Argument', *National Tax Journal*, vol. XXX11, no. 1, 1979, pp. 87-91.

[5] M.F. Morley, *The Fiscal Implications of Inflation Accounting*, The Institute for Fiscal Studies and the Institute of Chartered Accountants in England and Wales, London, 1974, presents a comprehensive analysis of the effects of inflation on assets and liabilities in company accounts.

[6] See Institute of Chartered Accountants in Ireland, *Current Cost Accounting*, Statement of Standard Accounting Practice, no. 16, Institute of Chartered Accountants in Ireland, Dublin, 1980.

[7] Using Statement of Standard Accounting Practice, no. 16. The total number of companies publishing inflation adjusted accounts and included in this study is shown in Table 4.1. A small number of companies which published inflation adjusted accounts wete omitted, as insufficient detail relating to these inflation adjustments was shown in their accounts

[8] That is the *Report of the Inflation Accounting Committee*, Inflation Accounting, Cmnd. 6225, H.M.S.O. London, 1975.

[9] J.R. Hicks, *Value and Capital*, 2nd edition, Oxford University Press, Oxford, 1946, p. 172. The quotation is from the Sandilands Report, p. 29.

[10] Meade Committee, *The Structure and Reform of Direct Taxation*, The Institute for Fiscal Studies and George Allen and Unwin, London, 1978, pp. 31-32, and 105

[11] G. Whittington, *Inflation Accounting: An Introduction to the Debate*, Oxford University Press, Oxford, 1983. See also W.T. Baxter, *Inflation Accounting*, Philip Allan, Oxford, 1984, especially pp. 17-24.

[12] The Sandilands Report, op. cit . p. 29

[13] The Sandilands Report, op. cit. p. 161.

[14] The Sandilands Report, op. cit. p. 162.

[15] The Sandilands Report, op. cit. p. 162, For further criticisms of the Sandilands Report see J.A. Kay, 'Inflation Accounting - A Review Article', *Economic Journal*, no. 346, 1977, pp. 300-311.

[16] Sandilands Report, op. cit. p. 162.

[17] Statements of Standard Accounting Practice are prepared by the Institute of Chartered Accountants of England and Wales, Scotland, and Ireland. These Statements do not have the rule of law, but failure to prepare accounts in accordance with the Statements may result in accounts not being endorsed by auditors, as 'true and fair'.

[18] See W.T. Baxter, ibid, for a clear discussion of the gearing adjustment especially pp. 59-64.

[19] For example, a firm could make real capital gains resulting from the appreciation in value of land and buildings. These real capital gains could then be realised and the firm could relocate in an area with lower land and building values. A possible argument is that real capital gains or holding gains should be included in income only if the fundamental nature of the business has not changed by realising them. However such real holding gains increase their owners potential for future consumption, while maintaining the value of capital intact, and as such would constitute part of income in the Hicksian sense. H.C. Simons, *Personal Income Taxation*, University of Chicago Press, Chicago, 1938, pp. 152-153, recognises that real capital gains are part of income but concludes, that as regards taxation of profits, 'the realization criterion must be accepted as a practical necessity'. In contrast Kaldor argues that real capital gains whether anticipated or not should be treated as part of taxable capacity. N. Kaldor, *An Expenditure Tax*, George Allen and Unwin, London, 1955, pp. 68-69.

[20] B. Moore, 'Equity Values and Inflation: The Importance of Dividends', *Lloyds Bank Review*, July, 1980, pp. 1-15.

[21] See also the criticisms of Moore ibid, by G.H. Lawson and A.W. Stark, 'Equity Values and Inflation: Dividends and Debt Financing' in *Lloyds Bank Review*, January 1981, pp. 41-59. There is also a reply by Moore and comments by P.J.O. Wiles in the same issue.

[22] F. Modigliani and R.A. Cohn, 'Inflation, Rational Valuation and the Market', *Financial Analysts Journal*, March/April, 1979, pp. 24-44.

[23] S. Davidson and R.L. Weil, 'Inflation Accounting: Implications of the F.A.S.B. Proposal', in H.J. Aaron (ed.) *Inflation and the Income Tax*, The Brookings Institution, New York, 1976.

[24] Financial Accounting Standards Board, *Financial Reporting in Units of General Purchasing Power*, Proposed Statement of Financial Accounting Standards Exposure Draft, Stamford, Connecticut: F.A.S.B.1974.

[25] J.I. Bulow and J.B. Shoven, 'Inflation, Corporate Profits, and the Rate of Return to Capital', in R.E. Hall (ed.) *Inflation*, University of Chicago Press for the National Bureau of Economic Research, Chicago, 1982.

[26] J.A. Kay and C. Mayer, *Inflation Accounting*, Institute of Fiscal Studies, Report Series no. 10, Institute of Fiscal Studies, London, 1984.

[27] J.A. Kay and C. Mayer, ibid. p. 25.

[28] J.A. Kay and C. Mayer, ibid. p. 8.

[29] T.N. Tideman and D.P. Tucker, 'Tax Treatment of Business Profits

Under Inflationary Conditions', in H.J. Aaron (ed.) *Inflation and the Income Tax*,The Brookings Institution, New York, 1976.

[30] T.N. Tideman and D.P. Tucker, ibid. p. 47.

[31] T.N. Tideman and D.P. Tucker, ibid. p. 67.

[32] J.R. Hicks, 'The Concept of Income in Relation to Taxation and to Business Management' *Greek Economic Review*, vol. 1, no. 2, 1979, pp. 1-14.

[33] B. Moore, (1980) op. cit.

[34] F. Modigliani and R.A. Cohn, op. cit.

[35] F. Modigliani and R.A. Cohn, op. cit. p. 27.

[36] The Sandilands Report, op. cit. pp. 198-200.

[37] Green Paper, *Corporation Tax*, Cmnd. 8456, H.M.S.O. London, 1982, pp. 43-49.

[38] M. Feldstein and L. Summers, 'Inflation and the Taxation of Capital Income in the Corporate Sector', *National Tax Journal,* vol. XXXII, 1979, pp. 445-469.

[39] M.A. King and D. Fullerton, op. cit. pp. 244-245.

[40] See J.S. Edwards and C.P. Mayer, *Issues in Bank Taxation*, Institute for Fiscal Studies, London, 1983, especially Chapter 5 for a further discussion of this point.

[41] See Chapter 3.

[42] M. Feldstein and L. Summers, 1979, op. cit. footnote 13.

[43] Although as noted by G.L. Bach and J.B. Stephenson, 'Inflation and the Redistribution of Wealth', *Review of Economics and Statistics*, 1975, no. 1, pp. 1-13, in a study relating to the United States, these redistributional effects may be quite complex. See also E. Nowotny, 'Inflation and Taxation: Reviewing the Macroeconomic Issues', *Journal of Economic Literature*, vol. XVIII, 1980, pp. 1025-1049, for a review of the effects of inflation and the tax system on resource allocation.

[44] Tideman and Tucker, op. cit. p. 36.

[45] D.W. Carlton, 'The Disruptive Effects of Inflation on the Organization of Markets', in R.E. Hall (ed.) *Inflation: Causes and Effects*, University of Chicago Press and National Bureau of Economic Research, Chicago, 1982, pp.139-152.

[46] P. Cagan and R.E. Lipsey, (1978) op. cit. pp. 13-27.

[47] J.A. Kay and M.A. King, *The British Tax System*, 3rd ed. Oxford University Press, Oxford, 1983, p. 162. See also pp. 181-183 for a further discussion of changes in stock relief in the U.K.

[48] The stock adjustment was estimated by calculating the average of opening and closing stocks, as they appear in the Balance Sheet, and deflating this sum by the annual rise in the wholesale price index. Calculating an average is a crude way of allowing for physical changes in stocks. raw materials, goods in process, etc. as they appear in the Balance Sheet. Another problem is that wholesale prices may also not be an accurate indicator of the rise in the price of raw materials and intermediate goods.

[49] Taxable profits as defined in Table 4.5 do not include dividends received from associated companies, and hence there is a slight

difference between taxable profits and gross internal cash flow.

[50] The percentage rise in the Consumer Price Index over the preceding year was 8.7, 11.4, 20.9, 18.0, 13.6, 7.6, 13.2, 18.2, 20.4, 17.2, 10.5, and 8.6 for the period 1972-84. G. Meeks, 'Profit Illusion', *Bulletin of the Oxford University Institute of Economics and Statistics*, vol. 36, 1974, pp. 267-285, has estimated that for the period 1967-72 in the United Kingdom 25.6 per cent of conventional profits were pre-empted in maintaining the physical volume of stocks.

[51] Modigliani and Cohn, (1979) op. cit.

5 The distribution of tax rates and aggregate corporate tax payments in O.E.C.D. countries

This chapter examines the distribution of tax rates amongst firms and also considers trends in aggregate tax payments in Ireland and other countries. It is useful to consider the distribution of tax rates amongst individual companies because the size distribution of firms is such that aggregated data will be dominated by the profits and tax payments of the larger firms.

5.1 **The distribution of tax rates**

Table 5.1 shows a cumulative frequency distribution of the ratio of 'cash tax payments' to current taxable profits for firms in the study during the period 1964-84. One feature of this table is the increase from 15 per cent in 1964 to 66 per cent in 1984 of the proportion of firms for which the level of current taxable profits paid in current 'cash tax payments' was under 10 per cent. Some of this increase is due to an increased number of firms reporting losses in one or more of the years 1971-84, and then offsetting these losses against taxable profits in subsequent years. For the period 1973-84 between 21 per cent and 32 per cent of all companies, in one or more years, either paid zero tax or had tax already paid subsequently refunded, resulting in a net cash inflow. A similar distribution of rates of 'cash tax payment' can be found in other countries[1]. If share capital profit is used as the base 8 per cent of companies in 1964 compared with 51 per cent 1984 had a ratio of 'cash tax payments' to share capital profits of under 10 per cent (Table 5.2), and for one or more of the years 1973-84, between 18 per cent and 28 per cent of companies in the study either had tax rates of zero or received a cash refund.

Table 5.1
The proportion of taxable profits (P) paid in 'cash tax payments' (T)*
shown as a cumulative frequency distribution 1964-84

per cent of firms

Tax Paid (per cent)	1964	1965	1966	1967	1968	1969	1970	1971	1972	1973	1974
≤ 0	3.1	3.7	5.1	5.1	4.3	12.8	6.7	12.1	15.2	25.5	30.3
<10	14.6	12.6	15.2	11.7	21.0	25.6	18.2	25.0	35.7	44.5	49.0
<20	33.8	31.1	29.7	22.6	40.6	43.6	40.5	44.8	54.5	64.5	61.2
<40	80.0	77.0	71.0	65.0	77.5	86.5	74.4	76.7	75.0	91.8	82.7
<100	97.7	98.5	94.2	97.1	99.3	99.2	100	95.7	95.5	100	95.9
No. of firms	130	135	138	137	138	133	121	116	112	110	99

Tax Paid (per cent)	1975	1976	1977	1978	1979	1980	1981	1982	1983	1984
≤ 0	21.8	21.3	21.6	26.1	22.7	23.7	24.3	22.2	30.9	31.9
<10	48.3	58.4	52.3	58.7	61.4	46.1	57.1	59.3	52.7	66.0
<20	72.4	73.0	63.6	71.7	77.3	59.2	72.9	74.1	74.5	76.6
<40	90.8	94.4	90.9	92.4	90.9	94.7	95.7	98.1	96.4	93.6
<100	97.7	98.9	98.9	98.9	98.9	100	98.6	100	100	95.7
No. of firms	87	89	88	92	88	76	70	54	55	47

(*) Calculated for only those firms with taxable profits

Table 5.2
The proportion of share capital profits (P - C) paid in 'cash tax payments'(T)*
shown as a cumulative frequency distribution 1964-84

per cent of firms

Tax Paid (per cent)	1964	1965	1966	1967	1968	1969	1970	1971	1972	1973	1974
≤ 0	3.1	3.8	5.2	4.5	4.4	11.5	5.9	12.1	15.9	23.8	26.6
<10	7.8	10.5	10.4	8.3	14.8	20.0	11.8	23.3	29.9	38.1	40.4
<20	20.9	19.5	19.3	13.5	28.1	31.5	24.4	32.8	44.9	52.4	54.3
<40	65.1	58.6	56.3	46.6	65.9	73.1	54.6	61.2	69.2	83.8	76.6
<60	86.8	88.7	80.7	73.7	90.4	91.5	81.5	81.9	84.1	95.2	83.0
<100	93.8	97.0	91.9	90.2	97.8	97.7	97.5	90.5	92.5	98.1	92.6
No. of firms	129	133	135	133	135	130	119	116	107	105	94

Tax Paid (per cent)	1975	1976	1977	1978	1979	1980	1981	1982	1983	1984
≤ 0	20.7	20.2	21.4	27.9	21.7	18.8	20.6	22.0	28.0	27.9
<10	40.2	51.2	47.6	53.5	51.8	37.7	46.0	50.0	42.0	51.2
<20	58.5	66.7	60.7	67.4	73.5	46.4	61.9	68.0	54.0	69.8
<40	81.7	91.7	89.3	87.2	85.5	79.7	77.8	82.0	72.0	86.0
<60	89.0	97.6	95.2	93.0	95.2	88.4	87.3	94.0	80.0	90.7
<100	93.9	97.6	98.8	96.5	97.6	94.2	92.1	98.0	94.0	97.7
No. of firms	82	84	84	86	83	69	63	50	50	43

(*) Calculated for only those firms with positive share capital profits
P = taxable profits; T = cash tax payments; C = accounting depreciation

Such a distribution of tax rates has considerable implications for the growth of leasing, which is explored further in Chapter 6 and may also result in a number of anomalies arising from asymmetries in the tax system. This is because in general only firms making profits may benefit from specific provisions of the tax code such as interest deductibility.

Table 5.1 also shows that in some cases the ratio of current 'cash tax payments' to current taxable profits exceeds 50 per cent and in some cases 100 per cent. This occurs because current 'cash tax payments' are largely based on profits in the preceding one or two year period. Hence a fall in reported profits has the effect of increasing the level of 'cash tax payments'. Table 3.1, Chapter 3 showed that a reduction in taxable profits, such as in 1979, or 1973-74, for an almost identical population of firms, in both periods had the effect of increasing the overall level of 'cash tax payments' thus adding to likely liquidity problems resulting from the decline in reported profits. Overall Balance Sheet tax liabilities may also be reduced for reasons other than a fall in profitability, for example a decline in investment, and hence accelerated depreciation allowances, which would increase the level of 'cash tax payments'.

It is also of interest to examine the distribution of tax rates by size of profits. Mayer[2] found, for a sample of 276 firms selected from various manufacturing industries in the U.K. for the period 1965-76, that companies with smaller absolute profits appear to have a higher tax rate than companies with larger absolute profits. A possible reason for this is that larger firms may be better able to reduce their tax payments by access to greater expertise, or by their ability to pursue various tax reduction strategies through, for example, a policy of diversification, or in Ireland, by selecting an appropriate financial strategy as is described in Chapter 6.

Table 5.3 shows the distribution of tax rates by size of firm (as measured by pre-tax profits), for companies in the study for the four years 1964, 1970, 1980 and 1984. The Table shows that for the year 1964 for all size clases, except the largest size class which had only three firms, the largest single group of firms had tax rates in the range 20 per cent to 40 per cent. In contrast for the years 1980 and 1984 the largest group of firms for all size classes had tax rates less than 20 per cent. In general Table 5.3 confirms a general shift towards lower tax rates.

A second point of interest is that tax rates appear to be spread fairly evenly amongst different size classes of firm for each year examined. For example for 1980, 3 out of 5 firms with profits <IR£ 50000 had tax rates less than 20 per cent compared with 4 out of 7 for firms with profits > IR£ 5 million.

Table 5.3
The distribution of tax rates by the size of company profits for the years, 1964, 1970, 1980 and 1984[a]

Tax Rate (per cent)	Size of Profits[b] 0 - 50	50 - 100	100 - 1000	1000 - 5000	>5000
	Number of firms				
1964					
< 20	16	10	17	1	
20 - 40	17	14	27	2	
> 40	13	6	7	0	
Total	46	30	51	3	
1970					
< 20	7	14	20	8	
20 - 40	7	15	17	2	
> 40	11	4	16	0	
Total	25	33	53	10	
1980					
< 20	3	5	20	13	4
20 - 40	2	1	13	4	3
> 40	0	0	5	3	0
Total	5	6	38	20	7
1984					
< 20	2		11	17	6
20 - 40			1	6	0
> 40	1		2	1	0
Total	3		14	24	6

Notes to Table 5.3

(a) Calculated for only those firms with taxable profits. T and P are measured as for Table 3.1, Chapter 3.

(b) IR£' 000.

Table 5.4
The distribution of tax rates by size of company profits for the periods, 1964-70, 1971-75, 1976-80, 1981-84[a]

	Size of Profits[b]				
	0 - 50	50 - 100	100 - 1000	1000 - 5000	5000
			Number of firms		
			1964-70		
Tax Rate (per cent)					
< 20	71	80	144	26	
20 - 40	103	99	174	10	
> 40	99	52	72	2	
Total	273	231	390	38	
			1971-75		
< 20	30	43	180	46	8
20 - 40	16	27	64	19	1
> 40	24	21	41	4	0
Total	70	91	285	69	9
			1976-80		
< 20	15	22	159	83	20
20 - 40	3	9	50	28	6
> 40	6	2	25	4	1
Total	24	33	234	115	27
			1981-84		
<20	5	4	74	61	24
20 - 40	1		13	17	1
> 40	1	1	13	11	0
Total	7	5	100	89	25

Notes to Table 5.4

(a) Calculated for only those firms with taxable profits. T and P are measured as for Table 3.1 Chapter 3.

(b) IR£' 000.

Table 5.4 shows the distribution of tax rates by absolute size of profits for companies in the study group for the four periods 1964-70, 1971-75, 1976-80, and 1981-84[3]. The same trends are evident as for Table 5.3. The largest group of firms for all profit categories had tax rates less than 20 per cent for the periods 1976-80 and 1981-84 compared with 20 - 40 per cent for the period 1964-70. One of the features of Table 5.4 is that smaller firms tend to have higher tax rates than larger firms in the period 1964-70, for example, 26 per cent of firms in the smallest size category had tax rates under 20 per cent compared with 68 per cent in the largest size category. However for more recent years all size categories of firm tend to have similar proportions with tax rates under 20 per cent.

Finally Table 5.5 shows some simple Ordinary Least Squares regressions relating tax rates (T/P) to the size of firm as measured by taxable profits (P), for the four years 1964, 1970, 1980 and 1984. While P is always positive the ratio T/P may sometimes be negative as tax is repaid. For all three years a negative but non- significant relationship was obtained. The relationship between tax rates and the size of firm as measured by net assets plus short term borrowing (K) was also estimated using Ordinary Least Squares, and again the coefficient of K, while negative, was not statistically significant. A possible relationship between size of company as measured by capital employed and the use of fiscal incentives is explored in Chapter 6

Table 5.5
Regression coefficients for tax rates (T/P) against taxable profits (P) for the four years 1964, 1970, 1980 and 1984

Year	N*	Constant	Coefficient of taxable profits (P)	F	R^2(adj.)
1984	47	0.228	-0.00113 (0.00135)	0.70	-
1980	76	0.179	-0.00031 (0.00057)	0.30	-
1970	121	0.299	-0.0065 (0.0039)	2.71	.014
1964	130	0.32	-0.0107 (0.0073)	2.11	.009

Note to Table 5.5
(*) N is the number of firms. Only firms with positive taxable profits have been included. T/P may be negative for example where tax payments are repaid. Standard errors are in brackets.

In conclusion, while there is some evidence that smaller companies had higher tax rates in the earlier years of this study, for more recent years there appears to be no relationship between tax rates and size of firm.

5.2 Aggregate corporate tax payments in Ireland and other O.E.C.D. countries

Aggregate data for taxable profits, or for share capital profits as defined in Chapter 3, are not currently published. However other aggregate information concerning tax payments by the corporate sector in Ireland is published. In addition to the firms included in this study, the corporate sector would include financial companies and banks, certain State owned organisations, foreign owned firms, and various private companies. Table 5.6 shows direct taxation of the corporate sector as a percentage of total tax revenue for the period 1955-57, and 1965-1984. Table 5.6 also shows aggregate tax payments by the corporate sector, and aggregate capital grant payments to the corporate sector for 1965-84. Taxation payments are on a cash basis, but aggregate capital grant payments appear to be partly on an accrued basis and partly on a cash basis.

The trend of direct taxation of the corporate sector as a percentage of total tax revenue has shown a general decline over the period examined; concurrently there has been a trend towards higher payments of capital grants and other subsidies. Company direct taxation as a proportion of total tax payments fell from 8.8 per cent in the period 1955-57, to 7.2 per cent in 1965-67, 4.38 per cent in 1975-77, and to 3.86 per cent for the period 1982-84[4]. Capital grant payments rose from 31 per cent of tax payments in the period 1965-67 to 41.0 per cent in the period 1982-84.

For comparative purposes Table 5.7 shows similar data for the United Kingdom. Comparing Tables 5.6 and 5.7 it can be seen that company direct tax payments as a proportion of total tax revenue were higher for the U.K. in the period 1955-57, were generally lower than in Ireland for the period 1965-69, and then rose above the ratio in Ireland for the period 1971-84. For more recent years tax revenues from the U.K. corporate sector reflect North Sea oil corporate taxation and also the effects of the introduction of A.C.T. The proportion of tax revenue returned to the corporate sector in the form of capital grants, while higher in the U.K. for the earlier years declines below the level in Ireland for more recent years. Capital grants data for the U.K. include public sector enterprises, which account for more than 50 per cent of grant payments for some years. Whereas capital grant payments to public sector enterprises are a lower proportion of the capital grants data for Ireland shown in Table 5.6.

Table 5.6
Tax paid and capital grants received for the company sector in Ireland 1965-84

IR£ million

Year	Company Direct Taxation as a Percentage of Total Tax Revenue	Amount Paid in Direct Taxation by Companies	Capital Grants Received
	(1)	(2)	(3)
1955-57	8.80	n.a.	n.a.
1965	9.06	22.62	5.9
1966	8.18	22.03	6.3
1967	7.04	22.28	8.6
1968	7.74	28.06	11.2
1969	7.94	34.05	18.7
1970	8.80	44.54	22.6
1971	6.09	36.49	30.2
1972	5.59	38.75	23.2
1973	5.56	46.85	19.0
1974	6.93	65.51	25.9
1975	4.83	57.74	35.3
1976	4.39	71.37	40.1
1977	4.10	77.72	37.2
1978	5.00	106.06	40.5
1979	5.71	140.74	49.7
1980	4.54	144.56	85.0
1981	4.99	199.64	97.1
1982	4.72	231.80	87.5
1983	3.79	214.86	104.7
1984	3.26	209.63	77.1

Sources:- Columns (1) and (2), Expenditure Trends in O.E.C.D. Countries 1960-80, Table A10, O.E.C.D. Paris, 1972, and Revenue Statistics of O.E.C.D. Member Countries 1965-85, Table 13, and Table 47 O.E.C.D. Paris, 1986. Column (3), U.N. Yearbook of National Accounts Statistics 1977, Table 11, National Income and Expenditure, 1981, C.S.O. Dublin, 1982, Table A19, and National Income and Expenditure 1985, C.S.O. Dublin, 1986, Table A21. Capital grant payments derived from the National Income Accounts were defined as being payments by the I.D.A plus payments to S.F.A.D.Co. and Udaras na Gaeltachta.

Table 5.7
Tax paid and capital grants received for the company sector in the U.K. for the period 1965-84

Stg £ Million

Year	Company Direct Taxation as a Percentage of Total Tax Revenue	Amount Paid in Direct Taxation by Companies	Capital Grants Received
	(1)	(2)	(3)
1955-57	15.5	n.a.	n.a.
1965	6.27	629	536
1966	6.02	717	32
1967	8.13	1002	251
1968	7.55	1103	526
1969	7.43	1178	1916
1970	9.17	1751	867
1971	8.12	1635	670
1972	7.52	1616	889
1973	8.64	2007	1075
1974	9.63	2819	585
1975	6.20	2330	1043
1976	5.11	2262	788
1977	6.45	3264	1020
1978	7.46	4145	1113
1979	7.61	4892	929
1980	7.84	6353	1196
1981	9.25	8539	4886
1982	9.71	10522	2307
1983	10.95	12441	
1984	11.47	14056	

Sources:- Columns (1) and (2), Expenditure Trends in O.E.C.D. Countries 1960-80, Table A10, O.E.C.D. Paris, 1972, and Revenue Statistics of O.E.C.D. Member Countries 1965-81, Table 13, and Table 59, O.E.C.D. Paris, 1982. Column (3), United Nations National Accounts Statistics, 1982, Table 3.23, Yearbook of National Accounts Statistics 1981, Table 11, and 1975, Table 13, United Nations, New York.

Table 5.8 shows direct taxes on companies as a percentage of total current tax revenues for the O.E.C.D. group of countries for the periods 1955-57, 1965-67, 1975-77, and 1982-84. There are difficulties in making inter-country comparisons because, for example, the corporate sector is of varying importance in different economies, and because inter-country data may not be strictly comparable for a variety of reasons. However Table 5.8 illustrates that direct taxes on companies as a percentage of total tax revenue has declined in importance for most countries. Only four countries recorded an increase in this ratio between 1955-57 and 1982-84 (Greece, Italy, Japan and Norway).

Table 5.8
Company direct taxation as a percentage of total tax revenue for O.E.C.D. countries

Country	1955-57	1965-67	1975-77	1982-84
Australia	n.a.	15.42	12.01	9.33
Austria	6.9	5.15	3.74	2.95
Belgium	6.7	5.97	6.60	6.01
Canada	19.0	13.28	12.17	7.96
Denmark	5.6	3.73	3.35	3.72
Finland	12.6	7.53	4.34	4.47
France	6.4	4.99	5.56	4.46
Germany	9.3	6.88	4.88	5.20
Greece	2.0	3.63	3.28	2.89
Ireland	8.8	7.52	4.38	3.86
Italy	5.9	6.9	6.71	9.24
Japan	17.9	18.04	20.45	20.19
Luxembourg	17.9	10.99	17.46	15.98
Netherlands	13.5	7.22	7.11	6.19
New Zealand	n.a.	20.74	11.55	7.68
Norway	9.9	3.73	4.06	15.85
Portugal	n.a.	n.a.	n.a.	n.a.
Spain	20.7	9.76	6.41	4.89
Sweden	12.2	5.17	3.50	3.48
Switzerland	8.9	7.33	7.42	6.00
Turkey	n.a.	4.35	4.77	11.48
United Kingdom	15.5	6.49	6.03	10.74
United States	19.8	16.44	10.91	6.57

Sources:- For 1955-57, Expenditure Trends in O.E.C.D. Countries, 1960-80, Table A10, O.E.C.D., Paris 1972. For 1966-67, Revenue Statistics of O.E.C.D. Member Countries, 1965-74 , Paris, O.E.C.D. 1976. For 1975-84, Revenue Statistics of O.E.C.D. Member Countries, 1965-85, Paris, O.E.C.D. 1986.

King[5] comments that for most countries the ratio of tax to G.N.P. has been rising over this period. O'Hagan[6] has demonstrated the same trend for Ireland. This implies that direct taxation of the corporate sector has become relatively less important as a source of tax revenue. A decline in the proportion of company direct tax in total tax may be due to corporate tax rates falling or remaining constant, while other rates rise, or rising, but at a lower rate than other taxes, or it could be due to falling profit shares. From the evidence presented in Chapter 3[7] it would appear that the fall in company tax as a proportion of total tax in Ireland is due to a fall in tax rates because of the growth and diffusion of fiscal incentives. King[8] argues that the downward trend in tax rates found for the U.K. is also found in other countries

(Germany, Japan, France and the United States) but that tax rates have not fallen by quite as much as in the United Kingdom.

Hill[9] has examined rates of return and profit shares for the industrial and transport sectors for various countries for the years 1955-76. These sectors were used as a proxy for the non-financial corporate sector. The data was obtained from National Accounts which as Hill[10] acknowledges may not be comparable between countries, particularly for estimates of the capital stock. In addition the Wilson Report[11] has drawn attention to some of the difficulties in estimating gross trading profits for the U.K. corporate sector. These estimates are based on data provided by the Inland Revenue, but because of stock relief and accelerated depreciation allowances a large proportion of trading profits are not taxed, and often go unrecorded. A similar problem has arisen in Ireland.

Hill found profit shares to be highest in Japan, Denmark, and Germany, and lowest in the United Kingdom, Sweden and the United States, with Canada, Australia, Italy, and the Netherlands in an intermediate position. There was no evidence of a decline in profit shares for four countries, Canada, Japan, Australia, and Denmark, but quite strong evidence for the other countries examined. Hence for Canada, Japan, Australia and Denmark, a falling proportion of company direct taxation in total tax payments must be largely due to a falling relative tax burden, assuming the non-financial corporate sector maintained its relative proportion of total corporate profits. For the United States and various European countries a fall in the proportion of company direct tax as a proportion of total tax may be due to a combination of falling profit shares and a fall in the relative tax burden, again assuming the non-financial corporate sector maintained its relative share of total corporate profits.

Comparative data for capital grant payments to the corporate sector are available for only some O.E.C.D. countries and generally no distinction is made between public and private sector enterprises. Hence the means used to finance investment by public sector enterprises (for example, capital grants versus loans) may invalidate inter-country comparisons. However, the available data reinforces the conclusion of a generally declining relative net tax burden for most countries. For example, in the period 1978-80 capital grant receipts as a percentage of corporate tax payments were 12.1 per cent for Sweden and 144.4 per cent for Austria, for the period 1976-78[12]. For the period 1965-67, capital grant receipts as a percentage of corporate tax payments were 2.4 per cent for Sweden and 63.7 per cent for Austria. In contrast capital grant payments as a percentage of corporate tax payments fell in Finland from 7.22 per cent in 1965- 67 to 2.3 per cent in 1978-80.

Finally it can be seen from Table 5.8 that Ireland moved from 8th position in 1965-67 to 18th position in 1982-84 in a ranking of countries by the size of company direct tax payments as a per cent of total Government tax revenues.

In summary, many companies in the study had tax rates of under 10 per cent for more recent years, and at least 25 per cent of firms in the study appear to have paid no tax or to have had tax refunds in one or more of the years 1973-84. The corporate sector in Ireland appears to have one of the lowest levels of company direct taxation as a proportion of total tax receipts amongst O.E.C.D. countries. It is also likely that the corporate sector in Ireland receives one of the highest proportions of capital grants as a percentage of tax revenues, although comparable data is available for only a minority of O.E.C.D. countries. These trends in Ireland may be partially explained by a growing proportion of export-oriented foreign firms in the total, which are tax exempt, and which may also receive higher capital grants. Furthermore the trend in Ireland is likely to be one of a continuing reduction in the proportion of taxable profits paid in tax because of the introduction of a general 10 per cent tax rate on manufacturing profits tax in 1981, and because of other factors leading to a continuing diffusion of fiscal incentives[13].

The next two chapters examine the effect of fiscal incentives on corporate financing.

Notes

[1] J.T. Winkler, 'Corporatism', *European Journal of Sociology*, vol. 17, 1976, pp. 100-136, cites evidence that 43 per cent of 115 of the largest British companies pay virtually no United Kingdom profits tax. Volvo, the Swedish car, firm paid no Swedish corporate tax on profits equivalent to Stg.£ 43 million in 1974, 'Swedish Query over Volvo Tax Position', The Times, 15 August, 1975. A recent study states '...in practice many Swedish corporations do not pay any corporation income tax', M.A. King and D. Fullerton (eds.), *The Taxation of Income From Capital*, University of Chicago Press and National Bureau for Economic Research, Chicago, 1984 pp. 139-140. See also J.A. Kay and M.A. King, The British Tax System, Oxford University Press, Oxford, 1983, pp. 183-184.

[2] C. Mayer, 'The Structure of Corporation Tax in the U.K.' *Fiscal Studies*, vol. 3, no. 2, 1982, pp. 121-141.

[3] The number of firms refers to the profits and tax payments of one firm for one accounting period, in most cases a twelve month period.

[4] This increase is partly accounted for by increased profits and tax payments by oil companies operating in Ireland. See Chapter (3).

[5] M.A. King, *Public Policy and the Corporation*, Chapman and Hall, London, 1977, p. 45.

[6] J.W. O'Hagan, 'An Analysis of the Growth of the Public Sector in Ireland, 1953-77', *Journal of the Statistical and Social Inquiry Society of Ireland*, vo. XXIV, 1979-80, pp. 69-98, Tables 9 and 10.

[7] See Chapter 3, Table 3.2.

[8] M.A. King, 'The United Kingdom Profits Crisis: Myth or Reality?', *Economic Journal*, vol. 85, 1975, pp. 33-54 and M.A. King ,1977, op. cit. p. 46.

[9] T.P. Hill, *Profits and Rates of Return*, O.E.C.D., Paris, 1979, Chapter 6.

[10] T.P. Hill, ibid. p. 113.

[11] Wilson Report, *Committee to Review the Functioning of Financial Institutions*, Appendix 9, 'Further Improvements to Financial Statistics', by P. G. Moore and M.T. Jones, pp. 573-589, Cmnd. 7937, H.M.S.O. London, 1980.

[12] Source:- United Nations Yearbook of National Accounts Statistics, 1981, and 1970 for various countries.

[13] See Chapter 1 pp. 3-11.

6 Fiscal incentives and corporate financing: financial strategies

Chapter 1 has shown that fiscal incentives aimed at the corporate sector in Ireland have become both more numerous and more generous. In many instances the increased scope of fiscal incentives is a result of planned Government action. In some cases it appears to result from an unplanned diffusion or extension of tax reliefs. A similar situation has also arisen in other countries[1]. Fiscal incentives also interact with one another. This chapter, using a partial equilibrium framework, focuses on tax minimisation strategies pursued by firms in the study population, within a time period determined by the life of an investment project. This chapter focuses on the use of debt finance and leasing. The following chapter examines other forms of finance such as share issues. It is assumed that the firm wishes to maximise post tax profits, and the firm has already decided on its export level and investment. This is because, for the majority of firms export levels are fixed in the short run, and in many cases may be fixed for the life of an investment project. A decision to export may also require additional, or new investment. Developing export markets may take a considerable amount of time, as well as high expenditures. Hence exports are not likely to be very responsive to annual changes in the firm's tax position, whereas the form of financing, and the use of leased assets, may be more easily adjusted to take account of annual changes in the firm's tax liabilities.

It is also assumed that firms in the financial and non-financial sectors face the same nominal tax rate. Given these prior decisions and assumptions it is argued that the firm focuses on leasing and financing decisions. On the basis of these assumptions and also assuming a constant rate of return on assets, so that profits are known, it is possible to predict the proportion of depreciation allowances used by the firm, or in other words the extent of leasing, and also the form of external finance.

The chapter is divided into three main sections. In section (1), given certain investment rates or export levels, alternative tax minimisation strategies which firms might pursue are developed. In section (2) the effects on alternative tax reduction strategies of a reduced rate of corporate tax and inflation are assessed, and finally in section (3) some policy implications are discussed.

6.1 **Alternative tax reduction strategies**

From 1956 until 1980 firms eligible for the benefits from various fiscal incentives in Ireland had two main possibilities in attempting to reduce tax payments:- (a) increase the proportion of output exported, and/or (b) increase accelerated depreciation allowances. During this period all manufacturing firms in Ireland must have benefitted in varying degrees from accelerated depreciation allowances, particularly following the extension in value of accelerated depreciation allowances in 1971. Companies engaged in distribution and various service industries may also have benefitted from accelerated depreciation allowances, and because of diversification into manufacturing activities, could also have benefitted from tax relief on exports[2].

Tax relief on the increase in the value of stocks due to inflation, though of considerable importance in reducing tax payments in 1975, the year of its introduction, and subsequent years, is not considered as the increase in the value of stocks due to inflation is largely outside the control of firms. However, at the margin, stock relief is a form of free depreciation for current assets[3]. That is, a marginal increase in stocks (ΔS) has the same effect as a marginal increase in investment (ΔI), as both ΔS and ΔI may be deducted in assessing profits liable to tax.

Post 1981 manufacturing companies could choose to be taxed at a rate of 10 per cent rather than avail of export sales relief, although as shown in chapter 1, export sales relief and accelerated depreciation allowances remain the main form of tax relief.

In Ireland, as in other countries, interest payments can be offset against tax payments, and hence can be regarded as a form of subsidy to debt finance, assuming no shifting effects, compared with the use of equity finance where dividends are not tax deductible by the firm. The introduction of debt into the capital structure would reduce the overall cost of capital[4], which would allow a reduction in shareholder funds and higher profits per equity share, but a reduced absolute profit. This proposition assumes the rate of interest as reduced by a tax offset is less than the rate of return on capital, and that the rate of return on assets remains the same. If it is assumed that the introduction of debt is used for additional investment so that the absolute size of profits increases, the effective tax rate would be directly affected only if taxation on company profits were progressive.

This is because higher absolute profits would face a higher nominal tax rate. Corporate taxation in Ireland is not, however, progressive except for low absolute profits[5]. There may however be indirect effects on tax rates (T/P) depending on what the additional finance is used for.

King[6] argues that under a fiscal system where interest is tax deductible and free depreciation is permitted the tax system is distortionary in the sense that an increase in the tax rate increases the value of tax allowances, and reduces the cost of capital. Hence an increase in the tax rate could lead to an increase in the stock of capital in the corporate sector. The argument presented by King depends, amongst other things, on there being no constraints on a firm`s financial policy, and more importantly, that profits are always large enough to enable tax allowances to be claimed, or alternatively that firms with excess tax allowances receive a refund. The arguments presented in this chapter largely hinge on the existence of surplus tax allowances, with no refund of excess tax allowances.

Given that debt is tax deductible, which reduces the cost of debt compared with equity financing, a prediction from the Modigliani-Miller model[7] is that new equity financing would never be issued. However as Gordon and Malkiel[8] argue the implications of the Modigliani-Miller model are 'counterfactual'. New equity continues to be issued in economies whose fiscal systems allow debt to be tax deductible, such as the United States, the United Kingdom, and Ireland. Various reasons have been advanced to explain this phenomenon. Modigliani[9] has summarised these arguments into four categories:- (1) Bankruptcy costs[10], where increased risk of bankruptcy results from increasing levels of debt, and hence the use of equity finance. (2) Agency costs, in which the equity shareholders and debt holders are viewed as the principal, and the management of the firm as agents. Agency costs increase as debt is introduced into the capital structure, because, for example, of the costs of writing contracts, and increased monitoring costs[11]. (3) A third argument relates to the problem of valuing future growth opportunities, which may imply high risk and equity financing compared with financing existing assets which are already in place, and imply low risk and debt financing[12]. (4) A fourth argument and the one which is closest to the tax strategies described in this chapter is that developed by DeAngelo and Masulis, which hinges on firms using debt only up to the point where 'there is zero probability of losing any corporate tax shield'[13]. DeAngelo and Masulis only consider debt, whereas this chapter includes leasing as well as debt. In addition some predictions are made in this chapter concerning the use of share financing, and 'section 84' loans, where interest payments are treated for tax purposes as a dividend distribution.

For companies operating in Ireland, for any given tax rate, for the period 1964-80, the rate of tax payments (T/P) for each accounting period will be largely determined by the export/sales ratio (E/S), and the depreciation allowances ratio (D/P), where the base P, is taxable profits, that is profits liable to corporation tax if no tax allowances are claimed, and accelerated depreciation allowances or free depreciation allowances (D) are a measure of the amount of tax deferred due to accelerated depreciation or free depreciation allowances. Most tax allowances for investment are in the form of accelerated depreciation allowances. The size of the firm may also indirectly influence the level of tax payments, if, for example, larger firms are better able to benefit from various fiscal incentives including accelerated depreciation allowances, or because they are better able to export, or have access to better tax advice than smaller firms[14]. A number of problems arise if an attempt is made to estimate the effect of these variables on tax payments, for example, the problem of measuring deferred tax due to depreciation allowances, and the effect of lags on payment of taxes[15].

The export sales ratio (E/S) can vary between zero and one. The ratio of accelerated depreciation allowances to taxable profits (D/P) may be zero, if no accelerated depreciation allowances are claimed, but will rarely exceed one, as accelerated depreciation allowances not used may be either held in reserve (carried forward in company accounts), or sold by leasing assets to another firm with taxable profits. Surplus tax allowances carried forward do not earn interest, hence their present value reduces as a function of the length of time they remain unused. This asymmetric treatment by the tax system of tax allowances also applies to profits or losses[16]. Johansen[17] has analysed the effects of accelerated depreciation for both a growing rate of investment (+q), a firm with constant investment ($q = 0$), and a firm with a falling rate of investment ($q < 0$). In the former two cases accelerated depreciation results in a permanent reduction in tax, whereas in the latter case the tax is merely redistributed through time. This of course leads to a reduction in the present value of tax. The relationships between exports, accelerated depreciation allowances, and leasing are more formally expressed in the appendix 1 to this chapter.

The proportion of debt in the capital structure (the gearing ratio), which is measured in this chapter as interest payments/(taxable profits + interest payments), may have indirect effects on the tax rate. If borrowing is used to finance capital expenditure, and leads to allowances for accelerated depreciation, or if it is used to finance investment whose output is exported, there will be a negative association between the gearing ratio and the tax rate. However, if all or nearly all output is exported, firms may reduce their gearing, as debt becomes a relatively more expensive form of finance[18]. This is because if all output is exported, corporate tax is zero and interest payments cannot be offset against tax payments, thus resulting in an increase in the overall cost of debt capital. Firms in this position, or where profits are only partially exempt from taxation because of exports, may substitute preference shares for debt. Dividends on preference shares in an exporting company in Ireland would be either tax free or taxed at a lower rate to the recipient, depending on the ratio of exports to sales, and hence preference shareholders would be willing to accept a lower payment gross of tax. Similarly, if firms pay no corporation tax because of depreciation allowances, interest payments cannot be offset against tax payments. Such firms may choose some other form of external finance depending on relative costs. Changes in corporate tax law in 1976 (Corporation Taxes Act, 1976) allowed interest payments on loans referred to as 'section 84' loans[19], to be treated for tax purposes as a dividend on which tax is deducted at source, and the lender is generally not liable to any further tax[20]. The rate of interest charged on such loans is thus correspondingly lower. Post 1976 'section 84' loans largely replaced preference share financing as a form of tax based lending[21].

Companies with high E/S may also have issued equity share capital, rather than preference shares, or, subsequent to 1976 'section 84' loans. However equity share capital is not redeemable, whereas preference shares and 'section 84' loans can be issued with medium term maturity (<5 years). The use of share finance is examined in the following chapter in the context of a flow of funds analysis.

From the foregoing it may be deduced that firms can reduce their tax payments in a number of different ways, and the means used affects other financial decisions within the firm. For example, firms benefit from depreciation allowances only to the extent that current profits are taxed. Capital expenditure which leads to allowances for accelerated depreciation can be financed wholly or partly with debt , and hence result in an increase in gearing. Firms may follow, therefore, a tax reduction strategy of combining the use of accelerated depreciation allowances with gearing, and/or one of exporting, but will avoid a position where total tax relief exceeds tax payable. These options give rise to a number of alternative tax reduction strategies, of which four essentially static cases are examined in this chapter. It is assumed that the level of investment, and hence total depreciation allowances, and the level of exports have already been decided, that is, they are exogenous.

(1) *Accelerated depreciation allowances only* $(P = D)$

In this case depreciation allowances are assumed to be greater than, or equal to, taxable profits, and as a result additional interest payments can no longer be offset against tax payments. Hence the firm is more likely to use external share financing or retentions as a source of finance. It is possible, though unlikely, that the firm could retain excess depreciation allowances, or lease assets, and shift to a position where interest payments, or increases in interest payments, can be offset against tax payments. This latter decision will be determined by the costs and benefits of the outcome, for example, the post tax cost of debt $i(1 - T)$, where i is the rate of interest, and T is the tax rate. This decision will also be influenced by the rate at which excess depreciation allowances carried forward in the Balance Sheet are discounted[22]. If a strategy of maximising depreciation allowances is used, the firm will be able to use 'section 84' loans, although the benefits may not be as great as in the case of a firm with a high exports/sales ratio, as some liability to income tax above the standard rate may arise for the ultimate owners of debt.

(2) *Depreciation allowances with interest deductibility* $(D < P)$

In this case depreciation allowances are assumed to be less than profits before deduction of interest and tax, allowing interest payments or increases in interest payments to be tax deductible. Using this strategy the firm will be eligible to receive capital grants. 'Section 84' loans would be of no benefit to the firm in this case, unless the combination of tax deductible interest plus depreciation allowances was equal to or exceeded taxable profits.

(3) *Depreciation allowances with export tax relief*

In this case expansion finance is more likely to be by share financing, as dividends will be taxed at a lower rate, which varies with the proportion of exports in sales. The higher the level of exports the more likely that external financing will be by share financing, as the tax rate on dividends will also be correspondingly lower. The decision to use share financing rather than debt financing will also be influenced by whether total tax allowances are equal to taxable profits. If they are not, gearing could be introduced or additional debt could be issued. The firm will be eligible to receive capital grants as described in Chapter 1. Since 1976 the firm may also benefit from the use of 'section 84' loans, if the combination of exports and depreciation allowances is equal to or greater than taxable profits.

(4) *Export tax relief only (E = S)*

In the case where all output is exported, resulting in profits being exempt from corporate tax, accelerated depreciation allowances are likely to be low or zero, as assets eligible for such allowances can be leased. The firm may rely largely on retentions, or share financing (preference or equity) as a source of long term finance. To the extent that fixed assets are leased the firm is not eligible to receive capital grants. Since 1976 the firm can also avail itself of 'section 84' loans.

The time period in which alternative tax strategies are followed has a considerable influence on the choice between different tax strategies. As mentioned earlier in this chapter, in the very short run it may not be possible to switch from one strategy to another, because developing export markets, for example, or planning and implementing capital investment may take a number of years. However firms have considerable short run flexibility in relation to other policies, such as the use of leasing, or the extent of gearing. Table 6.1 summarises the various tax strategies described.

Changes in interest rates, which in turn affect the level of gearing, may have a direct effect on the extent of leasing. This is apart from the effect of changes in interest rates on investment and economic activity. A rise in interest rates can reduce profits directly and hence the amount of depreciation allowances necessary to ensure zero tax payments. Rather than purchase assets which may result in excess depreciation allowances, the firm may lease assets. Similarly a fall in interest rates may reduce the use of leasing.

Table 6.1
Summary of tax strategies

D/P = 1 (1)	D/(P+i) + i(P+i) = 1 (2)	D/P + E/S = 1 (3)	E/S = 1 (4)
no gearing	gearing	no gearing (?)	no gearing
`section 84 loans	`section 84' loans (?)	`section 84' loans (?)	`section 84' loans
capital grants	capital grants	capital grants	no capital grants
leasing	leasing (?)	leasing (?)	leasing
		equity or preference shares (?)	equity or preference shares

The tax strategies described also assume that there is no effective limit to external funds available to the corporate sector. That is, that companies are always in a position to obtain external finance in the form of debt, preference shares, etc. This is probably a fairly realistic assumption for all except loss making concerns whose financial decisions are likely to be tightly constrained and less influenced by tax considerations.

The tax strategies described suggest the following propositions:-

H.1: That as the value of the export/sales ratio (E/S) approaches one, the value of the accelerated depreciation allowances/taxable profits ratio (D/P) approaches zero, or may be negative. Conversely firms with a high D/P ratio will have a low E/S ratio;

H.2: That there is a relationship between the gearing ratio (i/(P + i)) and D/P, although this relationship may be positive or inverse. Where a firm has no borrowing, gearing may be introduced into the firm's capital structure until P = D. In the case where the firm already has debt, additional gearing may be introduced into the firm's capital structure until P + i = D + i (where $i \geq 0$). However if the firm is not in equilibrium, that is $i_m < p_m$ (marginal cost of debt is less than the marginal rate of return on assets), the firm could still introduce additional debt into the capital structure, even though this debt is not tax deductible, in order to finance additional assets, and this would result in additional profits. Depending on what assets are purchased with the debt, there could also be extra depreciation allowances (increased D);

H.3: That up to 1976 there is likely to have been an inverse relationship between the gearing ratio and the export ratio, as debt finance is unlikely to be used to finance assets which produce output for export, because the profits (if any) on such output would be tax free, and debt finance would be relatively more expensive. This proposition depends on the existence of suitable administrative arrangements, for example, a separate exporting company which is financed independently of the parent company;

H.4: That since 1976 firms with high export ratios or high depreciation allowances ratios may have introduced debt into the capital structure in the form of 'section 84' loans;

H.5: That there may be a positive relationship between the size of firm as measured by capital employed (K), and the use of various fiscal incentives. This could occur if larger firms have better access to tax advice, or if larger firms are more able to benefit from depreciation allowances because they have a higher ratio of investment to capital employed. A higher than average ratio of investment to capital employed is not sufficient to ensure that accelerated depreciation allowances result in a continuous fall in annual tax payments. For example, if the capital stock is given, and if a fixed proportion of capital is replaced each year, and if prices and profits remain constant, after a time lag the introduction of free depreciation will result in the same annual tax payments as if depreciation were based on constant annual amounts. However if the stock of capital eligible for depreciation allowances is increasing, or if prices of capital equipment increase more than other prices, free depreciation will result in a continuously falling tax rate on annual profits. In the case where depreciation allowances exceed prices of eligible assets, similar but more pronounced results follow[23]. Conversely if the stock of capital is falling, or if prices of capital goods fall more than other prices, the existence of free depreciation will result in an increase in tax rates, as the stock of deferred tax is reduced, that is, as the tax carried forward in a company's balance sheet due to accelerated depreciation falls.

Some of these relationships and tax strategies may be illustrated using Figure 6.1.

Figure 6.1

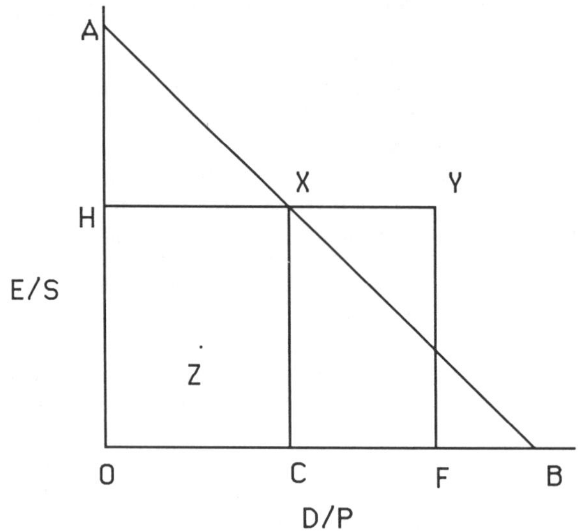

Figure 6.1 shows various combinations of the export/sales ratio and depreciation allowances/taxable profits ratio, that a firm may choose. At point A, exports = sales, and at point B depreciation allowances used by the firm = taxable profits. AB shows the locus of tax reduction strategies resulting in zero tax payments. A point to the right of AB, such as Y, represents a firm which has no tax payments and also has surplus tax allowances. A point to the left of AB, such as Z, represents a firm which has some positive tax payments, and some export and depreciation allowances. Point B corresponds to strategy (1) and point A to strategy (4). Any point along AB, except points A and B corresponds to strategy (3) if a firm has zero tax payments. The optimum post-tax profit maximising position for a firm is on the 'zero tax frontier' AB. A central proposition of this chapter is that a firm which found itself for example, at point Y could move to position X by selling tax allowances (leasing assets), thus reducing the ratio D/P from F to C,while keeping the same ratio of exports to sales (E/S) at point H. In other words, assuming a firm is in a position to benefit from both export tax relief and accelerated depreciation allowances, the firm will always operate so that $E/S + D/P \leq 1$ (see appendix to this chapter).

6.2 The effect of a reduced rate of corporation tax and inflation

(i) *A reduced rate of corporation tax*

In 1981 corporation tax for manufacturing firms in Ireland was reduced to 10 per cent, although distributions to Irish shareholders was also subject to income tax. Distributions to non-resident shareholders are not subject to income tax, nor is there any form of with-holding tax. Reducing the corporate tax rate to 10 per cent does not change the slope of the 'zero tax frontier', that is the relative proportions of exports and depreciation allowances necessary to ensure zero tax payments, but it is likely to reduce the relative proportion of depreciation allowances used by a firm subject to a 10 per cent tax rate. This is because these allowances are more valuable to a firm with higher rates of tax. The ability of firms to use both export tax relief and to avail of a 10 per cent tax rate will also depend on suitable administrative arrangements, for example, the formation of a separate manufacturing company. Similarly net of tax interest charges will be higher, which may lead to substitution of other forms of finance for debt by manufacturing firms.

Tax concessions are most valuable to firms with the highest marginal rate of tax. Hence with a 10 per cent tax rate on companies in the manufacturing sector, fiscal incentives such as accelerated depreciation allowances are more valuable to firms in the service sector such as banks. Increased demand for leasing will be limited by the extent of taxable profits in the banking sector, and is likely to result in a much less favorable distribution of tax savings between lessor and lessee. Under certain circumstances income from 'section 84' loans is worth less to the lender, for example where formerly a tax credit of 45 per cent might be claimed, this is now restricted to 10 per cent. Hence 'section 84' loans may become more expensive to borrowers. These factors may in turn encourage the internalisation of tax concessions through diversification - that is the benefits of tax concessions would be transferred within a group of companies to high tax activities (non-manufacturing activities) via group relief.

In addition to these factors a form of withholding tax on dividends, equivalent to Advance Corporation Tax (A.C.T.) in the United Kingdom was introduced in Ireland in June 1983, subsequent to a recommendation by the Commission on Taxation[25]. However tax concessions to exporting companies will not be affected by the introduction of A.C.T. Subsequent to the introduction of A.C.T., accelerated depreciation allowances became less valuable, even with leasing, as a firm must make a minimum payment of Corporation Tax (= to tax credit on dividends). For the same reason, for non-exporting companies, 'section 84' loans will become less valuable, but will continue to be issued. Prior to the introduction of A.C.T. there was rapid growth of 'section' 84 lending. From December 1982 to May 1983 'section 84' lending increased by IR£ 120 million to IR£ 637 million. Following the introduction of A.C.T. in June 1983, 'section 84' lending continued to increase, but at a much reduced rate so that by May 1984 'section 84 lending amounted to IR£ 741 million, and in May 1986 IR£ 807 million[26]. Advance Corporation Tax, coupled with fiscal incentives which largely exempt manufacturing companies from paying Corporation Tax, constitutes a form of differential profits tax, as companies that do not pay dividends will not pay A.C.T. There is considerable controversy relating to the effects of a differential profits tax. Rubner[27] argued that the post- war differential profits tax in the U.K. had little effect on company saving ratios. This conclusion was criticised by Feldstein[28] who argued that the differential profits tax increased corporate saving, and this viewpoint is now generally accepted, although for a more recent period Briston and Tomkins[29] argue that the differential profits tax had little effect on retentions as companies wished to maintain dividends at the same post-tax level to shareholders. Feldstein[30] has also argued that although total corporate saving may have increased, high retained earnings depressed personal saving, resulting in a slightly higher overall saving ratio. Controversy has also arisen relating to whether corporate savings are efficiently invested[31]. In Ireland, a post-tax profit maximising strategy would result in a higher retention rate (in the limit the retention rate would be 100 per cent) and hence result in a capital gain for shareholders. This is because effective rates of capital gains tax in Ireland are low, even in the short run, and if an asset is held longer than 21 years, the effective capital gains tax rate will be zero.

(ii) *Inflation*

It has been argued in Chapter 4 that inflation may not have much effect on aggregate profits but inflation does change the composition of profits by reducing the relative share of trading profits and increasing the relative share of capital gains in corporate profits. Because capital gains are infrequently realised, inflation reduces cash flows generated by the firm's operations. Effective tax rates on trading profits are raised, because trading profits are overstated due to historical cost accounting, and if capital gains are taxed, effective tax rates on overall profits may be higher with inflation, compared with a situation of constant prices.

Fiscal incentives are directed towards trading income, although the favourable treatment of capital gains in Ireland may bias firms to obtain income in the form of a capital gain rather than as trading income. In relation to figure 6.1 the main effect of inflation compared with constant prices is likely to be an increase in the proportion of accelerated depreciation allowances used by the firm, and a reduction in the use of leasing. Hence inflation may make it more difficult for firms to reach the 'zero tax frontier' AB in figure 6.1.

The rate of inflation also affects the loss in value from carrying forward unused tax allowances. The higher the rate of inflation the greater the real reduction in the value of unused tax allowances. Conversely at low rates of inflation, the real value of unused allowances, though continuing to fall, does so at a reduced rate. Hence at low rates of inflation firms may be less averse to carrying forward unused tax allowances.

6.3 Conclusion and implications for economic policy

It has been argued in this chapter that given exports and investment, and assuming a constant rate of return on assets, the proportion of depreciation allowances used by the firm, and the amount of leasing may be predicted for the firm. Depreciation allowances and export tax relief, in conjunction with leasing possibilities, permit firms to pursue a number of alternative tax reduction strategies in order to minimise tax payments. The tax strategy chosen in turn affects other financial decisions within the firm, for example the form of external finance.

A number of policy implications may also be drawn from this chapter:-

(1) One policy implication relates to the effect of accelerated depreciation allowances on the growth of leasing. The main benefit of accelerated depreciation allowances, where a firm has no tax liabilities, is through lower (or no) charges on leased assets, and secondly through reduced costs of finance;

(2) The growth of leasing (a market for depreciation allowances) has also helped diffuse fiscal incentives throughout the corporate sector and is partly responsible for the declining proportion of corporate tax revenues in Ireland, and in other countries such as the United Kingdom;

(3) A third implication arises from the chanelling of fiscal incentives via leasing, through financial institutions operating in imperfect markets. This may bias investment decisions towards assets which are more suitable for leasing, for example, homogeneous and non-specific assets, as assets with these properties will be more marketable in the event of default (for example office and transport equipment)[32]. This implies that the stream of earnings for different investment projects adjusted for risk may differ between the banking sector, which is considering the purchase of assets for leasing and their possible resale value in the event of default, and the non-banking sector which evaluates a project with the assumption of continuing operation. This divergence in valuation between potential lessor and potential lessee is most likely to occur in the case of projects with high asset specificity which require specialised knowledge and decision skills. Such knowledge and skills may often be unique to a firm, or in short supply, and are likely to be costly for a leasing agency to acquire. The resulting information bias gives rise to the problem of 'moral hazard', and also gives rise to possible future agency costs in the event of the leasing agency taking control of the assets. Both of these factors may result in differences in valuation[33]. There may also be a bias towards leased assets which represent a lower proportion of total firm assets, as again there is a lower risk of default, for example in the case of an M.N.C. subsidiary operating in Ireland;

(4) The Irish banking sector is highly concentrated and a recent study has concluded that there has been little change in concentration in recent years[34]. The Banking sector in the U.K. is also concentrated. It is unclear in a sector dominated by oligopolistic firms what the distribution of tax benefits between lessor and lessee is likely to be[35]. A recent study of 103 lease agreements in the U.K. by Edwards and Mayer[36] concluded that on average 83 per cent of the benefits were passed on to the lessee, although there was considerable variation for individual leases . The Edwards and Mayer study also examined leases which were not eligible for regional assistance grants. In Ireland the effective limit on leasing and tax based lending is the absolute size of profits in the banking sector (as little leasing

takes place outside the banking sector). Because the demand for tax based lending and leasing is likely to exceed this limit due to the introduction of a general 10 per cent tax rate, the banking sector may be in a position to retain a portion of the tax savings through higher charges (and hence higher profits) rather than pass on all tax savings. Eventually though, there may be a build up of unused tax allowances as has happened in the U.K.[37]. The introduction of Advanced Corporation Tax in Ireland may also encourage the build up of unused tax allowances, as it reduces the amount of taxable profits which may be offset aginst depreciation allowances. For more recent years a number of companies in the study have disclosed surplus depreciation allowances;

(5) Some companies may avoid these market biases by internalising the market for tax allowances, for example, through diversification and using surplus allowances within the group. Subsidiaries of multinational companies may switch taxable profits to subsidiaries in Ireland in order to 'mop up' any surplus tax allowances.

A policy option, assuming it is desirable to retain the current fiscal incentives, would be to remove restrictions in the present market for tax allowances by making it easier to sell tax allowances to other companies. Such a procedure has recently been attempted in the United States. The Economic Recovery Act of 1981 in the U.S. removed restrictions on the sale of surplus depreciation allowances, and the provisions are referred to generally as 'Safe Harbor Leasing'. Under this Act a firm buying assets with the intention of leasing them was treated as the owner of the assets for tax purposes only. The financial transactions between lessor and lessee consisted of an initial payment only. Other transactions were balanced by loan repayments and interest charges on a fictional loan which were set to equal leasing charges. The lessor thus benefitted from depreciation allowances as well as tax deductions for fictional interest payments. This measure has been subject to a number of criticisms[38], for example, the extent of benefits which accrue to the lessee[39]. In addition while leasing does reduce inequalities in benefits from accelerated depreciation allowances, between companies making losses or business start ups, and companies making profits, it is not compatible with various concepts of competitive neutrality between firms. Auerbach and Warren[40] argue competitive neutrality is desirable to provide equivalent benefit to different firms and to avoid market distortions, such as tax induced mergers. However the concept of 'competitive neutrality' is ambiguous. For example, it could mean equality in capital costs, or equality of subsidies, or equality of incremental subsidies; that is, those derived from a specific measure and ignoring the effects of existing tax provisions. It is also not clear, given Government intervention because of market imperfections, that 'competitive neutrality' is a desirable objective of Government.

'Safe harbor leasing' was also used in a variety of unintended ways; for example to offset tax liabilities in previous years, and to use foreign tax credits which would otherwise have been unused to offset against U.S. corporate tax. For these reasons Auerbach has described 'safe harbor leasing' as a legislative fiasco[41].

A further criticism is that unnecessary risk is introduced into the transaction, for example if the lessee becomes bankrupt. Instead it is argued surplus allowances should be converted into the tax equivalent and paid to the owners of the assets[42]. In the U.K. and Ireland this would be equivalent to increasing the grant rate on fixed assets. The U.S. measure was repealed in the Tax Equity and Fiscal Responsibility Act of 1982.

The study of leasing in the U.K. by Edwards and Mayer[43] argued that provided all benefits were passed on to the lessee leasing has the advantage that it subjects the firm 'to an external test of creditworthiness'. However this argument ignores the selective nature of leased assets in the U.K. A large proportion of assets which might potentially be leased are not in fact leased. In 1980 in the U.K. leased assets amounted to 22.5 per cent and in 1981 26.75 of net investment in plant, machinery, and vehicles for companies in the manufacturing, distributive and service sectors[44]. Edwards and Mayer recommend a system where assets carried forward in the Balance Sheet are marked up by the net of tax rate of interest. In future years in the U.K. the build up of unused allowances is likely to be reduced by the phasing out of accelerated depreciation allowances announced in the Budget Statement of 1984[45]. In Ireland the 1984 Budget announced restrictions on assets which will qualify for tax allowances, if leased, to machinery or plant which qualified for grants from certain State agencies and in 1986 depreciation allowances were limited to their net of grant cost. These provisions may also have some effect on the growth of unused depreciation allowances in Ireland by reducing investment in assets which are less attractive to lessors[46].

The following chapter examines the effect of fiscal incentives on corporate financing in the context of a flow of funds analysis.

Appendix 1

The relationship between leasing, exports, and investment

This appendix sets out more formally the relationship between leasing, exports, and investment. It is assumed that the firm has already decided on export levels and investment, that there is a constant rate of return on assets, and that all firms face the same nominal tax rate. Assuming a given investment the firm knows the stream of depreciation allowances that may be claimed. Granted all firms face the same nominal tax rate, the difference between total tax allowances available to the firm and taxable profits will equal the amount of depreciation allowances associated with leasing. That is:-

$$D_T - (P - A) = D_L \qquad (A.1)$$

D_T represents total depreciation allowances available, P is taxable profits, A is all other allowances and DL is the depreciation allowance on leased assets, which are claimed by the leasing agency, such as a bank. This argument assumes that there are surplus depreciation allowances, that is $D_T > (P - A)$.

Example:- If $D_T = 15, P = 10, \text{ and } A = 5,$

$$D_L = 15 - (10 - 5) = 10$$

Dividing A.1 by P, where P is taxable profits,

$$D_T/P - (P - A)/P = D_L/P \qquad (A.2)$$

Equation (A.2) may be rewritten as,

$$D_T/P = D_L/P - A/P + 1 \qquad (A.3)$$

For a firm that exports only and claims no other allowances except depreciation allowances,

$$A/P = E/S \qquad (A.4)$$

Substituting A.4 in A.3,

$$D_T/P = 1 - E/S + D_L/P \qquad (A.5)$$

That is given D_T and E/S, D_L/P is determined as a residual.

If other tax allowances, in addition to depreciation allowances, are used by a firm, given D_T and E/S, D_L may be only approximately estimated. However other tax allowances are relatively much less important than export tax relief and accelerated depreciation allowances.

Total depreciation allowances on investment may be subdivided into those depreciation allowances claimed by the firm, plus depreciation allowances on leased assets,

$$D_T = D + D_L \qquad (A.6)$$

Dividing A.6 by P,

$$D_T/P = D/P + D_L/P \qquad (A.7)$$

Substituting A.7 for D_T/P in A.5,

$$D/P + D_L/P = 1 - E/S + D_L/P \qquad (A.8)$$

That is,

$$D/P = 1 - E/S \qquad (A.9)$$

Equation (A.9) states that depreciation allowances used by the firm are negatively related to the export ratio. Equation (A.9) assumes firms have taxable profits, but where tax allowances $\geq$ taxable profits, resulting in zero tax payments. If other tax allowances, in addition to export tax relief, are assumed equal to A_X/P then,

$$D/P = 1 - E/S - A_X/P \qquad (A.10)$$

Assuming the firm has some positive tax payments,

$$D/P < 1 - E/S - A_X/P \qquad (A.11)$$

Combining (A.10) and (A.11),

$$D/P \leq 1 - E/S - A_X/P \qquad (A.12)$$

In addition, if r is the nominal tax rate, and T/P is the actual tax rate, and assuming E/S and D/P are the only tax allowances, and that there are no lags in tax payments.

$$r - r.E/S - r.D/P = T/P \qquad (A.13)$$

$$r(1 - E/S - D/P) = T/P$$

$$1 - E/S - D/P = (T/P)/r \qquad (A.14)$$

Example (1):-

Assuming $r = 0.5$ and $T/P = 0.1$
$D/P = 1 - 0.2 - E/S = 0.8 - E/S$

Example (2):-

Assuming $r = 0.5$ and $T/P = 0.45$
$D/P = 1 - 0.9 - E/S = 0.1 - E/S$

Example (3):-

Assuming $r = 0.1$ and $T/P = 0.05$
$D/P = 1 - 0.5 - E/S = 0.5 - E/S$

So that for low actual tax rates (T/P) compared with nominal tax rates, the value of the intercept approaches unity. If the nominal tax rate were reduced to 10 per cent,the actual tax rate would have to fall to almost zero in order for the intercept a, to equal to 1 in the expression,

$$D/P = a - E/S.$$

Notes

[1] See for example J.A. Kay and M.A. King, *The British Tax System*, Oxford University Press, Oxford, 1983, especially chapter 12; Clark Joel, 'Tax Incentives in Central American Development', *Economic Development and Cultural Change*, vol. 19, 1971, pp. 229-252, and J. Siegfried, 'Effective Average U.S. Corporation Income Tax Rates', *National Tax Journal*, vol. XXVII, 1974, pp. 245-259.

[2] Normally firms using both export tax relief and accelerated depreciation allowances would form separate exporting and manufacturing companies and transfer tax allowances to a holding company using group relief.

[3] See W.A. Thomas, *The Finance of British Industry*, Methuen, London, 1978, p. 232. M.A. King and D. Fullerton (eds.), *The Taxation of Income From Capital*, University of Chicago Press and National Bureau of Economic Research, Chicago, 1984, p. 44.

[4] F. Modigliani and M.H. Miller, 'Taxes and the Cost of Capital: A Correction', American Economic Review, vol. 53, nos. 3-5, 1963, pp. 433-443.

[5] Commission on Taxation, *Direct Taxation*, Pl. 617, Stationary Office, Dublin, 1982, p. 332.

[6] M.A. King, 'Taxation, Corporate Financial Policy, and the Cost of Capital', *Journal of Public Economics*, vol. 4, 1975, pp. 271-279; and M.A. King, *Public Policy and the Corporation*, Chapman and Hall, London, 1977, pp. 228-235.

[7] F. Modigliani and M. Miller, 'The Cost of Capital, Corporation Finance and the Theory of Investment', *American Economic Review*, vol. 48, 1958, pp. 261-297, and F. Modigliani and M. Miller, 1963, op. cit.

[8] R.H. Gordon and B.G. Malkiel, 'Corporation Finance', in H.J. Aaron and J.A. Pechman (eds.), *How Taxes Affect Economic Behaviour*, Brookings Institution, Washington D.C., 1981, pp. 131-192.

[9] F.Modigliani, 'Debt, Dividend Policy, Taxes, Inflation and Market Valuation', *Journal of Finance*, 1983, vol. 37, no. 2, pp. 135-138.

[10] R.H. Gordon and B.G. Malkiel, 1981, op. cit. pp. 131-192. There is some debate as to the size of bankruptcy costs and there may also be scale effects, the larger the firm the lower the costs of bankruptcy. J.R. Warren, 'Bankruptcy Costs: Some Evidence', *Journal of Finance*, vol. XXXII, no. 2, 1977, pp. 337-347.

[11] M.C. Jensen and W.H. Meckling, 'Theory of the Firm: Managerial Behaviour, Agency Costs and Ownership Structure', *Journal of Financial Economics*, vol. 3, no. 4 1976, pp. 305-360.

[12] S.C. Myers, 'Determinants of Corporate Borrowing', *Journal of Financial Economics*, vol. 5, 1977, pp. 147-175.

[13] H. DeAngelo and R.W. Masulis, 'Optimal Capital Structure Under Corporate and Personal Taxation', *Journal of Financial Economics*, vol. 8, no. 1, 1980, pp. 3-29. The quotation is on p. 16.

[14] For some evidence that larger companies in terms of size of assets

have lower tax rates, see G. Meeks and G. Whittington, 'Giant Companies in the United Kingdom', *Economic Journal*, vol. 85, pp. 824-843. C. Mayer in 'The Structure of Corporation Tax in the U.K.', *Fiscal Studies*, vol. 3, no. 2, pp. 121-141, argues that for a sample of U.K. companies, companies with larger profits tend to have smaller tax rates than companies with smaller profits. In Chapter 5 of this book it is argued that for more recent years for firms in this study, there appears to be no relationship between size of firm, as measured by profits or capital employed (p.90), and tax rates.

[15] Some empirical work is in progress on ways of measuring the value of deferred tax due to accelerated depreciation allowances in each accounting period.

[16] See A.J. Auerbach, 'Taxation, Corporate Financial Policy and the Cost of Capital', *Journal of Economic Literature*, vol. XXI, 1983, pp. 905-940, especially pp. 934-935. See also the comments by Auerbach on a paper by I. Cooper and J.R. Franks, 'The Interaction of Financing and Investment Decisions When the Firm has Unused Tax Credits', *Journal of Finance*, vol. 38, 1983 , pp. 571-583, and A.J. Auerbach, ibid, pp. 606-608.

[17] L. Johansen, *Public Economics*, North-Holland Publishing Company, Amsterdam, 1971, pp. 240-256.

[18] This gives rise to the same prediction, H.3, p. 21 of DeAngelo and Masulis (1980) op. cit. except they refer to decreases in depreciation deductions, or investment tax credits, rather than tax allowances relating to exporting.

[19] For a description of 'section 84' loans see Commission on Taxation (1982) op. cit. p. 579.

[20] No further tax liability can arise if profits are earned solely from exporting. Otherwise additional tax may be payable if the ultimate debt owner (for example, a shareholder) is liable to income tax above the standard rate.

[21] See Commission on Taxation, 1982, op. cit. p. 579.

[22] For a discussion of the appropriate discount rate see E.E. Williams and M. Chapman Findley III, 'Discounting Tax Liabilities: Some Clarifying Comments', *Journal of Business Finance and Accounting*, vol. 2, no. 1, 1975, pp. 121-133.

[23] See E.D. Domar, 'Depreciation, Replacement and Growth', *Economic Journal*, vol. 63, 1953, pp. 1-32, or A.R. Prest, 'Replacement Cost Depreciation', *Accounting Research*, vol. 1, no. 4, 1948-50, pp. 365-402, for a comprehensive discussion of the relationship between price changes and depreciation allowances.

[24] Commission on Taxation in Ireland , 1982, op. cit. p. 371.

[25] J.R. Gallagher, 'Advance Corporation Tax (ACT) - Finance Act 1983', *Irish Banking Review*, June 1983, pp. 9-19.

[26] Central Bank of Ireland, 'Monetary Developments in Ireland', *Quarterly Bulletin of the Central Bank of Ireland*, September 1983, p. 23. 'Section 84' lending as a percentage of aggregate bank Balance Sheets with respect to residents, amounted to 4.5 per cent, 5.4 per cent, and 5.6 per cent, respectively for December 1982, May 1983,

ERSITY COLLEGE Library CORK

and May 1984. This data was not collected prior to December 1982. Source: Central Bank of Ireland *Quarterly Report* September 1983 and September 1984, Table C 3. For more recent years 'section 84' lending has been extended to borrowing in foreign currencies, for example French and Belgium Francs, from banks located outside the State.

[27] A. Rubner, 'The Irrelevancy of the British Differential Profits Tax', *Economic Journal*, vol. 74, 1964, pp. 347-359.

[28] M.S. Feldstein, 'The Effectiveness of the British Differential Profits Tax', *Economic Journal*, vol. 77, 1967, pp. 947-953.

[29] R.J. Briston and C.R. Tomkins, 'The Impact of the Introduction of Corporation Tax Upon the Dividend Policies of U.K. Companies', *Economic Journal*, vol. 80, 1970, pp. 617-637.

[30] M.S. Feldstein and G. Fane, 'Taxes, Corporate Dividend Policy and Personal Savings: The British Postwar Experience', *Review of Economics and Statistics*, vol. LV, no. 4, 1973, pp. 399-411.

[31] G. Whittington, *Company Taxation and Dividends*, I.F.S. Lecture Series, no. 1, Institute for Fiscal Studies, London, 1974.

[32] For 1981 in the U.K. only 38 per cent of all assets leased were classified as plant and machinery. The rest consisted largely of transport and office equipment. See *Bank of England Quarterly Bulletin*, 'Recent Developments in Equipment Leasing', September 1982, p. 386.

[33] See G.A. Akerlof, 'The Market for Lemons: Quality Uncertainty and the Market Mechanism', *Quarterly Journal of Economics*, 1970, pp. 398-501. B. Klein and R.G. Crawford in 'Vertical integration, Appropriable Rents, and the Competitive Contracting Process', *Journal of Law and Economics*, vol. 21, 1978, pp. 297-326, argue that leases are less common 'for assets with specialized quasi rents that could be appropriated by the lessee or lessor' by what they describe as 'post-contractual opportunistic behaviour'. Goodhart provides another reason why specific assets such as chemical and steel plants are rarely hired, and that is the difficulty of transmuting the asset so that it may be used to produce some other product or in some other way. The value of a specific asset is thus largely a function of the expected returns from its first intended use. Hence there may be greater uncertainty relating to the value of a specific asset. See C.A.E. Goodhart, *Money, Information and Uncertainty*, MacMillan, London, 1975, p. 88. See also D. Flath 'The Economics of Short-Term Leasing', *Economic Inquiry*, vol. XVIII, 1980, pp. 247-259 for a discussion of short term leasing.

[34] R.P. Kinsella, 'The Measurement of Concentration in Irish Banking', *Journal of the Statistical and Social Inquiry Society of Ireland*, vol. XXIV, Part III, pp. 31-60. Kinsella (p. 40) found that 85 per cent of bank output was accounted for by the four largest banks and their subsidiaries.

[35] The relationship between concentration and oligopolistic behaviour in the U.K. banking sector has been questioned by G. Davies and J. Davies, 'The Revolution in Monopoly Theory', *Lloyds Bank Review*, July 1984, pp. 38-52, on the basis of the ease of entry and

exit for potential competitors. See also W.J. Baumol, 'Contestable Markets: An Uprising in the Theory of Industry Structure', *American Economic Review*, vol. 72, no. 1, 1982, pp. 1-15.

[36] J.S.S. Edwards and C.P. Mayer, *Issues in Bank Taxation*, The Institute for Fiscal Studies, London, 1983, p. 42.

[37] *The Green Paper on Corporation Tax*, London: H.M.S.O. 1982, Cmnd. 8456, p. 90, estimated unused tax allowances at Stg.£ 30 billion and that these allowances were increasing at a rate of Stg.£ 5 billion per annum. One third of these unused tax allowances are estimated to be due to stock relief and the rest to capital allowances. One way of preventing the accumulation of unused allowances would be to pay a sum equal in amount to unused allowances multiplied by the tax rate. Such a procedure appears to have occurred in a number of instances in the case of 'section 84' loans in Ireland. Source Irish Press, February 15, 1982.

[38] A.C. Warren and A.J. Auerbach, 'Transferability of Tax Incentives and the Fiction of Safe Harbor Leasing', *Harvard Law Review*, vol. 95, no. 8, 1982, pp. 1752-1786; H. Bierman, comments on a paper by F.J. Fabozzi and U. Yaari, 'Valuation of Safe Harbor Tax Benefit Transfer Leases', *Journal of Finance*, vol. 38, no. 2, 1983, pp. 571-583. The comments by Bierman are on pp. 611-612. See also the comments by C.S. Shoup in 'The United States Economic Recovery Tax Act of 1981', *British Tax Review*, no. 5, 1982 pp. 301-314, especially pp. 307-308.

[39] Warren and Auerbach, ibid. p. 1767, cite a Treasury Department Report that 84 per cent of the benefits of leasing under the Economic Recovery Act passed through to the benefit of lessees in 1981. Bierman, op. cit. cites a study by the Staff of the Joint Committee on Taxation of Congress that the lesee receives on average 76 per cent of the intended benefits.

[40] Warren and Auerbach, ibid. p. 1759.

[41] A.J. Auerbach, 'Corporate Taxation in the United States' in W.C. Brainard and G.L. Perry (eds.) *Brookings Papers on Economic Activity*, vol. 2, Brookings Institution, Washington, 1984.

[42] Both Warren and Auerbach, ibid., and Bierman, ibid., comment that under such an arrangement the benefits would increase and the costs reduce.

[43] J.S.S. Edwards and C.P. Mayer, 1983, op. cit. p. 53.

[44] See Green paper, 1982, op. cit . p. 90 and *Bank of England Quarterly Bulletin*, vol. 22, no. 3, pp. 382-389.

[45] Budget Speech by the Chancellor of the Exchequer, Mr. Lawson, *Financial Times*, March 14, 1984.

[46] *White Paper on Industrial Policy*, p. 43, Pl. 2491, Stationary Office, Dublin, 1982.

7 Fiscal incentives and corporate financing: a flow of funds analysis

This chapter examines the effect of fiscal incentives on corporate financing in the context of flow of funds beginning with some problems involved in preparing flows of funds data. The overall importance of different sources is then examined and finally some effects of fiscal incentives on corporate financing are considered.

7.1 Some technical problems with flows of funds

The sources of funds in this chapter are classified according to sector of issue. The three main sectors identified are the Capital Market, State Institutions and Commercial Banks. Few companies in the study appear to rely on foreign borrowing, the total identified amounting to just under IR£ 20 million for the period examined. Where disclosed such borrowing has been attributed to the Commercial Banks. Certain loans from State agencies may also represent foreign borrowing under a State administered scheme, where the exchange rate risk is borne by the State. The Capital Market refers to sources of funds such as equity shares, preference shares and quoted debt. Long term sources of funds (equity and debt) from the parent company in the case of subsidiary companies, included in the study, are also included under this heading. This is because, in general, equity shares cannot be redeemed or repurchased under Irish company law. It is also likely that that there is a considerable difference in the flexibility with which long term loans can be repaid versus short term loans that arise from intra-subsidiary trading. This is likely to be particularly true in the case of majority owned subsidiaries. In the case of subsidiaries of multinational companies included in the study, intra-group short term borrowing from the parent company or fellow members of the group is also separately identified as a source of funds. This largely relates to trade credit received and given. State Institutions are subdivided into two sources of funds: capital grants and borrowing (both short and long term). Borrowing from the third sector, Commercial Banks, is subdivided into long term (maturity longer than one year) and short term. There are alternative classifications for example those described by Bain[1], who suggests classification by the nature of the financial instrument, for example debt or equity, and also suggests that assets may be classified by liquidity. However Bain stresses that the key features in classifying flows of funds data should be homogeneity and importance[2].

The following are the main problems encountered in attempting to classify financial liabilities according to sector of issue:-

(1) If State Institutions purchased equity or preference shares, the relevant amounts could be shown as originating from State Institutions as with capital grants, or from the Capital Market. In this paper such amounts are shown as originating from the Capital Market;

(2) Many companies do not disclose the origin of debt in the Balance Sheet. Unless specifically identified, debt has been attributed to borrowing from the Commercial Banks. Hence in some cases, debt provided by a State Institution may be wrongly attributed to a Commercial Bank. In addition, no adjustment was made for a small number of cases where long term debt provided by a State Institution was subsequently converted into preference shares or equity;

(3) Because many companies do not disclose the origin of debt, some bank borrowing may have taken place outside Ireland. Where foreign borrowing is disclosed it has been attributed to the Commercial Banks rather than create a separate category;

(4) Insurance companies provided a small number of loans prior to 1970, known generally as mortgage loans, although the origin of these loans is not disclosed in company accounts. Generally these loans were of 5-10 years duration. In all cases these loans have been regarded as issuing from the Commercial Banks;

(5) Equity, debt, etc. issued to shareholders or quoted on the Capital Market was only included if issued in exchange for cash. Debt or equity issued in connection with mergers or takeovers was not included. In some cases this may lead to anomalous results, for example where a company issues shares for cash and then immediately purchases another company with the proceeds;

(6) Changes in short term borrowing and cash balances were estimated as the difference between Balance Sheet stocks in time period t_0 and t_1. In the case of mergers/takeovers or where subsidiaries are sold off this may also lead to anomalous results, for example where two companies already in the study population merge this shows up as an increase in the flow of bank borrowing by the surviving company even though the aggregate of bank borrowing by both companies before the merger is the same as post merger. Hence in those cases where companies already in the study merged/took-over other companies the change in short term bank borrowing

and in cash balances was treated as the difference between aggregate Balance Sheet totals prior and post the merger/takeover. A corollary of this procedure is that merging/taking over companies not already included in the study population results in an inflow of any short term bank borrowing by the taken over company/merged company to the surviving company, and divesting of a subsidiary results in a repayment of short term loans[3]. In some cases companies that merged or took-over other companies were omitted for a particular year because cash flows, such as tax payments, could not be accurately estimated from Balance Sheet data;

(7) As far as was possible changes in long term loans resulting from mergers/takeovers of companies already included in the study population were also excluded;

(8) Finally, changes in trade credit have been ignored.

The population of firms included varies from year to year. Hence in some cases changes in the pattern of financing may be partly due to the inclusion of different firms, rather than changes in the financing of the same firms. The data presented must also be interpreted in the light of varying rates of inflation from year to year.

7.2 Sources of internal and external finance

Table 7.1 shows sources of internal finance for companies in the study for the years 1964-84. Gross Internal Finance (depreciation plus retentions, column (6)) is a positive source of finance for each year, although Table 7.1 shows that there have been considerable variations in pre-tax profits particularly in the latter part of the period. Aggregate dividends show a generally rising trend through time, and as is suggested by the Lintner hypothesis[4] are much more stable than pre-tax profits. Hence fluctuations in profits become reflected in fluctuations in corporate saving. If a stock adjustment (S) and historical cost depreciation as it appears in company accounts (D) are deducted from gross internal finance, an estimate of funds available for additional investment is obtained. Column (9) shows that this amount is positive though more unstable than pre-tax profits for the period 1964-73, but becomes negative in the recession years 1974-76, and at the start of a new recession in 1980.

Table 7.2 shows various sources of external finance, the total of external finance and the sum of external and internal financing. There is some evidence that different sources of external finance appear to be used in a contra-cyclical fashion. For example, the fall in corporate profits in 1974-75 was associated with a rise in short term bank borrowing in 1974 and in long term bank borrowing in 1975-76. A fall in profits in 1980-81 was also associated with an increase in short term borrowing. The recovery of profits in 1975-76 was associated with a reduction in short term bank borrowing. While the recovery in profits in 1983-84 was associated with a reduction in short term borrowing in 1983, although short term borrowing was also reduced in 1982. Raising funds from shareholders or on the Stock Exchange tended to be associated with rising corporate profits, as in the period 1971-73, 1976, 1979 and 1984[5].

Table 7.1

Sources of internal finance 1964-84

IR£ Million

Year	N[a]	Pre-Tax[b] Profits (1)	Depreciation (2)	Gross Internal Cash Flow (3) (1+2)	Cash Tax Payment (4)	Dividends (5)	Gross Internal Saving (6) (3-4-5)	Net Profits Available for Distribution (7) (1-4)	Stock[c] Adjustment (8)	Internal Funds for new investment (9) (6-8-2)
1964	117	16.501	6.141	22.642	5.773	4.457	12.412	10.728	2.463	3.808
1965	136	17.444	7.381	24.825	6.394	5.157	13.274	11.050	1.916	3.977
1966	143	16.840	8.577	25.417	6.897	5.519	13.001	9.943	1.112	3.312
1967	140	18.149	9.011	27.160	7.734	5.607	13.819	10.415	1.625	3.183
1968	139	23.650	10.049	33.699	7.766	6.006	19.927	15.884	3.793	6.085
1969	137	25.445	10.407	35.852	7.176	7.217	21.459	18.269	5.159	5.893
1970	127	23.336	10.394	33.730	7.919	6.446	19.365	15.417	3.924	5.047
1971	130	28.954	11.952	40.906	8.408	7.503	24.995	20.546	4.725	8.318
1972	121	41.981	14.727	56.708	9.329	9.240	38.139	32.652	9.677	13.735
1973	114	61.953	18.431	80.384	9.036	11.348	60.000	52.917	22.138	19.431
1974	112	46.052	22.347	68.399	12.546	16.486	39.367	33.506	24.467	-7.447
1975	111	40.632	22.098	62.730	8.130	14.241	40.359	32.502	42.321	-24.060
1976	108	59.392	22.189	81.581	8.547	14.873	58.161	50.845	39.460	-3.488
1977	101	86.828	24.326	111.154	13.884	18.693	78.577	72.944	41.521	12.730
1978	95	104.639	31.302	135.941	14.435	23.292	98.214	90.204	27.060	39.852
1979	90	127.691	37.396	165.087	20.417	27.609	117.061	107.274	43.011	36.654
1980	88	95.258	44.184	139.442	21.684	33.981	83.777	73.574	44.547	-4.954
1981	79	84.609	50.384	134.993	19.086	35.650	80.257	65.523	73.027	-43.154
1982	77	72.284	57.224	129.508	16.887	39.757	72.864	55.397	51.864	-36.224
1983	72	72.164	60.663	132.827	13.872	42.406	76.549	58.292	29.362	-13.476
1984	66	85.407	56.192	141.599	12.360	42.867	86.372	73.047	34.103	-3.923

Table 7.2
Sources of external finance and total funds available 1964-84
IR£ Million

Year	Stock[a] Exchange or Share-holders (10)	Intra-Group[b] Borrowing (11)	State[c] Institution (12)	Capital Grants (13)	Long Term[d] Commercial Bank (14)	Short Term[e] Commercial Bank (15)	Total External Finance (16)	External[f] plus net Internal Finance (17) (7-5+16)	External plus gross Internal Finance (18) (6+16)
1964	2.419	0.885	-0.023	0.911	0.010	2.607	6.809	13.080	19.221
1965	5.672	1.463	0.924	1.623	0.288	2.113	12.083	17.976	25.357
1966	5.134	1.702	-0.756	1.771	0.244	3.886	11.981	16.405	24.982
1967	-0.089	0.658	0.106	2.219	0.300	1.623	4.817	9.625	18.636
1968	0.736	-0.286	0.139	1.293	0.676	8.072	10.630	20.508	30.557
1969	3.626	1.934	0.394	3.393	1.646	10.449	21.442	32.494	42.901
1970	1.235	9.733	-0.497	2.870	6.819	7.611	27.771	36.742	47.136
1971	5.710	-3.305	1.101	3.069	9.340	-8.125	7.790	20.833	32.785
1972	5.986	-6.717	0.771	3.851	11.317	18.107	33.315	56.727	71.454
1973	12.453	2.983	0.933	3.598	20.016	18.921	58.904	100.474	118.901
1974	1.828	2.237	2.752	3.739	7.392	29.209	47.157	64.177	86.524
1975	9.383	6.179	-0.252	5.938	30.622	-11.402	40.468	58.729	80.827
1976	17.196	-6.323	0.458	5.069	25.564	-7.886	34.078	70.050	92.239
1977	3.278	2.896	2.204	3.780	6.599	4.051	22.808	77.059	101.385
1978	8.591	2.042	-0.260	5.047	7.172	39.030	61.622	128.534	159.836
1979	36.934	-0.600	0.227	3.861	20.649	19.982	81.053	160.718	198.114
1980	7.254	3.297	0.090	7.383	36.980	31.261	86.265	125.858	170.042
1981	13.278	2.230	0.541	11.852	36.327	49.208	113.436	143.309	193.693
1982	20.400	-13.491	5.883	7.882	15.466	-14.279	21.861	37.501	94.725
1983	36.560	2.832	-0.113	5.124	22.877	-5.615	61.665	77.551	138.214
1984	66.230	-8.916	0.244	5.799	24.221	1.488	89.066	119.246	175.438

Notes to Table 7.1

(a) N is the number of firms included
(b) P is defined as in Chapter 3 plus dividends from associates.
(c) Estimated by subtracting from the average of opening and closing stocks for the current year, average stocks, deflated by the rise in the wholesale price index.

Source: Annual Reports of Companies.

Notes to Table 7.2

(a) Net issues for cash of long term debt, preference shares and equity
(b) Defined as Current Liabilities minus Current Assets
(c) Defined as long term loans from the Industrial Credit Company and Foir Teoranta - a State rescue agency. Preference and equity shares purchased by these agencies are included in column (10).
(d) Loans with maturity longer than one year.
(e) Loans with maturity less than one year.
(f) Net of accounting depreciation.

Source: Annual Reports of Companies

As in the case of pre-tax profits and company saving, aggregate external finance appears to show a cyclical pattern although the cycle appears one to two years out of phase with changes in pre-tax profits. When external finance was at a cyclically low point, for example in the years 1976-77, corporate profits were recovering from the trough of 1974-75. Conversely the recession years 1974-75 and 1980-81 were characterised by relatively large flows of external finance to the companies included in the study.

A.D. Bain[6] also draws attention to a cyclical pattern in reviewing empirical evidence relating to corporate liquidity in the U.K. for the period 1958-67. R.C.O. Matthews (writing in 1959) suggests the cycle (both real and monetary) as an explanation of corporate financing and corporate liquidity[7]. Matthews states (p. 144) '... share finance as a rule becomes more attractive relative to bond finance when trade improves'. More recently the Wilson Committee[8] did not explicitly refer to a trade cycle as an explanation of changes in external corporate financing, but rather referred to the use of external funds as depending on a favorable market (par. 500) and to a need to reduce high gearing levels (par. 516).

In order to examine the relative importance of various sources of funds it is convenient to divide the period 1964-84 into four subperiods, coinciding with significant changes in fiscal incentives, that is the introduction of 100 per cent depreciation allowances in 1971, 'section 84' loans in 1976, and a 10 per cent tax rate for manufacturing companies in 1981. Table 7.3 shows sources of funds as a percentage of total external sources for the Stock Exchange/shareholders, commercial bank long term loans, total commercial bank loans and other sources.

Table 7.3
Sources of external finance as a percentage of total external finance*

Period	Stock Exchange or shareholders	Commercial Bank Long Term Loans	Total Commercial Bank Borrowing	Other Sources
	(1)	(2)	(3)	(4)
1964-70	19.61	10.45	48.51	31.88
1971-76	23.70	47.02	64.53	11.77
1977-80	22.27	28.36	65.83	11.90
1981-84	47.71	34.57	45.34	6.95
1964-84	30.85	33.28	56.70	12.45

* Columns (1 + 3 + 4) = 100 per cent

By far the largest component of external finance over the period 1964-84 consisted of borrowing from the commercial banks, which provided 56.7 per cent of external funds (Table 7.3)[9]. Approximately 58.7 per cent of commercial bank borrowing was in the form of long term loans. Next in importance were funds from shareholders or funds raised on the Stock Exchange (that is equity shares, preference shares and long term debt) with 30.85 per cent of total external finance, of which approximately 13 per cent was raised by one company in 1979 (Cement Roadstone). Summing data over time may not be very meaningful because of varying rates of inflation from year to year. The rate of inflation as measured by the Consumer Price Index for the period 1964-70 and 1971-76 amounted to approximately 45 per cent and 120 per cent respectively, although the rate of inflation as measured by the C.P.I. for the period 1977-80 and 1981-84 is similar at about 64 per cent and 69 per cent respectively. Deflating the data by a price index such as the Consumer Price Index or the Wholesale Price Index may also not be very meaningful as firms are likely to raise funds to purchase capital goods rather than consumer goods. Deflating by a capital goods index would be more useful but could be misleading when applied to a subsector of the economy as a whole. Hence it is important to examine the relative importance of sources of finance on a year to year basis. For most years the Commercial Banks appear to be the largest single source of funds and for every year for the period 1972-82.

The Stock Exchange and shareholders appear to be significantly more important in the period 1981-84 compared with the earlier periods. This may be partly explained by the inclusion of State funding of Dublin Gas amounting to IR£ 22.5 million in 1984 and also two pharmaceutical companies who raised approximately IR£ 15.5 million on U.S. stock markets in 1983-84. Bank lending was highest as a per cent of external finance in the periods 1971-76 and 1977-80. Table 7.2 shows that for all years in the period 1964-70 short term bank lending was larger than long term bank lending. In contrast for 10 of the 14 years 1971-84, long term bank lending is larger than short term bank lending. Long term bank loans amounted to 72.9, 43.1 and 76.2 per cent of total bank lending in the periods 1971-76, 1977-80, 1981-84 respectively compared with 21.5 per cent for the period 1964-70.

It is also of interest to note that total equity and preference shares issued for cash amounted to IR£ 243.9 million for the period 1964-84, of which IR£ 4.60 million net consisted of preference shares. This latter figure excludes IR£ 5.2 million issued as preference shares and subsequently converted into equity shares. Over the period as a whole there were net redemptions of quoted debentures, and quoted long term debt. There were also net redemptions of long term loans from the parent company in the case of M.N.C. subsidiaries included. Currently most long term borrowing is from the commercial banks. There has also been a shift from quoted long term debt to short and medium term bank borrowing in the U.K. A recent U.K. study noted that for five of the years 1973-80 bond redemptions exceeded new issues[10]. Several reasons have been advanced to explain the shift from quoted long term debt, for example, increased uncertainty resulting from inflation; a decline in corporate profitability; and opposition by regulatory authorities to the issue of index linked securities. A study of the financing of U.K. Industrial and Commercial companies for the period 1971-76 found net redemptions of preference shares[11]. This was largely due to tax changes in the U.K. in 1965 which made interest on debt finance a tax deductible expense against corporation tax, whereas dividends were not tax deductible and in addition were subject to income tax.

State Institutions (Industrial Credit Company and Foir Teoranta) do not appear to be a major source of finance for companies in this study. However in some cases bank lending shown in company Balance Sheets is not identified according to the lending institution. Hence a certain proportion of lending by State Institutions in Table 7.2 may have been incorrectly ascribed to commercial bank lending.

Finally intra-group borrowing in the case of subsidiaries of M.N.C.s appears to be a positive, if variable, source of finance for most years.

Table 7.4 shows a Sources and Uses of Funds Statement for the period 1964-84. Total sources are defined as in Table 7.2, column (18). A similar problem to that of calculating the change in short term borrowing in cases were firms merge, take-over other firms, or sell subsidiaries, arises in relation to changes in cash balances and in stocks, and the same procedure of adjusting the data where firms merged or took-over firms already included was used.

Table 7.4
Total sources and uses of funds 1964-84

IR£ million

Year	Sources[a]	Uses		
		Change in[b] Cash Balances	Changes in Stocks	Other[c] Uses
	(1)	(2)	(3)	(4)
1963[d]	7.635	1.695	2.382	3.558
1964	7.473	-0.264	2.446	5.291
1964[e]	19.221	-0.503	4.752	14.972
1965	25.357	0.677	3.370	21.310
1966	24.982	0.557	4.565	19.860
1967	18.636	-0.632	3.971	15.297
1968	30.557	1.347	8.503	20.707
1969	42.901	1.085	9.721	32.095
1970	47.136	13.282	3.299	30.555
1971	32.785	-15.684	3.853	44.616
1972	71.454	5.283	14.482	51.689
1973	118.901	7.870	51.610	59.421
1974	86.524	-7.144	57.284	36.384
1975	80.827	19.185	-9.797	71.435
1976	92.239	13.291	61.556	17.392
1977	101.385	6.860	37.311	57.214
1978	159.836	4.198	48.487	107.151
1979	198.114	1.674	94.652	101.788
1980	170.042	5.455	55.240	109.346
1981	193.693	17.655	42.507	133.531
1982	94.725	1.326	-9.019	102.418
1983	138.214	35.591	7.666	94.957
1984	175.438	68.514	10.976	95.948

Notes to Table 7.4

(a) Table 7.2 column (18).
(b) Defined as cash plus short term bank deposits.
(c) Column (1) minus (column (2) plus column (3).
(d) Calculated for 50 firms for which comparable data was available for 1963 and 1964.
(e) For all firms for 1964 and subsequent years.

One of the features of Table 7.4 is a periodic negative movement in cash balances (for example 1964, 1967, 1971, and 1974) and the change in cash balances in 1979 and 1982, though positive, is low compared with immediately preceeding and succeeding years. For four of these years (1967, 1971, 1974 and 1982), the reduction or small increase in cash balances, was associated with a fall in total sources of funds. A small group of companies (50) published comparable Balance Sheet data prior to 1964 (the year in which standard company accounts were required by law). If this subgroup of companies were compared for the years 1963 and 1964, a slight fall in total sources of funds and in pretax profits and a larger fall in cash balances was found for 1964 compared with 1963. The fall in cash balances in the years 1971 and 1974 was followed by a substantial increase in cash balances during the following two years. The fall in aggregate profits from 1979 to 1983 was associated with growing cash balances. The largest increase in absolute terms in cash balances occurred in 1984 which was also the year in which funds from shareholders/stock exchange also reached a peak in absolute terms. Another feature of Table 7.4 is the absolute fall in the nominal value of stocks in 1975 followed by a rebuilding of stocks in 1976. There was also an absolute fall in stocks in 1982. Previous falls in aggregate profits in 1966-67 and 1970 were associated with smaller increases in the absolute value of stocks compared with previous years, and a slight fall in other uses of funds compared with previous years. Other uses of funds (fixed investment, company takeovers, and changes in trade credit) reached a low point in 1976, two years after the fall in cash balances, although in 1982 the low point for other uses of funds was coincidental with a small increase in cash balances. On average for the period 1964-84 changes in cash balances were a net use of funds, absorbing approximately 9.3 per cent of total sources, although there is considerable variation from year to year. Increases in stocks absorbed 26.3 per cent of total funds, leaving 64.4 per cent of total funds for other purposes, such as fixed investment.

Table 7.5 shows various savings ratios, and self financing ratios, for the period 1964-84. The table shows that all ratios of internal to external finance reached low points in the years 1965-66, 1970, 1974-75, and 1981, and on the narrowest definition of savings (column 4) became negative for the years 1974-76, and for 1980-84. Falls in the savings ratio also coincided with falls in pre-tax profits (Table 7.1). Conversely the pay-out ratio (column 3) was higher than average in the years 1966-67, 1974-75 and in 1982-83.

Table 7.5
Savings ratios and the ratio of internal to external financing 1964-84

Year	Internal/[a] Total Financing (1)	Net Savings/[b] Net Savings + External Finance (2)	Dividends/[c] Profits net of Tax and Depreciation (3)	Investible Funds/[d] Investible Funds + External Finance (4)
	%	%	%	%
1964	64.58	47.94	41.55	35.87
1965	52.35	32.78	46.67	24.76
1966	52.04	26.97	55.51	21.66
1967	74.16	49.95	53.84	39.79
1968	65.21	48.17	37.81	36.40
1969	50.02	34.01	39.50	21.56
1970	41.08	24.42	41.81	15.38
1971	76.24	62.61	36.52	51.64
1972	53.38	41.27	28.38	29.19
1973	50.46	41.37	21.44	24.81
1974	45.31	26.52	49.20	-18.75
1975	49.93	31.09	43.82	-146.64
1976	63.05	51.35	29.25	-11.40
1977	77.50	70.40	25.63	35.82
1978	61.45	52.06	25.82	39.27
1979	59.09	49.57	25.74	31.14
1980	49.27	31.46	40.56	-6.10
1981	41.44	20.85	54.41	-61.41
1982[e]	76.92	41.71	71.77	-
1983	55.38	20.48	72.75	-27.96
1984	49.23	25.31	58.68	-0.046
1964-70[f]	54.24	34.94	44.06	24.68
1971-76	54.07	40.24	33.05	2.84
1977-80	60.00	48.85	30.11	25.08
1981-84	52.49	24.25	63.70	-51.14
1964-84	55.54	38.38	41.54	2.87

Notes to Table 7.5

(a) Defined as Gross Internal Financing/(Gross Internal plus External Financing), Columns 6/18 of Tables 7.1 and 7.2.

(b) Defined as Net Retentions/(Net Retentions plus External Financing), columns (7 - 5)/17, Tables 7.1 and 7.2.

(c) Defined as Dividends/(Profits net of Tax and Accounting Depreciation), columns 5/7, Table 7.1.

(d) Defined as Net Retentions minus a Stock Adjustment/(Net Retentions minus a Stock Adjustment plus External Financing), columns (9/(9 + 16)), Tables 7.1 and

7.2.

(e) Column (4) could not be calculated for 1982 as both numerator and denominator were negative.

(f) Calculated as Internal Financing/ Gross Financing where both numerator and denominator are separately calculated by summing across all firms and years for the relevant interval. A similar calculation was performed for columns (2), (3), and (4).

The year 1947 was the first year for which comprehensive National Income Accounts were prepared for Ireland. The period 1947-68 has been examined by Kennedy and Dowling[12]. Aggregate company savings for the economy as a whole reached low points in the years 1952, 1957, and 1966. There was also a slight fall in company saving in 1964[13]. Aggregate profits also fell in the period 1951-52, 1956-57, and also by a small amount in 1966. Overall Kennedy and Dowling[14] conclude that 'there was comparative stagnation in company profits from 1949-57 followed by a strong and relatively upward trend from 1957-68'. It is also of interest to note from the study by Kennedy and Dowling that company profits as a per cent of National Income fell in 1964 and 1966. More recently Vaughan[15], using aggregate National Income profit figures expressed in current prices, calculates net retentions after making an allowance for stock appreciation for the period 1960-75, with estimates for the years 1976-78. Net retentions as calculated by Vaughan fell in the years 1964, 1966, 1970, and 1974. These aggregate profit and savings figures, as noted in the earlier part of this paper are not directly comparable with the data presented in this paper, but they confirm the downturn in 1965-66, 1970, and 1974, and also the slight fall in corporate profits in 1964.

Apart from cyclical elements in the payout ratio and savings ratios, there also appeared to be a trend towards higher corporate saving, and a lower payout ratio until the most recent recession when payout ratios reached a peak of 72.75 per cent in 1983. This can be illustrated by grouping the data into periods, for example 1964-70, 1971-76, 1977-80, and 1981-84. Table 7.5 column (3) shows that dividends as a proportion of profits net of tax and depreciation fell from 44.06 per cent in 1964-70 to 30.11 per cent in the period 1977-80 and then rose again to 63.7 per cent in the period 1981-84. If retentions are adjusted for the increase in the value of stocks (Table 7.5, column 4) a slightly different conclusion is reached. The rate of corporate savings is positive in the period 1964-70 at 24.68 per cent, fell to 2.84 per cent in the period 1971-76, rose to 25.08 per cent in the period 1977-80 and became negative for the period 1981-84. Hence conclusions relating to corporate savings ratios appear quite sensitive to the defintions used.

Finally, if the data is divided into three subperiods 1964-70, 1971-76 and 1977-84 the variability of the ratios shown in Table 7.5 appears highest in the period 1977-84 compared with the earlier periods. For column (1), for example, the standard deviation (S.D.) was 10.47 for 1964-70 and 10.38 for 1971-76, compared with 12.15 for 1977-84. For column (2) the S.D. for 1964-70 was 9.96 and 12.05 for 1971-76, compared with 16.55 for 1977-84. For column (3) the S.D. for 1964-70 was 6.49 and 9.51 for 1971-76 compared with 18.93 for 1977-84. Although for column (4) the

S.D. was highest in the period 1971-76 (64.9) compared with the other two periods.

Table 7.6 shows the total stock of bank borrowing by companies in the study (excluding borrowing from State Institutions and foreign borrowing) and also shows the total stock of bank lending within Ireland (excluding lending by State Institutions) for the period 1972-84. The year 1972 was the first year for which aggregate data for lending by the banking sector became available. Table 7.6 may be used to illustrate two main points. Firstly long term bank borrowing within Ireland was an increasing proportion of the total stock of bank borrowing by companies in the study, until 1977 when it reached 50.2 per cent. It then fell slightly, before rising to 58.3 per cent in 1984. Secondly, columns (6) and (7) of Table 7.6 show that companies in the study appeared to increase their share of bank lending to the manufacturing and services sector until 1975 and their share of aggregate lending until 1974 but that their share of bank lending has fallen continuously since then. This implies that other companies in the manufacturing and services sector (mostly multinational companies and companies in the State sector) reduced their share of total bank lending and may even have reduced their absolute amount of domestic bank borrowing in this period. This may indicate that companies in the study were affected to a greater extent by the recession of 1974-75 than foreign owned companies operating in Ireland.

Table 7.6
Total stock of bank lending to companies in the study as a proportion of total bank lending
IR£ million

Year	Short Term[a] Bank Borrowing (1)	Long Term[a] Bank Borrowing (2)	Total[a] Bank Borrowing (3)	Aggregate[b] Bank Lending to Manufacturing and Services (4)	Aggregate[b] Bank Lending Within Ireland (5)	(3/4) (6)	(3/5) (7)
1972	62.603	28.596	91.199	376.2	854.4	24.24	10.67
1973	81.120	47.905	129.025	433.0	1016.8	29.80	12.69
1974	113.085	51.699	164.784	505.3	1130.6	32.61	14.57
1975	98.127	77.821	175.948	531.6	1237.0	33.10	14.22
1976	87.922	87.070	174.992	717.2	1650.2	24.40	10.60
1977	88.442	89.269	177.711	787.5	1935.5	22.57	9.18
1978	128.103	102.517	230.620	1108.7	2683.4	20.80	8.59
1979	145.403	128.326	273.729	1503.0	3425.1	18.21	7.99
1980	177.067	163.446	340.513	2112.9	4306.1	16.12	7.91
1981	213.075	199.532	412.607	2497.8	5082.4	16.52	8.12
1982	210.016	204.327	414.343	3107.8	6330.5	13.33	6.55
1983	195.385	227.204	422.589	3428.0	6815.2	12.33	6.20
1984	179.529	251.032	430.561	4045.3	7716.0	10.64	5.58

Notes to Table 7.6

(a) Relates to firms in the study. This data excludes foreign borrowing.

(b) Relates to February of the following year. This data excludes installment credit and leasing agreements,as well as lending by State Institutions.

Source:- Central Bank of Ireland Annual Report. The year 1972 is the first year for which aggregate data is available.

An examination of the accounts of eleven State owned companies for the period 1970-84[16] in the Appendix to this chapter, also appears to show an increase in the share of domestic bank lending (both short and long term) as a proportion of total lending to the services and manufacturing sector between 1972 and 1975. Their share of domestic bank lending also appears to increase, although at a reduced rate between 1975 and 1981. This conclusion must however be interpreted with caution as the accounts examined do not show what proportion (if any) of short term borrowing originated outside the State. In addition, prior to 1979, and the split between the Irish Pound and the Pound Sterling, any Pound Sterling borrowing is not separately identified as foreign currency borrowing[17]. The main feature relating to the financing of State owned companies in the period 1970-84 was the increased reliance on foreign borrowing in the period 1978-83[18], coupled with pre-tax losses in the years 1980-81. Aggregate pre-tax profits were found to be positive in other years and to exhibit a coincident cyclical trend with public companies in the private sector. A reliance on foreign borrowing also appears to have had the effect of increasing cash balances with the domestic banking system. Hence it is likely that domestic companies increased their share of domestic bank lending in the period 1972-74, and the foreign owned corporate sector reduced its share of bank lending in the period 1972-74.

In conclusion, the proportion of finance provided internally varies considerably as between recession years and non-recession years, and also depending on the defintion of internal funds. So that for a non-recession year, for example, the year 1979, the broadest definition of internally generated funds amounted to 59.09 per cent of total funds, Table 7.5, column 1), the narrowest definition of internally generated funds amounted to just 31.14 per cent of total funds (column 4). For the entire period 1964-84 internally generated funds (including depreciation) provided 55.54 per cent of total funds. Excluding depreciation, internally generated funds provided 38.38 per cent of total funds, and excluding depreciation and a stock adjustment, 2.87 per cent of total funds. Bank borrowing was also found to vary considerably over the trade cycle, for example funds from commercial banks provided 88 per cent of external finance in 1972, 47.5 per in 1975, and 75.0 per cent in 1978.

There are no officially published estimates of flows of funds for the Irish economy. However some estimates of aggregate flows have been published[19], using four sectors:- personal sector, corporate sector, government sector and a foreign sector. One of these studies (Honohan, 1982) used existing published data and relied on a statistical estimating procedure to fill in any gaps. Such a procedure is subject to a wide margin of error, particularly as the author notes published data is sometimes of 'indifferent quality'. This aggregate study also found that bank borrowing was the main source of finance for the corporate sector. It is concluded (p. 192) that the financial position of the corporate sector appears to be 'countercyclical and slightly lagging activity'. The financial position is defined to be the accumulation of money and deposits plus bank borrowing. However, the data presented in this paper suggests a more complex picture. Changes in equity finance, short term bank borrowing and long term bank borrowing vary over the trade cycle. In addition the change in cash balances also appears to be cyclical. However different sources of finance vary in importance over the trade cycle. Aggregate data relating to the economy as a whole are likely to be dominated by flows of funds into and out of the foreign owned corporate sector.

There are considerable problems in making comparisons between countries of sources of corporate finance, because of differing accounting conventions. There are also difficulties in making comparisons between different studies even for the same country, because of differing conventions relating to the definition of internally generated funds, for example, whether tax payments relate to cash tax payments as in this chapter, or tax liabilities. However, if a stock adjustment is deducted from internally generated funds (Table 7.1, column 6 - column 8), a roughly similar measure of self financing is obtained for Irish companies as that contained in the Wilson Report for U.K. companies. One important difference is that the Wilson Report found that import and other credit amounted to between 3 and 7 per cent of total sources of funds for the period 1968-79, whereas trade and other forms of credit have been ignored in this study. From the Wilson Report[20], it appears that for each of the years 1968-79 U.K. companies have a higher ratio of self-financing than Irish companies. For example, for the years 1978 and 1979 the self financing ratios for U.K. companies were 67 per cent and 59 per cent respectively, compared with 53.6 and 47.7 for companies in this study. However bank borrowing appears to be higher as a percentage of total sources for companies in this study compared with U.K. companies. For the years 1978 and 1979 bank borrowing for firms in this study amounted to 34.8 and 25.2 per cent of total sources compared with 15 and 23 per cent for U.K. firms. Perhaps surprisingly, shareholders or the Stock Exchange appear more important for companies in this study compared with U.K. companies. For the same two years these sources provided 6.5 and 23.8 per cent of total sources compared with 4 per cent for U.K. firms for both years. Equity finance in the U.K. also contributed a low proportion of total sources of funds (defined in a similar way to column 18, Table 7.2) in the period 1970-79.

Equity finance provided 4.8 per cent of total funds in the U.S. for the period 1970-79, compared with 10.0 per cent for firms in this study for the same period[21]. The higher proportion found in Ireland compared with both the U.S. and the U.K. may be explained by the favorable tax treatment of dividends by exporting companies in Ireland and this hypothesis is examined further in the next section of this chapter.

An earlier study of U.K. quoted Commercial and Industrial companies, for the years 1948-71, by Meeks and Whittington[22] found that retained profits plus depreciation accounted for 83.1 per cent of total funds for the period 1948-64, and 78.1 per cent for the period 1964-71. For the period 1964-71 equity issues for cash amounted to 8.0 per cent of total funds and long term loans issued for cash amounted to 7.1 per cent of total funds[23]. However, this study referred to the average pattern of financing by companies, equal weight being given to each firm, rather than focussing on aggregate financial flows. In addition, shares issued in connection with mergers and takeovers were included as a source of funds (amounting to 8.2 per cent of total sources for 1964-71), short term bank borrowing was treated as a negative source, and there was no adjustment for inflation. A.D. Bain[24] reports an average figure of 72 per cent self financing, based on aggregate flows, for U.K. Industrial and Commercial companies for the period 1958 to 1967.

The self financing ratio for the Meeks and Whittington study is higher than that of firms in this study and of the Wilson Report. Issues of equity, preference shares and long term debt for cash amounted to 9.9 per cent for the period 1964-71 compared with 10.1 per cent for companies in this study for the same period.

Using similar definitions of internal and external funds, higher pay-out ratios (dividends/internal plus external funds) were found for companies in this study compared with Meeks and Whittington for the period 1964-71 (19.8 per cent compared with 14.7 per cent). Finally, in a study of trends in financing of all quoted U.K. manufacturing companies for the period 1950-73 by S.J. Prais[25], retentions were found to be 14 per cent of total funds for the period 1970-73, 19 per cent for 1965-69, 25 per cent for the period 1960-64, 28 per cent for 1955-59, and 21 per cent for 1950-54. Prais measured retentions net of depreciation and also subtracted an estimate of stock appreciation (p. 127). Prais also argues that larger firms tend to be more highly geared, a point also made by Meeks and Whittington in a study of large companies in the U.K.[26]. Prais argues that although interest was tax deductible against profits tax and Corporation Tax when it was introduced in the U.K. in 1965, restructuring the capital structure is subject to substantial 'frictional delays' (p. 105), because U.K. tax legislation prohibits changes in the capital structure of a company solely designed to reduce tax payments. Hence there may have been a delay of several years before companies adjusted their 'gearing ratio' to take account of the relative advantage of debt finance compared with equity finance following the introduction of Corporation Tax in 1965.

Meaningful comparisons with other European countries apart from the U.K. is difficult because of differing accounting conventions. Nevertheless several writers suggest that gearing ratios tend to be higher in European countries than in the U.K. and that borrowing from various banking institutions is the main source of external finance. Although new equity issues in France and Germany are similar or larger in absolute magnitude than funds raised in the U.K. Bayliss and Butt Philip show that for 1977 U.K. firms raised Stg£ 854 million, French companies Stg£ 1235 million and German companies Stg£ 501 million. Stonham concludes from a survey of corporate financing in E.E.C countries that 'British industry is still low geared compared with much of E.E.C. industry'[27] and hence it is likely that gearing ratios of Irish firms are also lower than those found in other European countries[28].

7.3. Flows of funds and fiscal incentives

The foregoing analysis of flows of funds has shown some of the effects of fiscal incentives on corporate financing. First of all, from Table 7.1 it can be seen that since 1973 aggregate dividend payments have been greater than aggregate tax payments. This result has not come about as a result of positive discrimination in favour of dividends, but rather from the increasing value of tax allowances. Although as noted earlier in this paper, the savings ratios shown in Table 7.5, while fluctuating considerably from year to year, appear to show a long run trend to increase up until the most recent recession, and conversely for the dividend pay-out ratio. The savings ratios and dividend pay-out ratios are also more variable in the period 1971-82, compared with 1964-70.

A second point which can be noted from Table 7.1 results from the payment of tax in arrears. This results in tax payments being procyclical. A fall in profits has the perverse effect of increasing the tax rate on profits, although recent tax changes have reduced the lag in corporate tax payments. In addition, in contrast to the U.K., firms in Ireland do not have an opportunity to pay tax in advance by the purchase of interest bearing tax certificates.

Capital grants provided about 10.5 per cent of external funds, for the period 1964-84 and appear rather unimportant as a source of funds. However compared with internal funds available for new investment, capital grants are more significant. For the period 1964-84 internal funds available for new investment amounted to IR£ 25.299 million compared with IR£ 90.072 million paid in capital grants. For eight years, 1974-76 and 1980-84 capital grants are larger than internally generated funds available for investment and are larger than funds raised by share issues for six years (1967-68, 1970 1974, 1977, 1980).

The effect of fiscal incentives on the form of external financing is more difficult to assess. The growth of long term debt finance after 1976 could be attributed to the growth of 'section 84' loans. Companies with high export ratios may also rely to a greater extent on issues of equity and preference shares because the dividends on these shares would be taxed at a lower rate or in the case of 100 per cent exporting companies, would be tax free. However it is also likely that companies issue share capital under a variety of circumstances, and not just in response to tax law. For example, Fama and Jensen[29] argue that equity shares are more likely to be issued where large amounts of wealth are required to finance specialised and hence risky assets. These assets are also likely to require specialised decision skills, which wealth owners are unlikely to possess. In this context it is interesting to note that approximately 38 per cent of all share issues were raised by one company with the sort of assets structure described by Fama and Jensen, that is a company which manufactures cement.

To a certain extent capital grants may also be a substitute for share issues. Companies that receive capital grants may either not need associated share issues, or else require reduced amounts. An examination of the data indicates that all companies (with one exception, Woodchester Investments) which issued shares (preference and equity) in the period 1964-84, also received capital grants, whereas not all companies that received capital grants issued shares[30]. It may be the case that for companies with profitable investment projects, (in the absence of capital grants) capital grants are a partial substitute for share isues, as the project could have been financed from other sources. `But for companies with investment projects dependent on the receipt of a capital grant to ensure private profitability, the effect of capital grants may be to increase demand for external sources of finance such as share issues. From a survey of the empirical evidence Marsh[31] recently summarised the factors affecting the choice between debt and equity. Companies that are small, or have high price/earnings ratios, or have high gearing ratios are more likely to issue equity. While companies raising large sums in relation to total assets are more likely to issue debt, companies with high market value/book value of assets are more likely to issue equity. In addition, equity issues are widely thought to follow Stock Market rises and the level of interest rates is thought to have considerable influence on the long term corporate debt market. A.D. Bain also argues that all companies except those with considerable financial problems, have considerable choice in relation to the timing of capital issues. Bain argues that this choice will depend on capital and credit market conditions, while the choice between equity and long term debt depends on Balance Sheet structure and relative costs[32].

Marsh also examines issues of equity and debt by U.K. quoted companies for the period 1959 to 1970. Marsh concludes (p. 142) that 'companies are heavily influenced by market conditions and the past history of security prices in choosing between equity and debt'. Marsh also found support for the proposition that companies have a target ratio for the proportion of long term debt in the capital structure and also for the ratio of short term debt to long term debt. These ratios are explained by company size, bankruptcy risk, and asset composition.

Marsh argues that while tax may be an important determinant of debt issues, all companies in a tax paying position are affected in the same way and hence tax cannot be used to explain cross sectional differences in debt/equity ratios. However if the companies examined included both tax paying and non-tax paying ones, tax effects are likely to be more important.

The relationship between the level of share issues and the export/sales ratio was examined for companies in this study using equations (1) and (2) below for the period 1964-70, 1971-76, 1977-80, and 1981-84. In summary, a positive but non-significant relationship was found between share issues (equity and preference shares) as a proportion of capital employed (I/K) and the export/sales ratio (E/S) and also between share issues expressed as a proportion of total external finance (I/F) and the export/sales ratio (E/S).

More specifically the following relationships were examined using an ordinary least squares regression procedure, on various subsamples of the study population selected according to the value of the export/sales ratio (E/S).

$$I/K = f(E/S) \qquad (1)$$

where,

I = share issues (equity and preference share issues)

K = capital employed is defined as fixed + net current assets + short term bank borrowing.

E = sales

$$I/F = f(E/S) \qquad (2)$$

F = total external finance, as in Table 7.2, column (16)

All the data were derived from annual Reports and Accounts prepared according to historic cost conventions. The data consist of pooled cross section data, which was divided into four subperiods 1964-70, 1971-76, 1977-80, and1981-84. Regression equation (1) was examined using an ordinary least squares regression procedure. If all cases were included the coefficient of E/S was found to be positive and significant at the 5 per cent level for the period 1980-84 (R^2 adj. = 0.023) and positive but not significant for the periods 1964-70, and 1977-80. The coefficient was found to be negative but not significant for the period 1971-76.

In a few cases the L.H.S. of equation (1) may be negative as preference shares are redeemed, and regression equation (1) was also examined omitting these negative cases. The L.H.S. of equation (1) is then constrained to lie between 0 and 1 and was transformed using a logit transformation to the form:- -log((1 -I/K)/(I/K))[33]. The coefficient of E/S was found to be positive but non-significant for all periods. Subsamples based on various values of E/S were also found to have a weak positive statistical relationship.

Aggregate values of I/K, that is :-

$$\sum_{t=1964}^{1970}\sum_{i=1}^{n} I_{it} / \sum_{t=1964}^{1970}\sum_{i=1}^{n} K_{it}, \quad \sum_{t=1971}^{1976}\sum_{i=1}^{n} I_{it} / \sum_{t=1971}^{1976} K_{it}, \quad \sum_{t=1977}^{1980}\sum_{i=1}^{n} I_{it} / \sum_{t=1977}^{1980} K_{it} \quad \text{and}$$

$$\sum_{t=1981}^{1984}\sum_{i=1}^{n} I_{it} / \sum_{t=1981}^{1984}\sum_{i=1}^{n} K_{it},$$ where n is the number of companies and t is the time period

were also examined for the periods 1964-70, 1971-76, 1977-80 and 1971-84. Table 7.7 shows the results.

Table 7.7 shows that share issues as a proportion of capital employed (I/K) are higher for exporting companies than for non-exporting companies for the periods 1964-70 and 1971-76. For the periods 1977-80 and 1981-84 share issues as a proportion of capital employed are higher for companies with export/sales ratios greater than 0.25. It also appears for these latter periods that the higher the level of exports, the higher the ratio I/K. The relationship between share issues as a proportion of external finance (I/F), and the export/sales ratio (E/S) is more complicated, than that between I/K and E/S because F (total external finance) may become negative, as loans and preference shares are repaid. I (preference and equity shares) may also be negative, due to repayment of preference shares. If all cases were included except cases where the denominator was negative, a positive and significant (at the 5 per cent level) relationship was found for equation (2) for the period 1964-70 with an R^2 (adj.) of 0.034. A positive but non-significant relationship was found for the period 1971-76, and a negative but non-significant relationship was found for the periods 1977-80 and 1981-84. If cases where negative values of both the numerator and denominator are excluded, I/F is then constrained to lie between zero and one[34]. As for equation (1), equation (2) was transformed using a logit transformation to the form:- -log((1 - I/F)/(I/F)). For all periods a positive but non-significant relationship was found. For example if all cases were included, except those where the numerator and denominator were negative and using a logit transformation, a positive significant coefficient was found for the period 1964-70 with an R^2(adj.) of 0.012. As for equation (1), subsamples based on higher values of E/S also had a weak positive statistical relationship.

Table 7.7 also shows a general increase in the ratio of aggregate share issues to aggregate external financing for the periods examined for subsamples based on different values of E/S. As for I/K, the highest value of the ratio I/F was obtained for a subsample based on E/S > 0.25 for the period 1964-70 and 1971-76, and for a subsample with E/S > 0.5 for the period 1977-80 and 1981-84.

These results appear to show that there is a positive relationship between the level of exports and share issues as a proportion of external finance. However the statistical relationship for individual companies on a yearly basis is weak. This may be explained by the spasmodic use of share issues as a source of external finance. Companies issue shares only on an occasional basis, and as shown earlier in this paper there appear to be strong cyclical influences. Debt, though more costly than share finance for an exporting company with taxable profits, is a much more flexible source of external finance. These results must also be interpreted with caution, as not all companies publish information relating to both exports and sales. This is particularly true of the period 1964-70. In addition the ratio of share issues to capital employed will be influenced by company policies relating to revaluation of assets in the Balance Sheet as well as by the general rate of inflation.

Table 7.7

Share issues as a proportion of capital employed and external finance for the period 1964-84 (per cent)

Shares Issues(I)/ Capital Employed (K) or External Finance (F)[a]	E/S=0[b]	E/S>0	E/S>0.25	E/S>0.5
	1981-84			
$\sum_{t=1981}^{1984}\sum_{i=1}^{n} I_{it} / \sum_{t=1981}^{1984}\sum_{i=1}^{n} K_{it}$	2.33	1.80	2.32	3.16
$\sum_{t=1981}^{1984}\sum_{i=1}^{n} I_{it} / \sum_{t=1981}^{1984}\sum_{i=1}^{n} K_{it}$	41.92	55.13	45.29	59.08
	1977-80			
$\sum_{t=1977}^{1980}\sum_{i=1}^{n} I_{it} / \sum_{t=1977}^{1980}\sum_{i=1}^{n} K_{it}$	0.48	0.40	0.68	1.13
$\sum_{t=1977}^{1980}\sum_{i=1}^{n} I_{it} / \sum_{t=1977}^{1980}\sum_{i=1}^{n} F_{it}$	8.40	8.42	13.54	19.60
	1971-76			
$\sum_{t=1971}^{1976}\sum_{i=1}^{n} I_{it} / \sum_{t=1971}^{1976}\sum_{i=1}^{n} K_{it}$	0.48	1.38	1.97	0.71
$\sum_{t=1971}^{1976}\sum_{i=1}^{n} I_{it} / \sum_{t=1971}^{1976}\sum_{i=1}^{n} F_{it}$	10.04	20.56	24.32	19.98
	1964-70			
$\sum_{t=1964}^{1970}\sum_{i=1}^{n} I_{it} / \sum_{t=1964}^{1970}\sum_{i=1}^{n} K_{it}$	0.47	0.63	1.96	1.23
$\sum_{t=1964}^{1970}\sum_{i=1}^{n} I_{it} / \sum_{t=1964}^{1970}\sum_{i=1}^{n} F_{it}$	9.42	8.28	15.96	12.90

Notes to Table 7.7

(a) One company, Cement Roadstone, which accounted for 34.7 per cent of all share issues over the period 1964-84, was excluded from Table 7.7 for the periods 1964-70, 1971-76, 1977-80, as exports amounted to between 3 and 5 per cent of sales. If the ratio I/K and I/F were calculated for all firms with E/S > 0 (including Cement Roadstone), the values obtained were 1.8 and 56.1 per cent for 1964-70, 1.7 and 23.3 per cent for 1971- 76, and 1.9 and 37.7 for 1977-80 respectively. Data relating to

exports was not published for the period 1981-84.
(b) E/S = value of exports/sales ratio.

7.4 Conclusion

This chapter examined flows of funds to companies included in the study. Overall Commercial bank borrowing accounted for more than 50 per cent of external finance in 11 of the years 1964-84 and provided approximately 57 per cent of total external finance over the entire period 1964-1984. Commercial bank borrowing as a proportion of external finance rose from 48.5 per cent in the period 1964-70 to 65.8 per cent in the period 1977-80 and then fell to 45 per cent in the period 1981-84. Funds from shareholders/Stock Exchange amounted to 19.6 per cent of external finance in the period 1964-70, were slightly higher in the periods 1971-76 and 1977-80 at 22 and 23 per cent respectively and reached a peak of 47.7 per cent in the period 1980-84. Fiscal incentives in the form of capital grants while not as important as other external sources of finance are larger for some years than internal sources if internal sources are adjusted for stock appreciation. This chapter also noted than since 1973 aggregate dividend payments have been larger than aggregate tax payments. Indeed aggregate dividend payments have remained positive even though aggregate savings adjusted for stock appreciation are negative. This may suggest that dividend payout ratios for companies in the study are too high. The introduction of Advance Corporation Tax (A.C.T.) means that companies are now faced with a type of differential profits tax, as A.C.T. only becomes payable on payment of a dividend, and this may have the effect of reducing payout ratios.

There appeared to be a positive but weak relationship between exporting and share issues. Apart from the effect of the fiscal system on the form of external finance, the fiscal system was found to have other effects on the financing of the corporate sector, for example, the payment of corporation tax in arrears appears to have a procyclical effect on cash flows.

Finally, because of the complexity and heterogeneous nature of the factors affecting corporate finance, it is dificult to separate cyclical factors from trend factors, and non-fiscal effects such as asset specificity from fiscal effects. Specific assets such as plant and machinery are likely to be specialised and hence more risky. They are also likely to require specialised decision skills, for example cement and chemical plants. As argued in Chapter 6 such plant is not suitable for leasing, because of possible difficulties with the value of collateral in the event of default, and may be more cheaply financed with equity rather than debt[35].

Appendix 1

Flows of funds to non-financial Semi-state companies 1970-84

Tables 7.8 and 7.9 Appendix show internal and external flows of funds to various companies in the Semi-state sector for the period 1970-84. Before discussing the main features of Table 7.8 and Table 7.9 appendix, it is important to note some problems encountered in interpreting the accounts of the companies included. Many of the problems encountered in preparing a flows of funds statement for companies in the private sector are also encountered with companies in the public sector. Many companies in the Semi-state sector have taken over companies in the private sector, for example the Irish Refining company by I.N.P.C. However the main additional problem relates to disclosure of foreign borrowing and to variations in the accounting treatment of foreign exchange gains/losses. In a number of cases Semi-State companies do not disclose the amount of foreign borrowing (Bord na Mona, B + I). In some cases it was possible to identify foreign borrowing from the annual report of the European Investment Bank. However because of nondisclosure of foreign borrowing, long term borrowing from domestic banks is overstated. As far as was possible foreign exchange gains or losses have been omitted from pre-tax profits. Finally accrued interest has not been included as part of short term borrowing. This mostly affects the E.S.B.

It also proved difficult to reconcile amounts shown as sources of finance in the Public Capital Programme for various years with receipts from the State by Semi-state companies as shown in their accounts. In particular, difficulty was found with amounts shown as 'capital restructuring and re-financing of borrowing'. There were also some other instances where the accounts of Semi-state companies do not show amounts received under the Public Capital Programme (P.C.P.), for example an amount of IR£ 10.7 million shown as paid to 'Air Lines' in 1976. In addition some companies have received far more by way of equity, grants and loans, than is shown in the P. C. P., for example, Irish Steel.

The main feature of Table 7.8 appendix is that pre-tax profits are small but positive for all but two of the years 1970-82 (1980-81) and show large increases for 1983-84 reflecting the profits of Bord Gais Eireann. Pre-tax profits for Semi-state companies also show coincident cyclical trends to public companies in the private sector, for example the downturn in profits in 1973-74 and a new recession beginning in 1979. There was also a downturn in profits of Semi-state companies in 1969 which is not shown in Table 7.8 appendix. Finally if depreciation allowances and a stock adjustment are subtracted from gross internal saving an estimate of internal funds available for net new investment is obtained (column 8). This is negative for the period 1972-75 and also for 1979-82, coinciding with a drop in pre-tax profits in 1974-75 and pre-tax losses in 1980-81. Table 7.9 shows how the deficit arising from trading activities and also how net new investment is financed. The fall in pre-tax profits in 1974 and in 1980-81 was associated with a rise in short term bank borrowing followed by a fall in short term bank borrowing and an increase in foreign borrowing and long term domestic bank borrowing.

Foreign borrowing was found to be the main source of external finance for the period examined. For all years except 1971, 1977, 1982 and 1984 foreign borrowing accounted for more than 50 per cent of external finance. For 1971 the State was the main source of external finance and for 1977, 1982 and 1984 the main source was borrowing from domestic banks. Approximately IR£ 51 million net was raised on the Stock Exchange over the period 1970-82.

The E.S.B. was the only company to issue securities directly on the Stock Market. The State provided approximately IR£ 406 million by way of equity, loans, and grants. This figure excludes current grants and subsidies.

Table 7.8 Appendix
Sources of internal finance for Semi-state companies 1970-84

IR£ million

Year	N[a]	Pre-tax[b] Profits	Depreciation	Gross Internal Cash Flow	Cash Tax Payment	Dividend[c]	Gross Internal Saving	Stock Adjustment	Internal[d] Funds Available for new Investment
		(1)	(2)	(3) (1+2)	(4)	(5)	(6) (3-4-5)	(7)	(8) (6-7-2)
1970	9	4.409	16.116	20.525	0.309	0.096	20.120	1.545	2.459
1971	9	2.789	17.480	20.269	0.156	0.095	20.018	1.857	0.681
1972	9	3.425	23.359	26.784	0.126	0.093	26.659	3.838	-0.632
1973	8	5.193	24.534	29.727	0.040	0.093	29.594	6.592	-1.532
1974	9	0.727	29.511	30.238	0.033	0.092	30.113	7.653	-7.051
1975	8	3.818	31.384	35.202	0.0	0.0	35.202	10.635	-6.817
1976	9	13.826	38.149	51.975	0.060	0.107	51.808	13.644	0.015
1977	9	27.271	41.852	69.123	0.449	0.143	68.531	12.876	13.803
1978	10	18.555	43.425	61.980	0.420	0.126	61.434	8.831	9.178
1979	10	2.543	54.604	57.147	0.137	0.169	56.841	16.097	-13.860
1980	10	-19.656	71.064	51.408	1.051	0.191	50.166	19.844	-40.742
1981	11	-10.105	89.143	79.038	0.024	0.0	79.014	39.220	-49.349
1982	11	32.207	104.520	136.727	0.492	33.000	103.235	27.606	-28.891
1983	10	82.313	118.117	200.430	13.076	63.000	187.354	15.596	53.641
1984	10	134.532	138.484	273.016	0.363	54.000	218.653	19.595	60.574

Notes to Table 7.8 Appendix

(a) Due to changes in accounting year end dates Irish Sugar was omitted for 1975 and N.E.T. for 1973.

(b) Pre - tax profits omiy foreign exchange gains or losses. Profits of the E.S.B. are defined as the surplus on trading plus interest on sinking funds.

(c) For 1970-80 refers to dividends paid on preference shares by Irish Sugar company and for 1982-84 to payments by An Bord Gais.

(d) Net deficit of C.I.E. includes current grant.

Table 7.9 Appendix
Sources of external finance for Semi-state companies 1970-84

IR£ million

Year	Stock Exchange or equity (10)	Loans from the State and State Institutions (11)	Capital Grants (12)	Long Term Commercial Bank (13)	Short Term Commercial Bank (14)	Foreign Borrowing (15)	Total External Finance (16)	Total External plus net internal finance (17)	Total External plus gross internal finance (18)
1970	5.626	-0.472	2.780	0.999	3.748	14.549	27.230	31.234	47.350
1971	11.258	13.642	1.713	4.399	3.182	4.823	39.017	41.555	59.035
1971	-1.556	-0.026	3.026	0.619	-8.679	51.932	45.316	48.522	71.881
1973	-4.501	2.140	1.518	4.182	-0.098	21.590	24.831	29.891	54.425
1971	-4.747	2.003	1.382	2.300	18.649	33.084	52.671	53.273	82.884
1975	3.766	0.652	2.328	4.199	5.506	50.091	66.542	70.360	101.744
1976	9.947	17.320	2.396	4.704	-6.617	68.642	96.392	110.051	148.200
1977	27.574	-0.021	3.953	25.213	1.424	-0.415	57.728	84.407	126.259
1978	13.011	6.958	2.573	18.022	7.578	95.731	143.873	161.882	205.307
1979	12.503	12.587	3.136	24.229	22.834	174.226	249.515	251.752	306.356
1980	8.905	12.047	6.496	49.611	74.008	213.932	364.990	344.101	415.165
1981	22.789	80.092	3.497	2.705	47.756	236.680	393.519	383.390	472.533
1982	5.771	3.043	12.740	102.399	78.511	160.935	363.399	362.114	466.634
1983	74.802	-5.679	0.0	86.314	-19.390	182.461	318.508	387.745	505.862
1984	82.211	-2.109	0.0	136.352	-31.131	0.995	186.318	266.487	404.971

Notes

[1] A.D. Bain, 'Surveys in Applied Economics: Flow of Funds Analysis', *Economic Journal* vol. 83, no. 332,, 1973, pp. 1055-1093.

[2] A.D. Bain, ibid. p. 1062.

[3] A similar adjustment is made in estimating sources and uses of funds for U.K. companies published in Company Finance, Business Monitor, MA3, H.M.S.O., London.

[4] Lintner found that the following gradual adjustment process explained a large proportion of the change in dividend payments for a sample of 28 U.S. Corporations: $D_{it} = A_{it} + C_i(R_iP_{it} - D_{i(t-1)}) + U_{it}$, where D_i = change in dividends, R_i = target payout ratio, P_t is the current years after tax profits, and C_i is the speed of adjustment coefficient. Lintner's study has been repeated numerous times, sometimes substituting cash flow for dividends, however in all cases an extremely good fit of the above equation has been obtained. J. Lintner, 'Distribution of Incomes of Corporations among Dividends, Retained Earnings and Taxes', *American Economic Review*, May 1956, pp. 97-113. For an example of Lintner's model fitted to U.K. data see T. Ryan, 'Dividend Policy and Market Valuation in British Industry', *Journal of Business Finance and Accounting*, vol. 1 Autumn, 1974, pp. 415-429.

[5] A.D. Bain describes the financing pattern of U.K. companies in the following terms in the *Control of the Money Supply*, Penguin Books, 1970, Harmondsworth, p. 113, 'U.K. companies demands on the capital and credit market have typically been light in the early stages of recovery, but have grown much heavier as economic activity quickened during the upswing'.

[6] A.D. Bain, ibid. pp. 108-114.

[7] R.C.O. Matthews, *The Trade Cycle*, Cambridge University Press, Cambridge, 1959.

[8] Wilson Report, *Committee to Review the Functioning of Financial Institutions*, Cmnd. 7937, H.M.S.O. London, 1980.

[9] This finding is also supported by flows of funds data prepared by T. O'Connell in 'The Flow of Funds 1960-1985', *Central Bank of Ireland Quarterly Bulletin*, Summer 1986, pp. 76-102. See also T. O'Connell 'The Flow of Funds, 1960-1985', paper read to the Statistical and Social Inquiry Society of Ireland 24 April , 1986. See also National Economic and Social Council, *The Role of the Financial System in Financing the Traded Sectors*, Report no. 76, Pl. 4450, Stationery Office, Dublin, especially Chapter 5.

[10] M.A. King and D. Fullerton, *The Taxation of Income from Capital,* University of Chicago Press and National Bureau of Economic Research, Chicago, 1984, p. 64. See also Wilson Report, op. cit., p. 79.

[11] G. Meeks and G. Whittington, *The Financing of Quoted Companies in the U.K.*, Royal Commission on the Distribution of Income and Wealth, H.M.S.O., London, 1976, p. 5.

[12] K.A. Kennedy and B.R. Dowling, *Economic Growth in Ireland: The Experience Since 1947*, Gill and MacMillan, Dublin, 1975.
[13] K.A. Kennedy and B.R. Dowling, ibid. 1975, p. 158.
[14] K.A. Kennedy and B.R. Dowling, ibid. 1975, p. 165.
[15] R.N. Vaughan, 'Profits, Finance and Growth', in B.R. Dowling and J. Durkan (eds.), *Irish Economic Policy: A Review of Major Issues*, Economic and Social Research Institute, Dublin, 1978.
[16] The eleven examined were:- Aer Lingus/Aerlinte, B + I, Bord Gais Eireann, Bord na Mona, C.I.E., Electricity Supply Board, Irish National Petroleum Corporation, Irish Shipping, Irish Steel, Irish Sugar, Nitrogen Eireann.
[17] Total foreign borrowing by State owned companies amounted to IR£ 490.2 million in December 1979, of which IR£ 92.4 million was due to the U.K. The year 1979 was the first year for which this data was published. Source: *Quarterly Bulletin of the Central Bank of Ireland*, Autumn, 1982, Table 8.
[18] Foreign borrowing by State owned companies increased from IR£ 490.2 million in December 1979 to IR£ 778.8 million in December 1980. By December 1983 this sum had increased to IR£ 1830 million. Source: *Central Bank of Ireland Quarterly Bulletin*, Autumn 1982, Table 8, and Summer 1984, Table D9.
[19] P. Honohan, 'The Flow of Funds 1972-1977', *Journal of the Statistical and Social Inquiry Society of Ireland*, vol. XXIV, part IV, 1981-1982, pp. 175-216
[20] Wilson Report, 1980, op. cit. p. 133.
[21] M.A. King and D. Fullerton, 1984, op. cit. pp. 237-238.
[22] G. Meeks and G. Whittington, op. cit. 1976.
[23] A breakdown between securities issued for cash and securities issued in relation to takeovers or mergers is not given for the period 1948-64.
[24] A.D. Bain, 1970, 0p. cit. p. 112.
[25] S.J. Prais, *The Evolution of Giant Firms in Britain*, Cambridge University Press, Cambridge, 1976, Table 5.8, p. 126.
[26] G. Meeks and G. Whittington, 'Giant Companies in the U.K. 1948-1969', *Economic Journal*, vol. 85 no. 340. 1975, pp. 824-838, esp. Table (4).
[27] See P. Stonham, *Major Stock Markets of Europe*, Gower, London, 1982, p. 122. See also J.M. Samuels, R.E.V. Groves and C.S. Goddard, *Company Finance in Europe*, Institute of Chartered Accountants in England and Wales, London, 1975.
[28] It is also argued in Chapter 4 that inflation is likely to reduce gearing in real terms.
[29] E.F. Fama and M.C. Jensen, 'Separation of Ownership and Control', *Journal of Law and Economics*, vol. XXVI, 1983, pp. 301-325.
[30] For each year and for the entire period examined a minority of companies issued share capital, but for most individual years and for the entire period a majority of the companies included in the study received capital grants.
[31] P. Marsh, 'The Choice Between Equity and Debt: An Empirical Study', *Journal of Finance*, vol. XXXVII, no. 2, 1982, pp. 121-144.

[32] A.D. Bain, 'A Model of U.K. Company Financial Behaviour', *The Manchester School*, 1977, pp. 345-370. See also A.D. Bain, C.L. Day and A.L. Wearing, *Company Financing in the United Kingdom*, Martin Robertson, London, 1975, especially Chapter 7.

[33] See S. Pindyck and D.L. Rubinfeld, *Economic Models and Economic Forecasts*, McGraw-Hill, London, 1981, pp. 287-300. The misspecification resulting from omitting these cases is likely to be small, as 5 out of 176 cases were omitted for the period 1980-84, 4 out of 223 cases for the period 1977-80, 4 out of 410 cases for the period 1971-76, and 4 out of 297 cases for the period 1964-70.

[34] The number of omitted cases for the period 1980-84 was 3 out of 109, 4 out of 153 for the period 1977-80, 3 out of 247 for the period 1971-76 and 3 out of 183 for the period 1964-70.

[35] Some implications of the dominance of the banking sector in the provision of external finance are discussed in J.C. Stewart, 'Fiscal Incentives and Corporate Financing: a Flow of Funds Analysis', forthcoming *Journal of the Statistical and Social Inquiry Society of Ireland.*

8 Summary and some policy implications

This chapter presents a summary of the main findings and also discusses some policy implications with particular reference to some of the reforms of the taxation system as discussed in the work of the Commission on Taxation in Ireland.

8.1 Summary

Chapter 1 of this book argued that the fiscal system for corporations in Ireland can be described in terms of a diffusion process - fiscal incentives once introduced tend to diffuse so that the definition of a development area is widened to include other areas not originally classified as development areas, or to include other sectors or industries. Specific fiscal incentives are often introduced in response to lobbying by affected interests. New fiscal incentives are often introduced without replacing the existing ones, for example a reduced rate of corporation tax of 10 per cent was announced as replacing export tax relief. In reality most firms may continue to benefit from both forms of tax relief until 1990. It is not surprising then that fiscal incentives and State aid to the corporate sector account for an increasing proportion of G.N.P. Excluding lending by State agencies, State aid to the corporate sector in Ireland, in so far as it was possible to identify and quantify this, rose from approximately 2.74 per cent of G.N.P. in 1978 to 6.08 per cent in 1984 (Table 1.9 appendix). The appendix to Chapter 1 also argued that total State aid to the corporate sector in Ireland was likely to be larger as a percentage of G.N.P. than in the U.K. or other E.E.C. countries.

Chapter 2 described the firms included in this study, which consist of non-financial public companies in Ireland during the period 1964-84. The accounts of these companies form the main data source used in this thesis. These companies accounted for at least 25 per cent of total trading profits in 1964, but by 1984 their share had fallen to about 5.8 per cent (Table 2.3). Chapter 2 also noted that employment for 20 companies included in the study for the entire period had also contracted in recent years, despite the receipt of IR£ 52.4 million in capital grants (Table 2.5).

The study population described in Chapter 2 was used to estimate average effective tax rates in Chapter 3 using historical data. Auerbach, and King, Fullerton and others, have argued that average effective tax rates may not indicate marginal tax rates and hence may not be used to predict returns on new investment. However average effective tax rates are useful in other contexts, for example estimating flows of funds in the corporate sector and corporate savings rates, and costing fiscal incentives. Average effective tax rates were shown to have fallen considerably over the period examined. The average tax rate for companies included in the study, using historical cost data, fell from approximately 29 per cent in the period 1964-66 to 10.7 per cent in the period 1981-83 (Table 3.3). It is also likely that the future trend for average tax rates will continue to fall, due to the general introduction of a 10 per cent tax rate for manufacturng companies in 1981.

Chapter 4 described various adjustments to company accounts in order to allow for inflation. Several empirical studies were reviewed which demonstrate the sensitivity of inflation adjusted profits to particular inflation adjustments. In general Chapter 4 argued that fully inflation adjusted profits are likely to result in higher profits than the partially inflation adjusted accounts currently published, although profits in different companies are affected to varying degrees and in different directions. It is concluded that company accounts for the corporate sector as a whole, if fully adjusted for inflation, would be also likely to show that effective average tax rates fell during the period 1964-84. The chapter also noted that the effects of inflation on company accounts last far longer than the actual period of inflation. Finally the chapter noted that inflation has other effects on the corporate sector, for example corporate liquidity may be reduced, as may liquidity within the economy as a whole.

Chapter 5 examined the distribution of tax rates and found that approximately 66 per cent of companies in the study had tax rates on taxable profits which were less than 10 per cent for 1984 and for the same year, 32 per cent of companies had tax rates of zero or received a tax refund. These figures compare with 15 per cent and 3 per cent respectively for 1964 (Table 5.1). Chapter 5 also showed that at least 25 per cent of all companies in the study had zero tax payments or tax refunds in one or more of the years 1973-84. This has had considerable implications for the development of leasing. Finally Chapter 5 argued that compared to other O.E.C.D. countries Ireland obtained a small proportion of total tax revenue from the corporate sector (3.86 per cent), and ranked 18th out of 22 countries in terms of the proportion of taxable revenue derived from taxation of profits (Table 5.8).

Chapters 6 and 7 examined the effects of fiscal incentives on corporate financial behaviour and corporate financing. Chapter 6 argued that fiscal incentives had led to a number of innovations in the way companies finance themselves, for example, the growth of leasing has arisen in order to prevent the accumulation of unused tax allowances. The chapter also argued that because of the way fiscal incentives interact with each other, companies have evolved a number of different financial strategies. For example, exporting companies will tend to rely on 'section 84' loans and share financing (preference or equity) as a source of external finance. They will also sell surplus tax allowances via leasing. In contrast non-exporting companies will not lease assets unless depreciation allowances are sufficiently large to ensure zero tax payments. They may also rely to a reduced extent on share financing. However, the form of external finance is likely to be influenced by other factors, apart from fiscal incentives, such as asset specificity. Chapter 6 concluded by arguing that the development of various financial strategies by firms in response to fiscal incentives has a number of different policy implications, relating to the diffusion of fiscal incentives, but also arising from the chanelling of fiscal incentives through financial intermediaries. This has two main effects. First of all, certain biases are introduced into the capital market. Investment decisions may be biased towards assets suitable for leasing, for example homogeneous and non-specific assets (office and transport equipment) as such assets are more marketable in the event of default. Secondly, it reduces the value of fiscal incentives to firms which lease capital equipment compared with firms who purchase capital equipment.

Chapter 7 examined flows of funds. Borrowing from the commercial banks was the largest external source of funds, providing almost 57 per cent of total external finance over the period 1964-84, with long term bank borrowing becoming more important in the latter part of the period. There also appeared to be a greater reliance on the Stock Exchange/shareholders for sources of external funds than, for example, in the U.K. In contrast savings ratios appeared lower than those found in the U.K. The chapter also noted the sensitivity of savings ratios to the definition of savings, for example including or excluding a stock adjustment. Chapter 7 also reported some empirical evidence relating to the effect of fiscal incentives on financial strategies of firms. A weak but positive statistical relationship was found between exporting and the use of share issues as a source of finance. However the chapter also noted strong cyclical influences on corporate profits and retentions and also on sources of external finance.

8.2 Some policy implications

The low average tax rates found for companies in this study were largely explained by the growth and diffusion of fiscal incentives. Indeed there appears to be a considerable gap between the announced intended effects of fiscal incentives and their operation in practice. The Commission on

Taxation in Ireland state that they 'have been unable to ascertain any coherent policy in relation to the granting of incentives in the past'[1]. There is a general argument that the tax system should be neutral between different economic activities. The Wilson Report states that 'neutrality is in our view best seen as a benchmark against which instances of non-neutrality, intentional or otherwise, need to be justified'[2]. The Green Paper on corporation tax in the U.K. states that 'as a general principle it may be argued that the tax system should not distort the market allocation of resources unnecessarily, or without good reason'[3], and this appears to be the view generally accepted in the U.K. as in for example in the White Paper on Regional Incentives[4].

There have also been various arguments and discussion of what a neutral tax system involves, for example, equality of capital costs, or equality of subsidy from fiscal provisions[5]. In contrast the Commission on Taxation in Ireland, while recognising the general principle of neutrality argue that 'efficiency may be improved by a departure from neutrality'[6]. The Commission go on to present a case for fiscal incentives in certain limited circumstances, for example the need to attract foreign direct investment. Similar arguments for fiscal incentives have also been used in other countries. Immediate difficulties are raised in relation to the definition of worthwhile activities, and the related need to prevent the diffusion of fiscal incentices to other activities. A further problem that arises is that the Irish corporate tax system departs from neutrality in several unintended respects.

The corporation tax system is not neutral in Ireland between different economic activities, between different sources of finance, or between incorporated and unincorporated entities. Further problems have arisen in Ireland and in other countries because of tax losses. Fiscal incentives are only of benefit to firms that pay taxes, but many firms in Ireland and other countries do not pay tax on profits. Hence further distortions arise between tax-paying and non tax-paying firms (firms making losses, business start-ups, and firms with surplus depreciation allowances).

Apart from issues of neutrality and the difficulties of identifying and defining areas thought to require special tax treatment, the system of corporation tax in Ireland has been extensively criticised in the context of reform of the tax system as a whole. The Commission on Taxation[7] has described the Irish tax system as 'unfair, muddled, and complicated'.

The two main problems with the corporation tax system identified in this book are low net yields and asymmetries in the treatment of different economic units, which may be engaging in similar economic activities. In other countries where similar problems have arisen, a possible solution suggested has been to abolish corporation tax. Auerbach[8] favours this solution in the U.S. Kay and King[9] also recognise that 'the simplest reform would be to abolish corporation tax altogether', but dismiss this solution for the U.K. Instead they suggest a tax based on cash flows, in which interest would not be tax deductible. A tax based on cash flows was also suggested by the Meade Committee[10], and a Green paper on Corporation Tax in the U.K. examined the implications of a tax based on cash flows, as well as other reforms such as taxing profits on the basis of Current Cost

Accounts[11].

The Commission on Taxation in Ireland recommended removal of many fiscal incentives and their replacement by a single lower rate of tax which would be set at the same rate for individuals and for capital gains tax. This follows from the Commission's belief 'that almost all the problems in the area of company tax arise because company profits are charged to tax at a flat rate while income tax on individuals is charged at progressive rates'[12]. The 1984 U.K. budget announced reforms in this direction in terms of a reduction in the value of depreciation allowances. Unfortunately, in Ireland, such reforms are more difficult because of existing contractual commitments in relation to export tax relief and a 10 per cent tax rate for manufacturing firms[13]. Indeed, accepting that existing incentives to attract foreign direct investment to Ireland are contractually binding rules out many reforms because firstly a number of distortions arise directly from these incentives. Companies that pay no tax because of export tax relief are in a position where interest payments are no longer tax deductible and accelerated depreciation allowances are of diminishing value the longer they remain unused. Hence pressures arise to develop alternative sources of finance (previously preference share financing, currently 'section 84' loans), and a market for surplus depreciation allowances. The proposals of the Commission to revalue losses and capital allowances in line with changes with the Consumer Price Index[14] will only partly solve this problem, as many companies may expect to remain in a position where tax allowances are greater than taxable profits. Secondly it is not possible to provide favorable tax treatment to foreign owned companies alone, and thereby exclude domestically owned companies. It is also difficult to restrict fiscal incentives to particular sectors or industries. Fiscal incentives thus become widely available to the corporate sector with resulting problems for the tax system as a whole, such as increased tax avoidance, through, for example, artificial incorporation.

A further difficulty with the reforms suggested by the Commission on Taxation relates to whether it is desirable that reforms should be introduced in total as the Commission expect[15], or piecemeal, as is likely in practice. Introducing single reforms may result in unintended consequences For example the Commission argued against a differential profits tax to increase corporate saving[16], and argued in favour of an advanced corporation tax (A.C.T.)[17]. However as argued in Chapter 6 of this study the effect of introducing A.C.T on tax exhausted companies, is similar to introducing a differential profits tax, (viewing the company and the shareholder as one unit) as the effective tax rate becomes proportional to the dividend pay-out ratio.

The Commission on Taxation consider that proposals to harmonise corporate tax within the E.E.C. are not 'a significant constraint on our recommendations'[18]. This is also the view of Kay and King in relation to U.K. tax reform[19] and the Green Paper on corporation tax in the U.K. does not even mention the E.E.C. draft proposals for harmonisation of corporate tax.

In general, reform of corporation tax in Ireland, towards a more neutral and simplified system, is dependent on shifting industrial policy from attracting foreign direct investment with fiscal incentives to some alternative, for example, emphasising indigenous industry and providing direct State aid, rather than aid directed through the fiscal system. Only to the extent that such a policy is pursued can existing tax reliefs aimed at the corporate sector be severely curtailed. In this context the proposals of the White Paper on Industrial Strategy, to limit aid to the corporate sector to selected firms, rather than provide general aid to all applicants through tax relief, if implemented, should facilitate tax reform[20].

Finally Feldstein has argued that the interaction between inflation and nominal tax rates has increased tax rates on real profits in the U.S. This in turn has reduced real investment as a proportion of G.N.P.[21] and has also adversely affected stock market values[22]. The Feldstein argument does not apply in Ireland, or most likely the U.K., because of low effective tax rates. King, Fullerton and others[23] also suggest a connection between the tax system and economic growth. They note that for the four countries examined (W. Germany, Sweden, United Kingdom and United States) there was an inverse relationship between effective marginal tax rates on income from capital and G.N.P. growth for the period 1960-80. West Germany had the highest effective tax rate and the highest growth rate and the opposite was true for the U.K.[24], but the particular feature of the tax system they emphasise is the dispersion of different tax rates, for an identical project, depending on, for example, the means of financing the project. This dispersion or variance of the four countries was found to be highest in the U.K. examined and lowest in W. Germany.

This study also argues that the corporate fiscal system in Ireland may adversely influence investment and economic growth . The work of the Commission on Taxation in Ireland implies that the corporate fiscal system results in a divergence between private profitability and macroeconomic efficiency. The Commission says[25]:- 'As a nation we spend far too much of our time ensuring that investment decisions maximise the after-tax return rather than ensuring that they are economically or socially efficient'. This book has argued that the complexity of the tax system encourages firms to pursue different tax stategies in order to maximise post-tax profits. This is inefficient because of the diversion of managerial resources and the growth of specialised firms in response to demand for advice and interpretation of complex tax legislation. It is also inefficient because it has resulted in the channelling of fiscal incentives through financial intermediaries (the banks in the case of the corporate sector, pension funds and insurance companies in the case of the personal sector) which is likely to result in certain capital market biases, for example towards less specific and more homogeneous assets. It is also likely that fiscal incentives, because they are increasingly channelled through financial intermediaries such as banks, are worth less to the companies at which they are targeted compared with fiscal incentives used directly by companies.

Notes

[1] Commission on Taxation, *Direct Taxation, Second Report of the Commission on Taxation*, Stationery Office, Pl. 1755, Dublin, Stationery Office, Pl. 1755, 1984, p. 18.

[2] Wilson Report, *Committee to Review the Functioning of Financial Institutions*, Cmnd. 7937, H.M.S.O.,London, 1984, p. 197.

[3] Green Paper, *Corporation Tax*, Cmnd. 8456, London, H.M.S.O. 1982, p. 20.

[4] White Paper, *Regional Industrial Development*, cmnd 9111, London: H.M.S.O. 1983, especially paragraph 18.

[5] See for example A.C. Warren and A.J. Auerbach, 'Transferability of Tax Incentives and the Function of Safe Harbor Leasing', *Harvard Law Review*, vol. 95, no. 8 1982, pp. 1752-1786; A.C. Harberger, 'Tax Neutrality in Investment Decisions, in H.J. Aaron and M.J. Boskin (eds.) *The Economics of Taxation*, The Brookings Institution, Washington, 1980, pp. 299-313.

[6] Commission on Taxation, 1984, op. cit. p. 84.

[7] Commission on Taxation, *First Report of the Commission on Taxation*, Stationery Office, Dublin, 1982, p. 29. More recently a report by the National Planning Board states :- 'The Existing tax system and especially the system of direct taxation is muddled, complicated and inefficient', in *Proposals for Plan 1984-87*, Prl. 2309, National Planning Board, 1984, Dublin, p. 69.

[8] A.J. Auerbach, 'Corporate Taxation in the United States', in W.C. Brainard and G.L. Perry (eds.) *Brookings Paper on Economic Activity*, Brookings Institution, Washington, D.C., 1984. Auerbach states, p. 497:- 'Given the low level of corporate revenues at present, abolition of the corporate tax has its appeal'.

[9] J.A. Kay and M.A. King, *The British Tax System*, 3rd edition, Oxford University Press, Oxford, 1983, pp. 184 - 189.

[10] Meade Committee, *The Structure and Reform of Direct Taxation*, Report of a committe chaired by J.E. Meade, Institute for Fiscal Studies, London, 1978, Chapter 12.

[11] Green Paper, *Corporation Tax*, Cmnd 8456, London: H.M.S.O. 1982, Chapters 6 and 7.

[12] Commission on Taxation, First Report, 1982, op. cit. p. 39.

[13] Commission on Taxation, Second Report, 1984, op cit. p. 137.

[14] Commission on Taxation, First Report, 1982, op. cit. p. 358.

[15] Commission on Taxation, Second Report, 1984, op. cit. p. 21.

[16] Commission on Taxation, First Report, 1982, op. cit. p. 365.

[17] Commission on Taxation, ibid. p. 371.

[18] Commission on Taxation, ibid. p. 380.

[19] J.A. Kay and M. King, 1983, op. cit. p. 189.

[20] White Paper , Industrial Policy, Pl. 2491, Stationery Office, Dublin, 1984, pp. 38-39. See also *Review of Industrial Performance 1986*, Stationery Office, Dublin, 1987, Chapters 2 and 5 for a further discussion of proposed changes in Government policy to industry.

[21] M. Feldstein, 'Inflation, Tax Rates and Investment: Some Econometric

Evidence', *Econometrica*, vol. 50, no. 4, 1982, pp. 825-862, especially p. 827.

[22] M. Feldstein, 'Inflation and the Stock Market', *American Economic Review*, vol. 70, no, 5, 1980, pp. 839-847. For a summary of Feldstein's views see M. Feldstein, 'Inflation, Capital Taxation and Monetary Policy', in R.E. Hall (ed.) *Inflation*, University of Chicago Press and the National Bureau of Economic Research, Chicago, 1982, pp. 153-167.

[23] M.A. King and D. Fullerton (eds.) *The Taxation of Income from Capital*, University of Chicago Press for the National Bureau of Economic Research, Chicago, 1984, pp. 301-302.

[24] M.A. King and D. Fullerton (eds.) ibid. , p. 301.

[25] Commission on Taxation, Second Report, 1984, op. cit. p. 39.

Bibliography

Aharoni, Y., *The Foreign Investment Decision Process*, Harvard School of Business, Boston, 1966.

Akerlof, G.A., 'The Market for Lemons: Quality Uncertainty and the Market Mechanism', *Quarterly Journal of Economics*, vol. 84,1970, pp. 398-501.

Allied Irish Banks, *Attitudes of Overseas Companies Towards Investment in Ireland*, Allied Irish Banks, Dublin, 1981.

Atkinson, A.B. and Stiglitz, J.E., *Lectures on Public Economics*, McGraw-Hill, London, 1980.

Auerbach, A.J., 'Taxation, Corporate Financial Policy and the Cost of Capital', *Journal of Economic Literature*, vol. XXI, 1983, pp. 905-940.

Auerbach, A.J., 'Corporate Taxation in the United States', in W.C. Brainard and G.L. Perry (eds.) *Brookings Paper on Economic Activity*, Brookings Institution, Washington, D.C. 1984.

Bach, G.L. and and Stephenson, J.B.,'Inflation and the Redistribution of Wealth', *Review of Economics and Statistics*, no. 1, 1975, pp. 1-13.

Bain, A.D., *The Control of the Money Supply*, Penguin Books, Harmondsworth, 1970.

Bain, A.D., Surveys in Applied Economics: Flow of Funds Analysis', *Economic Journal*, vol. 83, no. 332, 1973, pp. 1055-1095.

Bain, A.D., Day, C.L. and Wearing, A.L., *Company Financing in the United Kingdom*, Martin Robertson, London, 1975.

Bain, A.D., 'A Model of U.K. Company Financial Behaviour', *The Manchester School*, 1977, pp. 345-370.

Baxter, W.T., *Inflation Accounting*, Philip Allan, Deddington, Oxford, 1984.

Bayliss, B.T. and Butt Philip, A.A.S., *Capital Markets and Industrial Investment in Germany and France*, Saxon House, Farnborough, 1980

Bradford, D.F. and Fullerton, D., 'Pitfalls in the Construction and Use of Effective Tax Rates', in C.R. Hulten (ed.) *Depreciation, Inflation, and the Taxation of Income From Capital*, The Urban Institute Press, Washington, D.C., 1981.

Baumol, W.J., 'Contestable Markets: An Uprising in the Theory of Industry Structure', *American Economic Review*, vol. 72, no. 1, 1982, pp. 1-15.

Briston, R.J. and Tomkins, C.R., 'The Impact of the Introduction of Corporation Tax Upon the Dividend Policies of U.K. Companies', *Economic Journal*, vol. 80, 1970, pp. 617-637.

Bulow, J.I. and Shoven, J.B., 'Inflation, Corporate Profits, and the Rate of Return to Capital', in R.E. Hall (ed.) *Inflation*, University of Chicago Press for the National Bureau of Economic Research, Chicago, 1982.

Burgess, G. and Webb, A., 'Rates of Return and Profit Shares in the United Kingdom', *Lloyds Bank Review*, no. 112, April, 1974, pp.1-9.

Cable, J., 'Capital Market Imperfections and Industrial Performance: The Role of West German Banks', *Economic Journal*, vol. 95, no. 377, 1985, pp. 118-132.

Cagan, P. and Lipsey, R.E., *The Financial Effects of Inflation*, Ballinger Publishing Co. for the National Bureau of Economic Research, Cambridge,

Mass., 1978.
Carlsson, B., 'Industrial Subsidies in Sweden: Macro-Economic Effects and an International Comparison', *Journal of Industrial Economics*, vol. XXII, 1983, pp. 1-24.
Carlton, D.W., 'The Disruptive Effects of Inflation on the Organization of Markets', in R.E. Hall (ed.) *Inflation: Causes and Effects*, University of Chicago and National Bureau of Economic Research, Chicago, 1982.
Cooper, I. and Franks, J.R., 'The Interaction of Financing and Investment Decisions When the Firm has Unused Tax Credits', *Journal of Finance*, vol. 38, 1983, pp. 571-583.
Davidson, S. and Weil, R.L.,'Inflation Accounting: Implications of the F.A.S.B. Proposal', In H.J. Aaron (ed.), *Inflation and the Income Tax*, The Brookings Institution, New York, 1976.
Davies, G. and Davies J., 'The Revolution in Monopoly Theory', *LLoyds Bank Review*, July, 1984, pp. 38-52.
Davis, J.M., 'An Aggregate Time Series Analysis of the Short-Run Shifting of Company Taxation in the United Kingdom', *Oxford Economic Papers*, vol. 24, 1972, pp. 357-371.
DeAngelo, H. and Masulis, R.W., 'Optimal Capital Structure Under Corporate and Personal Taxation', *Journal of Financial Economics*, vol. 8, no. 1, 1980. pp. 3-29.
Domar, E.D., 'Depreciation, Replacement and Growth', *Economic Journal*, vol. 63, 1953, pp. 1-32.
Dusansky, R., 'The Short- Run Shifting of the Corporation Income Tax in the United States', *Oxford Economic Papers*, vol. 24, pp. 357-371.
Edwards, J.S.S., and C.P. Mayer, *Issues in Bank Taxation*, The Institute for Fiscal Studies, London, 1983.
Fabozzi, F.J. and Yaari, U., 'Valuation of Safe Harbor Tax Benefit Transfer Leases', *Journal of Finance*, vol. 38, no. 2, 1983, pp. 571-583.
Fama, E.F. and Jensen, M.C., 'Separation of Ownership and Control', *Journal of Law and Economics*, vol. XXVII, 1983, pp. 301-325.
Feldstein, M.S., 'The Effectiveness of the British Differential Profits Tax', *The Economic Journal*, vol. 77, 1967, pp. 947-953.
Feldstein, M.S. and G. Fane, 'Taxes, Corporate Dividend Policy and Personal Savings: The British Postwar Experience', *Review of Economics and Statistics*, vol. LV, no. 4, 1973, pp. 399-411.
Feldstein, M.S. and Summers, L., 'Inflation and the Taxation of Capital Income in the Corporate Sector, *National Tax Journal*, vol. XXXII, 1979, pp. 445-470.
Feldstein, M.S., 'Inflation and the Stock Market', *American Economic Review*, vol. 70, no. 5, 1980, pp. 839-847.
* Feldstein, M. S., 'Inflation, Tax Rates and Investment: Some Econometric Evidence', *Econometrica*, vol. 50, no. 4, 1982, pp. 825-862.
Feldstein, M., 'Inflation, Capital Taxation and Monetary Policy', in R.E. Hall (ed.) *Inflation*, University of Chicago Press and National Bureau of Economic Research, Chicago, 1982..
Feldstein, M. Dicks-Mireaux, L. and Poterba, J., 'The Effective Tax Rate

and the Pretax Rate of Return', *Journal of Public Economics*, vol. 21, 1983, pp. 129-158.

Financial Accounting General Standards Board, *Financial Reporting in Units of Purchasing Power*, Proposed Statement of Financial Accounting Standards Exposure Draft, F.A.S.B., Stanford, Connecticut, 1974.

Fisher, I., *The Theory of Interest*, MacMillan, London, 1930.

Flath, D., 'The Economics of Short Term Leasing', *Economic Inquiry*, vol. XVIII, 1980, pp. 247-259.

Fullerton, D. and Henderson, Y.K., 'Long Run Effects of the Accelerated Cost Recovery System', *National Bureau of Economic Research, Working Paper*, no. 828, National Bureau of Economic Research, New York, 1981.

Fullerton, D., 'Which Effective Tax Rate?', *National Tax Journal*, vol. XXXVII, no. 1, 1983, pp. 23-41.

Gallagher, J.R., 'Advance Corporation Tax (A.C.T.) - Finance Act 1983', *Irish Banking Review*, June 1983, pp. 9-19.

Goodhart, C.A.E., *Money, Information and Uncertainty*, London: MacMillan, 1975.

Gordon, R.H. and Malkiel, B.G., 'Corporation Finance', in H.J. Aaron and J.A. Pechman (eds.), *How Taxes Affect Economic Behaviour*, Brookings Institution, Washington, D.C., 1981, pp. 131-192.

Gravelle, J.G., Which Effective Tax Rate? A Comment and Extension', *National Tax Journal* , vol. XXXVIII, 1984, pp. 103-110.

Harberger, A.C., 'Tax Neutrality in Investment Decisions', in H.J. Aaron and M.J. Boskin (eds.) *The Economics of Taxation*, The Brookings Institution, Washington, 1980, pp. 299-311.

Hicks, J.R., 'Maintaining Capital Intact: A Further Suggestion', *Economica*, vol. IX, 1942, pp. 276-280.

Hicks, J.R., *Value and Capital*, 2nd. edition, Oxford University Press, Oxford, 1946.

Hicks, J.R., 'The Concept of Income in Relation to Taxation and to Business Management', *Greek Economic Review*, vol. 1, no. 2, 1979, pp. 1-14.

Hill, T.P., *Profits and Rates of Return*, O.E.C.D., Paris, 1979.

Honohan, P., 'The Flow of Funds 1972-1977', *Journal of the Statistical and Social Inquiry Society of Ireland*, vol. XXIV, Part IV, 1982-83, pp. 175-216

Industrial Development Authority, *Survey of Grant Aided Industry*, Stationery Office, Dublin, 1967.

Institute of Chartered Accontants, *Statement of Sources and Applications of Funds*, Statement of Standard Accounting Practice, no. 10, Institute of Chartered Accountants, Dublin, 1975.

Institute of Chartered Accountants, *Accounting for Depreciation*, Statement of Standard Accounting Practice, no. 12, Institute of Chartered Accountants, Dublin, 1977.

Institute of Chartered Accountants, *Current Cost Accounting*, Statement of Standard Accounting Practice, no. 16, Institute of Chartered Accountants, Dublin, 1980.

Jensen, M.C. and Meckling, W.H., 'Theory of the Firm: Managerial

Behaviour, Agency Costs, and Ownership Structure', *Journal of Financial Economics*, vol. 3, no. 4, 1976, pp. 337-347.

Joel, Clark, 'Tax Incentives in Central American Development', *Economic Development and Cultural Change*, vol. 19, no.2, 1971 pp. 229-252.

Johansen, L., *Public Economics*, North-Holland, London, 1971.

Kaldor, N., *An Expenditure Tax*, George Allen and Unwin, London, 1956.

Kaldor, N., '*Economics of the Selective Employment Tax*', in Reports on Taxation, vol. 1, Duckworth, London, 1980.

Kay, J. A., 'Inflation Accounting: A Review Article', *Economic Journal*, no. 346, 1977, pp. 300-311.

Kay, J.A. and King, M.A., *The British Tax System*, 3rd edition, Oxford University Press, Oxford, 1983.

Kay, J.A. and Mayer, C.P., *Inflation Accounting*, Institute of Fiscal Studies, Report Series, no. 10, Institute of Fiscal Studies, London, 1984.

Kennedy, K.A. and Dowling, B.R., *Economic Growth in Ireland: The Experience Since 1947*, Gill and MacMillan, Dublin, 1975.

King, M.A., 'The United Kingdom Profits Crisis: Myth or Reality?' *Economic Journal*, vol. 85, 1975, pp. 33-54.

King, M.A., 'Taxation, Corporate Financial Policy, and the Cost of Capital', *Journal of Public Economics*, vol. 4, 1975, pp. 271-279.

King, M.A., *Public Policy and the Corporation*, Chapman and Hall, London, 1977.

King, M.A. and Fullerton D. (eds.), *The Taxation of Income from Capital*, University of Chicago Press for the National Bureau of Economic Research, Chicago, 1984

Kinsella, R.P., 'The Measurement of Concentration in Irish Banking', *Journal of the Statistical and Social Inquiry Society of Ireland*, vol. XXIV, Part III, 1980-81, pp. 31-60.

Klein, B, Crawford, R. and A.A. Alchian, 'Vertical Integration, Appropriable Rents, and the Competitive Contracting Process', *Journal of Law and Economics*, vol. 21, 1978, pp. 297-326.

Lall, S., 'Transfer Pricing by Multinational Firms', *Oxford Bulletin of Economics and Statistics*, vol. 35, no. 3, 1973, pp.173-195.

Lawson, G.H. and Stark, A. W., 'Equity Values and Inflation: Dividends and Debt Financing', *Lloyds Bank Review*, January, 1981, pp. 41-59.

Lintner, J., The Financing of Corporations', in E.S. Mason (ed.) *The Corporation in Modern Society*, Harvard University Press, Cambridge, 1959.

Lintner, J., 'Distribution of Incomes of Corporations among Dividends, Retained Earnings, and Taxes', *American Economic Review*, 1956, pp. 97-113.

Lyons, F.S.L., *Ireland Since the Rising*, Collins and Fontana, Glasgow, 1973.

McGrath, J., 'New Tax Relief Aims to Spur Reinvestment', *Irish Times*, June 10th, 1980.

Marsh, P., 'The Choice Between Equity and Debt: An Empirical Study', *Journal of Finance*, vol. XXXVII, no. 2, 1982, pp. 301-325.

Matthews, R.C.O., *The Trade Cycle*, Cambridge University Press,

Cambridge, 1959.
Mayer, C.P., 'The Structure of Corporation Tax in the U.K.', *Fiscal Studies*, vol. 3, 1982, pp. 121-141.
Mayer, C.P. and Morris, C.N., *A Disaggregated Model of U.K. Corporation Tax*, Working Paper, no. 33, Institute for Fiscal Studies, London, 1982.
Meade Committee, *The Structure and Reform of Direct Taxation*, Report of a Committee chaired by J.E. Meade, Institute for Fiscal Studies, London, 1978.
Meeks, G., 'Profit Illusion', *Bulletin of the Oxford University Institute of Economics and Statistics*, vol. 36, 1974, pp. 267-285.
Meeks, G. and and Whittington, G., 'Giant Companies in the U.K. 1948-1969', *Economic Journal*, vol. 85, no. 340, 1975, pp. 824-838
Meeks, G. and and Whittington, G. *The Financing of Quoted Companies in the United Kingdom*, Royal Commission on the Distribution of Income and Wealth, H.M.S.O., London, 1976.
Modigliani, F. and Miller, M. 'The Cost of Capital, Corporation Finance and the Theory of Investment', *American Economic Review*, vol. 48, 1958, pp. 261-297.
Modigliani, F. and Miller, M.H., 'Taxes and the Cost of Capital: A Correction', *American Economic Review*, vol. 53, nos. 3-5, 1963, pp. 433-443.
Modigliani, F. and Cohn, R.A., 'Inflation, Rational Valuation and the Market', *Financial Analysts Journal*, March/April, 1979, pp. 24-44.
Modigliani, F., 'Debt, Dividend Policy, Taxes, Inflation and Market Valuation', *Journal of Finance*, vol. 37, no. 2, 1983, pp. 135-138.
Morley, M.F., *The Fiscal Implications of Inflation Accounting*, The Institute for Fiscal Studies and the Institute of Chartered Accountants in England and Wales, London, 1974.
Myers, S.C., 'Determinants of Corporate Borrowing', *Journal of Financial Economics*, vol. 5, 1977, pp. 147-175.
Nowotny, E., 'Inflation and Taxation: Reviewing the Macroeconomic Issues', *Journal of Economic Literature*, vol. XVIII, 1980, pp. 1025-1049.
Oakland, W.H., 'Corporate Earnings and Tax Shifting in U.S. Manufacturing', *Review of Economics and Statistics*, August 1972, pp. 235-244.
O'Connell, T., 'The Flow of Funds, 1960-1985', *Journal of the Statistical and Social Inquiry Society of Ireland*, forthcoming.
O'Connell, T., 'The Flow of Funds, 1960-1985', *Quarterly Bulletin of the Central Bank of Ireland*, summer , 1986, pp. 76-102.
O'Hagan, J.W., 'An Analysis of the Growth of the Public Sector in Ireland, 1953-1977', *Journal of the Statistical and Social Inquiry Society of Ireland*, vol. XXIV, 1979-80, pp.69-98.
Olson, M., *The Logic of Collective Action*, Harvard University Press, Harvard, 1965.
Olson, M., *The Rise and Decline of Nations*, Yale University Press, London, 1982.
Pindyck, S. and and Rubinfeld, D.L., *Economic Models and Economic*

Forecasts, McGraw-Hill, London, 1981.
Prais, S.J., *The Evolution of Giant Firms in Britain*, Cambridge University Press, Cambridge, 1976.
Prest, A.R., 'Replacement Cost Depreciation', *Accounting Research*, vol. 1, no. 4, 1948-1950, pp. 365-402.
Prest, A.R., *How Much Subsidy* ? I.E.A. Research Monograph, no. 32, Institute of Economic Affairs, London, 1974.
Prest, A.R. and Barr, N., *Public Finance*, 6th edition, Weidenfeld and Nicolson, London, 1979.
Reddaway, W.B., *Effects of the Selective Employment Tax*, First Report, H.M.S.O., London, 1970
Reddaway, W.B., *Effects of the Selective Employment Tax*, Final Report, Cambridge University Press, Cambridge, 1973.
Rosenberg, L. G., 'Taxation of Income from Capital by Industry Group', in A.C. Harberger and M.J. Bailey (eds.) *The Taxation of Income from Capital*, The Brookings Institution, Washington, 1969.
Rubner, A., 'The Irrelevancy of the British Differential Profits Tax', *Economic Journal*, vol. 77, 1967, pp. 947-953.
Ryan, T., 'Dividend Policy and Market Valuation in British Industry', *Journal of Business Finance and Accounting*, vol. 1, 1974, pp. 415-429.
Samuels, J.M. Groves, R.E.V. and Goddard, C.S., *Company Finance in Europe*, Institute of Chartered Accountants in England and Wales, London, 1975
Shoup, C.S., 'The United States Economic Recovery Tax Act of 1981', *British Tax Review*, no. 5, 1982, pp. 301-314.
Siegfried, J., 'Effective Average U.S. Corporation Income Tax Rates', *National Tax Journal*, vol. XXVII, 1974, pp. 245-259.
Simons, H.C., *Personal Income Taxation*, University of Chicago Press, Chicago, 1938
Singh, A. and and Whittington, G., Growth, *Profitability and Valuation*, Cambridge University Press, Cambridge, 1968.
Stewart, J.C., 'Multinational Companies and Transfer Pricing', *Journal of Business Finance and Accounting*, vol. 4, 1977, pp. 353-371.
Stewart, J.C., 'A Study of the Financing of Multinational Companies in Ireland 1964-1980', *Irish Business and Administrative Research*, vol. 4, no. 2, 1982, pp. 72-86.
Stewart, J.C., 'Some Aspects of the Financial Behaviour of Multinational Companies operating in Ireland', in J.H. Kelly and J. FitzPatrick (eds.) *Perspectives of Irish Industry*, Irish Management Institute, Dublin, 1985.
Stewart, J.C., 'Fiscal Incentives and Corporate Financing: A Flow of Funds Analysis 1964-1982', Forthcoming *Journal of the Statistical and Social Inquiry Society of Ireland.*
Stonham, P., *Major Stock Markets of Europe*, Gower, London, 1982
Sumner, M.T., *The Reform of Corporation Tax: A Review of the Green Paper*, Salford Papers on Economics, no. 5, 1982.
Thomas, W.A., *The Finance of British Industry*, Metheun, London, 1978.
Tideman, T.N. and Tucker, D.P., 'Tax Treatment of Business Profits

Under Inflationary Conditions', in H.J. Aaron (ed.) *Inflation and the Income Tax*, The Brookings Institution, New York, 1976.
United Nations, *Multinational Corporations in World Development*, Praeger Publishers, London, 1974.
United Nations Conference on Trade and Development, *Dominant positions of Market Power of Transnational Corporations*, TD/B/C2/167, United Nations, New York, 1978.
Vaughan, R.N., 'Profits, Finance, and Growth' in B.R. Dowling and J. Durkan (eds.) *Irish Economic Policy: a Review of Major Issues*, Economic and Social Research Institute, Dublin, 1978.
Warren, J.R., 'Bankruptcy Costs: Some Evidence', *Journal of Finance*, vol. XXXII, no. 2, 1977, pp. 337-347.
Warren, A.C. and Auerbach, A.J., 'Transferability of Tax Incentives and the Fiction of Safe Harbor Leasing', *Harvard Law Review*, vol. 95, no. 8, 1982, pp.1752-1786.
Whalley, J., 'Capital Gains Taxation and Interest Rate Changes: An Extension of Paish's argument', *National Tax Journal*, vol. XXXII, no. 1, 1979, pp. 87-91.
Whittington, G., *Company Taxation and Dividends*, I.F.S. Lecture Series no. 1, Institute for Fiscal Studies, London, 1974.
Whittington, G., *Inflation Accounting: An Introduction to the Debate*, Oxford University Press, Oxford, 1983.
Williams, E.E. and Findley, M.C. 'Discounting Tax Liabilities: Some Clarifying Comments', *Journal of Business Finance and Accounting*, vol. 2, no. 1, 1975, pp. 121-133.
Winkler, J.T., 'Corporatism', *European Journal of Sociology*, vol. 17, 1976, pp. 100-136.

United Kingdom Government Publications

Bank of England, 'Recent Developments in Equipment Leasing', *Bank of England Quarterly Bulletin*, September, 1982.
Department of Trade and Industry, *Regional Industrial Development*, White Paper, cmnd. 9111, H.M.S.O., London, 1983.
Inland Revenue, *Green Paper on Corporation Tax*, Cmnd. 8456 H.M.S.O. London, 1982.
Sandilands Report, *Inflation Accounting*, cmnd. 6225, H.M.S.O., London, 1975.
Wilson Report, *Committee to Review the Functioning of Financial Institutions*, Cmnd. 7937, H.M.S.O., London, 1980.

Irish Government Publications

Commission on Taxation, Direct Taxation, *First Report of the Commission on Taxation*, Stationery Office, Dublin, 1982.
Commission on Taxation, Direct Taxation, *Second Report of the Commission on Taxation*, Stationery Office, pl. 1755, Dublin, March 1984.

Department of Finance, *Committee of Inquiry into Taxation on Industry*, Pr. 3512, Stationery Office, Dublin, 1956.
Department of Finance, *Company Taxation in Ireland*, Prl. 2628, Stationery Office, Dublin, 1972.
Department of Finance, *Proposals for Corporation Tax*, Stationery Office, Prl. 3713, Dublin, 1974
Department of Industry Trade and Commerce, *Industrial Policy*, White Paper, Pl. 2491, Stationery Office, Dublin, 1984.
Department of Industry and Commerce, *Review of Industrial Performance 1986*, Pl. 4769, Stationery Office, Dublin, 1987.
National Economic and Social Council, *Regional Policy in Ireland: a Review*, Report, no. 4, Prl. 4147, Stationery Office, Dublin, 1975.
National Economic and Social Council, *The Role of the Financial System in Financing the Traded Sectors*, Report no. 76, Pl. 4450, Stationery Office, Dublin, 1984.
National Planning Board, *Proposals for Plan*, National Planning Board, prl. 2309, Dublin, 1984.
Revenue Commissioners, *Guide to the Corporation Tax*, Revenue Commissioners, Dublin, 1976.
Telesis, *A Review of Industrial Policy*, National Economic and Social Council, Report no. 64, Pl. 409, Stationery Office, Dublin, 1982.

Index

The Summary and Bibliography have not been indexed. References to tables are in italics.